# WINE, SOCIETY, AND GLOBALIZATION

# WINE, SOCIETY, AND GLOBALIZATION

## MULTIDISCIPLINARY PERSPECTIVES ON THE WINE INDUSTRY

*Edited by*
*Gwyn Campbell and Nathalie Guibert*

First published in 2007 by
PALGRAVE MACMILLAN™
175 Fifth Avenue, New York, NY 10010 and
Houndmills, Basingstoke, Hampshire, England RG21 6XS.
Companies and representatives throughout the world.

PALGRAVE MACMILLAN is the global academic imprint of the Palgrave Macmillan division of St. Martin's Press, LLC and of Palgrave Macmillan Ltd.
Macmillan® is a registered trademark in the United States, United Kingdom and other countries. Palgrave is a registered trademark in the European Union and other countries.

ISBN-10: 1-4039-8423-9
ISBN-13: 978-1-4039-8423-4

Library of Congress Cataloging-in-Publication Data

Gwyn Campell and Nathalie Guibert
  Wine, Society, and Globalization: Multidisciplinary Perspectives on the Wine Industry / edited by Gwyn Campbell and Nathalie Guibert.
        p. cm.
  Includes bibliographical references and index.
  ISBN 1-4039-8423-9 (alk. paper)
    1. Wine industry. 2. International trade. 3. Globalization—Economic aspects. I Campbell, Gwyn. II. Guibert, Nathalie.

  HD9370.5.G65 2008
  338.4'76632—dc22                                              2007020725

A catalogue record of the book is available from the British Library.

Design by Scribe Inc.

First Edition: December 2007

10 9 8 7 6 5 4 3 2 1

Printed in the United States of America.

# CONTENTS

# Tables and Figures

## Tables

## Figures

# CHAPTER 1

# INTRODUCTION
## THE HISTORY AND CULTURE OF WINE

*Gwyn Campbell and Nathalie Guibert*

Wine has, from early times, played a significant economic and social role in human history. Until relatively recently, the number of major wine-producing countries was limited. Of these, only France gained a universal reputation for its wines, and in consequence largely dominated the international trade in quality wines. Since the 1990s, in a context of globalization, this situation has changed radically. In non-wine-producing countries, wine consumption is spreading from the elite to the middle classes, and Old World producers, such as France, are fighting to meet the challenge in international markets from "New World" competitors such as Australia, California, and Chile. Moreover, a new wine-producing frontier is forming in regions benefiting from global warming and in high altitude regions in the tropics. Wine is making a greater contribution than ever before to a growing number of economies, including those of a number of developing countries. It is against this backdrop that the contributions to this volume present a number of studies in the history and culture of wine from different countries and different eras up to the present day.

## Historical Background

### The Old World

While there is debate about the precise origins of wine, there is general consensus that the wild Eurasian grapevine *(Vitis vinifera sylvestris)*, cutivars of which produce the vast majority of current wine grapes, was first domesticated by 5500 BCE[1] in the Caucasian region.[2] It quickly established a reputation as a luxury drink and by around 3000 BCE, following the development of bottle-necked pottery jars that facilitated both the storage and carriage of wine,[3] it was shipped long distances to supply urban-elite demand for this new luxury beverage. For example, the Ur-Nammu tablets, dated to 2300 BCE, mention slaves serving wine to members of the royal household in the Assyrian capital of Nimrod.[4] This elite, and elites elsewhere, encouraged experimentation in local wine production. Whereas the climate and soils of Mesopotamia proved inauspicious, vineyards were established early in Syria and Palestine, where they thrived, and by 2125 BCE in Egypt, where they survived in adverse climatic conditions only due to intensive care. From the eastern littoral of the Mediterranean, grape vine cultivation spread gradually westward to Crete, Greece, Italy, and France, where from 600 BCE it diffused further west to the Iberian peninsula, and to hinterland regions such as the Rhône Valley.[5] By the first centuries CE a considerable market for wine had developed in more northern regions of Europe that was supplied by a vibrant trading network from southern Europe.[6]

From the first century CE, French wines earned a high reputation in other markets, including wine-producing countries such as Italy.[7] This reputation grew as the wine-growing frontier in France spread north beyond the traditional olive-vine cultivation zone to more temperate climes. By the mid–first millennium CE, vineyards had been planted in the Bordeaux, Burgundy, Loire Valley, Parisian Basin, and Champagne regions, and by the sixth century in Brittany. Indeed, by the Middle Ages wine had become France's major export commodity. For the export market, transport was key, so a premium was placed on vineyards close to navigable waterways, which led to the predominance of the wine-growing regions of the Loire (via La Rochelle), the Ile de France (via Rouen), and Gascony (via Bordeaux) as the major producer regions supplying the prestige markets of northern Europe.[8]

Over succeeding centuries, the Old World wine-producing and marketing structure solidified. The Mediterranean littoral produced a huge variety of mostly cheap wines from small farms to meet a predominantly local mass market, while more northern French wine-growing regions shipped their produce to non-producer countries—especially Bordeaux wines (claret) to Britain, and Burgundy wines to Flanders, the Netherlands, and Scandinavia.[9]

Climatic change, notably the "Little Ice Age" (c.1300–1850), modified the structure of wine production and trade. As temperatures dropped, viticulture retreated from northern regions, and in new frontier areas such as Champagne, switched from the production of red to white wines. Climate change also encouraged the development of sweet wines in the Mediterranean region and during the peak of the "Little Ice Age" from 1692–95 when low temperatures ruined the Bordelais harvest, opened the door for Portuguese wines to find a niche on the British market.[10] Traders, chiefly from England, developed Porto, the fortified dessert wine named after the port of Oporto in northern Portugal that developed a large reputation in Britain.[11]

Enhanced demand for sweet wines in northern Europe also led to an acceleration of wine exports from France in the seventeenth century, notably from the Bordeaux region where Dutch mercantile investment stimulated the local production of sweet wines and brandy.[12] Bordeaux wine exports reached new heights in the eighteenth century due to an increased demand for sweet wine in Britain and the opening of a significant market in the newly independent United States.[13]

Nevertheless, a mass market for wine developed only in the later nineteenth century as a result of demand for cheap wine by the expanding working class and urban populations of northern France, combined with traditional demand for elite wines from the wealthier classes of northern Europe and the eastern seaboard of the United States. However, French viticulture and the wine trade were also hit hard by a series of catastrophes, notably *Oidium* (a vine mildew) from 1852–57, *Phylloxera* (a tiny louse that attacked vine roots) from the 1860s to the 1880s, and "Mildew" and "Black Rot" in the 1870s and 1880s. The only solution to *Phylloxera* proved to be the mass introduction of American hybrid vines in the 1890s, followed by the development of European hybrids at the start of the twentieth century.[14]

Due to French urban demand and the expansion of the railway system, the Languedoc plains had been transformed into a huge supply region of light red wines for the markets of northern France by the start of the twentieth century. In order to augment alcohol content and color, light red wines were reinforced with stronger wines from Algeria, where viticulture experienced, in consequence, rapid development.[15] In 1923, following the "Judgement of Châteauneuf-du-Pape" the *Appellation d'origine contrôlée* (AOC) system of regulations was established,[16] which in turn led, in 1935, to the creation of the *Institut national des appelations d'origine* (INAO), which aimed to define all French vintages by the application of similar criteria. These regulations subsequently formed the basis for similar controls in Germany, Italy, and Spain.[17]

France has maintained its position as the world's chief producer and supplier of wine, but by the close of the twentieth century its wine sector was clearly in crisis. While it produced 35.4 million hectoliters of wine or 16 percent of global wine production in the year 2000, the domestic market for wine was shrinking (per capita wine consumption almost halving between 1960 and 2000), as was the French share of foreign wine markets in the face of competition from New World wine producers, led by Australia. This is the subject of a contribution by Gwyn Campbell, who examines the historical trends in the domestic market for French and Australian wines, and the consequences in terms of export strategy, focusing upon their current competition for the British market.[18]

The other Old World wine producers—Portugal, Spain and Italy—have experienced very similar problems. Their reaction has been threefold: to appeal for more government and European Union subsidies and other assistance for domestic wine industries; to oppose New World production and marketing practices that are considered to undermine Old World norms;[19] and to adopt New World and other innovative strategies designed to improve efficiency in production and distribution and more effectively cater to the rapid expansion and changes in international demand for wine.

## The New World

From the late fifteenth century, the Portuguese and Spanish carried viticulture via the Atlantic islands (notably the Canary Islands and Madeira) to the New World, including Mexico (by the 1520s); Peru,

Bolivia and Columbia (1530s); Chile (1540s); Argentina (1550s); and California (1619). Just as religious orders had contributed to the development of viticulture in Europe, Jesuit priests played a major role in its diffusion in the Americas.[20] By contrast, in the 1650s, the Protestant Dutch introduced viticulture to South Africa, where it was consolidated from the 1680s by the arrival of French Huguenots fleeing religious persecution at home.[21] The British introduced vines to Australia in 1788 and New Zealand by 1819, although vineyards only became established there beginning in the 1830s.[22]

With the exception of California, viticulture in the New World was limited by relatively small local markets, poor technology, and difficulties of transportation until the 1980s, and notably the 1990s when, led by Australia, they adopted more efficient production, distribution, and marketing techniques that, in an era of globalization, enabled them to claim growing market shares in centers of world demand for wine, such as northern Europe, North America, and Southeast and East Asia.[23]

## WINE AND THE STATE

A number of contributions to this volume highlight the role of the state in wine culture. In her study of Napa Valley (California) wines, Kathleen Brosnan explores the importance of the state in deciding the appellation system that is, as reflected on bottle labels, critical to the status and thus the market price of wines.[24] Shortly after Napa Valley wine production took off in the 1870s, the state of California intervened and, in 1880, created seven wine districts. These districts were represented on the Board of State Viticultural Commissioners (BSVC) that promoted improvements in Napa Valley wine production and marketing. In the 1890s, the region was attacked by vine plagues (*Phylloxera* and Anaheim disease) and, although some replanting occurred, vineyards were affected again by Prohibition in 1919. Bootlegging, which was widespread, and legal loopholes that permitted home-made, sacramental, and "medicinal" wines, ensured continued demand for grapes. However, by 1925, supply outstripped demand, and the wine industry slumped. Moreover, most producers had reverted to the production of inferior quality red wines, so that when Prohibition was lifted in 1933, the industry was characterized by inadequate equipment and poor quality products.

Improvement was gradual, but the California wine industry participated in the post-1945 boom. Moreover, in the late 1960s when the vineyards of Napa Valley were threatened by property speculators and rapidly spreading urbanization, the state protected them through legislation restricting the sale of adjacent plots of land. By the early 1980s the local wine industry was further boosted by a state-regulated system of appellation on French lines based on *terroir*—a concept that embraces a combination of factors including soil type, water, degree of sunlight, climate, and grape varietals. This, and a booming domestic wine tourism trade, led to an expanded and modernized wine sector, producing high quality wines, that was well placed to take advantage of the forces of globalization beginning in the 1990s—albeit at considerable environmental cost.

In his contribution, Robert Ulin takes issue with those who extol the virtues of *terroir*, arguing that that "history and the hegemonic components of cultural representation" are as important to wine culture, and the evaluation of elite wines, as the essentially subjective criteria of climate and soil.[25] He contends that while, in the minds of consumers, *terroir* conjures up small family-based farms whose wines reflect a combination of wholesome natural factors and generations of traditional know-how, the concept has been hijacked and manipulated by elite estates, most of which are currently controlled by global corporations. Tracing the origins of the Western association of "natural" and "virtue" to the Enlightenment, he argues that it also became central to the ideal "imagined community" developed by the nation-state during the nineteenth century. This community forged by blood ties and rooted to the soil formed the core of the "nation," and epitomized its unique characteristics. In France, the ideal imagined community is that composed of peasant *viticulteurs*— a community that, like the vine from which it is inseparable, is nourished by uniquely French combinations of soil and climate. This in large part explains the outcry against using American hybrids to beat *Phylloxera* in the late nineteenth century, and current protests against foreign disregard for French wine-producing regulations. Attachment to this imagined community also gave rise to classifications of *terroir* into a hierarchy, first formalized in the Bordeaux region in 1855, and imitated in California in the 1880s, but often had little relation to the actual quality of wine produced.

The role of government is again prominent in the history of Argentinean wine production, presented here by Steven Stein.[26] In

1853, the Argentinean government founded the country's modern wine industry by importing French wine expertise and technology, as well as French grape stock to replace the *Uva Criolla* originally introduced by Spanish missionaries. The industry took off in the late nineteenth century when railways linked the wine-producing region of Mendoza to Buenos Aires. Consequently, wine production increased by 90 percent from 1901 to 1915, turning Argentina into the world's sixth largest wine producer. However, the demand established by predominantly poor Italian and Spanish immigrants was for strong low-quality wines. Reinforced by government protection in the form of tax reductions for wineries and tariff barriers against imported wines, this acted as a disincentive to investment in quality control and up-to-date equipment and techniques—all elements required to produce superior quality wines.

The industry slumped during the Depression, only to recover rapidly from 1945 due to domestic demand from a booming urban population and government assistance in the form of massive tax concessions, cheap credit, and high protective tariffs. High tariffs, combined with strict currency controls and barriers to the import of foreign equipment, acted as further disincentives on investment in the skill and technology required to produce quality wines, and induced producers to pull up French varietals and revert to the more productive *Uva Criolla* grape stock. This accentuated the predominance of poor quality wines, the production of which reached new peaks in the 1970s when Argentina became the world's second largest producer of wine. However, the sharp decline of domestic demand in the 1980s, due to a combination of recession and changing consumer preferences, precipitated a crisis of overproduction that in the 1990s forced the industry to radically re-evaluate strategy. Once again, the government proved instrumental through economic reforms beginning in the late 1980s that loosened import and export controls, stabilized the currency, and encouraged foreign investment and structural consolidation. As a result, the Argentinean wine industry overhauled its outdated technology, and started to produce quality wines that enabled it to seriously compete in international markets for the first time.

The role of the state is also central to the history of the Canadian wine industry. Canada was initially settled by the French mostly along the St. Lawrence River, a waterway running from 50° N at its mouth to almost 46° N at Niagara. The same latitudes in France run from just north of Dieppe on the English Channel (in the north) to a little north of Lyons (to the south)—a region in which some of the most celebrated of French vineyards are found (Champagne, Loire, Burgundy). This encouraged French settlers and priests to plant vines that were initially, however, largely laid waste by the harsh continental winters that characterize the region.

Nevertheless, wine industries have slowly developed in Canada where the state—federal and provincial—has been decisive. In their contribution, Linda Bramble, Carman Cullen, Joseph Kushner, and Gary Pickering analyze the rise of viticulture in Ontario, currently Canada's most internationally reputed wine industry.[27] Following the Prohibition era, the government established the Liquor Control Board of Ontario (LCBO), and encouraged a concentration of the industry by reducing the number of provincial producers from sixty-three to six. However, neither the government nor this group of privileged growers invested in "Research and Development" (R&D), and in consequence never realized the potential for the cultivation of the *V. vinifera* grape in the Niagara region where the lakes create a favorably mild microclimate. Instead, the small elite of producers used their virtual monopoly to produce chiefly poor quality "ports" and "sherries."

The situation changed in the 1970s with the 1973 Wine Content Act that permitted producers to use up to 75 percent of imported wines in bottles labeled "Canadian," and the 1975 lifting of the quasi-monopoly on production. Privileged wine producers were further hit by competition from California that followed the 1989 application of the North American Free Trade Act (NAFTA) rulings on agricultural goods. These measures, combined with the application from the mid-1990s of simple but effective New World technologies, such as temperature and hygiene controls, created the basis for the emergence of good-quality wines of truly local vintage. These developments have, moreover, been backed by government support as well as the establishment in 1997 of the Brock University Cool Climate Oenology and Viticulture Institute (CCOVI), the only North American centre dedicated to research into cool climate vine cultivation and wine production. As a result, Canadian wines are competing in the domestic market with foreign wines, and some Canadian products, notably ice wines, have earned an international reputation.

Marianne Ackerman also underlines the role of the state in shaping the wine industry in Quebec, the province with the highest per capita wine consumption in Canada. She relates how, ironically, Quebec viticulture took off during the Prohibition years, largely as a result of the Quebec provincial government's decision in 1919 to exclude wine (alongside beer and cider) from its liquor ban, which rather focused on spirits.[28] This exemption increased revenue for both local wine producers and the state, which imposed a monopoly on alcohol sales. However, in the late 1970s a revamped state monopoly, the *Société des alcohols du Quebec* (SAQ), started importing massive quantities of wine, and following the 1987 NAFTA treaty—when the tax advantages enjoyed by local producers was phased out—and the rapid increase in international competition from the 1990s, Quebec viticulture again declined. Nevertheless, growing domestic demand and the cultivation of "local" labels by regional vineyards has created a market niche for regional wines which, combined with a growth in wine tourism, appears to have guaranteed a future for Quebec wine producers.

Finally, the state has also been central to the development of the South African wine industry: "white" governments after World War I provided institutional support and underwrote efforts to ensure the supply of cheap "colored" labor to the Cape wine farms; while the new post-apartheid government is pushing white wine farmers to negotiate "voluntary" joint ventures with black farm workers in the context of a promised redistribution to blacks of 30 percent of all agricultural land by 2014.[29]

## WINE CULTURE

More than any other beverage, wine has been imbued through history with enormous cultural significance and value, in everything from religion to literature to sexual customs. From ancient times, it was an elected drink for the afterlife. Thus, in a tomb dating to the fourteenth century BCE of a Syrian mercenary who died in Egypt, there is a fresque that depicts an amphora from which the seated soldier is drinking wine. In ancient Greece, the three-day festival of *Anthestéria*, linked to the cult of Dionysus, was held to celebrate new wine, and at Rhodes, amphorae inscriptions refer to the priest of Helios.[30]

In Chapter 8, Patric Choffrut discusses the role of wine in the culture of the Jews of Provence, which was an independent kingdom until the late Middle Ages.[31] Wine had always been important to

Jews. Before the Diaspora *tirosh* (new wine) constituted one of the three staple productions of Israel, alongside grain and oil. Rabbis taught that wine, taken in moderation, induced appetite and a state of happiness, and had medicinal properties. Moreover, they prescribed it for the Sabbath and other important religious festivals, such as the Passover *Seder*, weddings, circumcisions, and funerals (to alleviate grief). Such traditions accompanied the Diaspora including the Jews who settled in Provence, France. There, members of the four Jewish communities at Carpentras, Avignon, Cavaillon, and L'Isle de Venisse adopted the Provencal language, which they used in everyday parlance and to express themselves in poetry and prose. They also found in Provence a culture that, like theirs, and unlike that of the Jews of Eastern Europe, was deeply influenced by wine. This communality of tastes helped foster in Provence—unlike the neighboring kingdoms of France (to the north) and Spain (to the west), from which their coreligionists were expelled in 1349 and 1492, respectively—relatively amicable relations with Christian neighbors.

## WINE AND WOMEN

Kathleen Brosnan, in her chapter, notes Euripides' declaration that "where there is no wine, there is no love."[32] However, it is not certain that this "amour" refers to love for women who, in the classical world, were forbidden to drink wine—sometimes under pain of death—unless prescribed for strictly medicinal purposes. In Rome, men of non-noble origin were forbidden to drink wine until the age of thirty.[33]

Most literature on wine has been from the perspective of males with whom the wine industry, from grape cultivation to wine consumption, has been overwhelmingly identified. This is starting to change as the growing influence of female wine consumers and wine writers demonstrates.[34] Julie Tolley elucidates the role of women in the South Australian wine industry.[35] In South Australian vineyards, as in agriculture generally in European-dominated regions, men owned vineyards on which there existed, theoretically at least, a division of labor, whereby the women were responsible for the domestic sphere (home management, child-rearing, and catering for the home needs of males), and men for taming "nature" outside. To this day, the *Australian Bureau of Statistics* has no data on women employed in the wine industry in South Australia.

However, Tolley cites a number of cases from the early and mid-nineteenth century where the involvement of women was such that they either established vineyards, or more frequently, following the death of their husbands, took over the management of vineyards. She also emphasizes the vital role played by wives in male-owned wine-producing units. When vineyards were first established, a minimum of three years was needed before vines bore sufficient fruit for wine making. During that period wives had to both assist with the foundation work, such as clearing, digging irrigation channels, root trimming, and vine planting, and secure part-time off-farm work in order to help generate the income required to support the establishment of a vineyard. Once the vineyards had become productive and off-farm work eased off—notably in the post-1945 era characterized by rising demand for wine—it was expected that farmers' wives assist even more in agricultural work, notably during busy periods, as when vines were pruned or grapes harvested. However, unlike hired hands, they were generally unpaid. Tolley thus underlines the need for more research into the role of women in the wine business. This is further underscored by current tendencies in the South African wine industry, whereby black women are assuming increasingly important roles as shareholders and vintners.[36]

## WINE, ECONOMIC DEVELOPMENT, AND INDIGENOUS PEOPLES

Most chapters here allude to the role that wine has played in the economic development of certain regions and countries. Vicente Pinilla and María-Isabel Ayuda, taking Spain as a case study, compare and contrast the developmental potential of wine and fruit export industries in the period 1850 to 1935. This was a period that, except in the 1880s and after 1929, was characterized by rapid growth in the international economy when demand for foods and raw materials from the industrial and industrializing countries offered primary producing countries the potential for export-generated economic growth.[37] However, demand for wine in industrialized countries was restricted to elites who consumed high-priced rather than table wine. The middle and lower classes, who could not afford high-priced wines, continued to consume traditional, locally-produced alcoholic beverages such as beer. Wine consumption was thus primarily confined to domestic markets within the wine-producing countries of Southern Europe and South America where demand for cheap table wines—the traditional drink of the middle and lower classes—soared as a result of expanding urban populations, rising living standards, and the advent of cheap transport in the form of the railways (coupled, in South America, with significant immigration from Southern Europe). By contrast, consumption of imported fruit in the industrialized countries of the north increased, as a growth in per capita income was reflected in a more diverse diet, and notably an increased demand for imported fruit. However, the sharp increase in fruit imports needs to be set in a context wherein imports of Mediterranean fruits prior to 1850 were at negligible levels. Also, before 1945, consumption of imported fruit in industrialized countries was largely restricted to upper-income groups.

Rupert Tipples, in Chapter 13, traces the historical development of the wine industry in New Zealand and examines the contribution of vineyards in the South Island province of Canterbury, and notably those of Waipura, to the development of both the regional economy and the New Zealand wine industry since the 1970s.[38] Vineyards were first established around Canterbury by French settlers in the 1840s. However, they lacked the capital to develop commercial vineyards, and instead produced mainly for household consumption. Although domestic demand for wine grew steadily from 1945, the commercial development of the regional wine industry only took off from the late 1970s. This was the result of a combination of factors. First, beginning in 1973, Lincoln College—an agricultural college in Canterbury—started to invest in vine planting on the basis that the region's dry and relatively cool climate would be ideal for the production of a German-style white wine. Experiments eventually proved successful, and the region started producing increasing quantities of good quality white wine beginning in the 1980s. Since the 1990s, wine production, and its developmental impact, has been strengthened from by the growth of a regional wine tourism industry that has encouraged both foreign investment and a further expansion of vineyards.

In new angles on the relationship between wine production and economic growth, two contributions explore the significance of wine on development amongst indigenous peoples. Campbell examines the role in the South African wine industry of nonwhites who—discriminated against economically, politically, and socially—traditionally worked as cheap and landless labor for a white-owned wine industry. Indeed, cheap labor was a major cause for both the profitability of South African vineyards and their lack of investment in modern labor-saving techniques. The end of apartheid and the rise of globalization in the 1990s had a major impact on this traditional structure, forcing the South African wine industry at all levels to grant decent working conditions and pay to its labor force, invest in modern techniques, and give Black Africans, for the first time, access to ownership and management of vineyards.[39]

In Chapter 11, Robert Anderson, Dianne Wingham, Robert Giberson, and Brian Gibson analyze the adoption of wine making by a group of Maori in New Zealand, and the Osoyoos Aboriginal community in Canada, who created the world's first and second indigenous-owned wineries—the Tohu Winery in New Zealand and Nk'Mip Cellars in Canada.[40] In both instances, these communities worked through trusts that enabled them to create wine-related businesses as a key aspect of their economic development strategy. They have developed modern wine-producing techniques, and have established successful sales strategies through encouraging a local wine tourism industry, and marketing their wine as specialized labels in niche foreign markets. Moreover, these strategies have enabled them to both participate in the global market and safeguard their traditional culture and values. This defies the conventional "development" paradigm in which modernization comes at the expense of tradition and thus serves as an important prototype for development projects amongst indigenous peoples elsewhere.

## NOTES

1. BCE = "Before the Common Era," or "BC"; CE = "Common Era," or "AD."
2. Hugh Johnson, *Story of Wine* (London: Mitchell Beazley, 1989), 14–23; "First Wine? Archaeologist Traces Drink to Stone Age," http://news.nationalgeographic.com/news/2004/07/0721_040721 _ancientwine_2.html.
3. "First Wine?"
4. Jack Goody, "Slavery in Time and Space" in *Asian and African Systems of Slavery*, ed. James L. Watson (Berkeley and Los Angeles: University of California Press, 1980), 18–19.

5. Dominique Bottani, *Le Guide des pays du Ventoux* (Lyons: La Manufacture, 1995), 72; Jancis Robinson, *Encyclopédie du vin* (Paris: Hachette, 1997), 434–35.

6. Guy Bertucchi, *Les Amphores et le vin de Marseille, VIes. avant J.-C.-IIes. après J.-C.* (Paris: CNRS, 1992), 21, 184; Robinson, *Encyclopédie du vin*, 434–35; Johnson, *Story of Wine*, 35–97.

7. Bottani, *Guide des pays du Ventoux*, 72; Robinson, *Encyclopédie du vin*, 434–35.

8. Robinson, *Encyclopédie du vin*, 435–36.

9. Ibid., 435–36.

10. Ibid., 269.

11. Darrell Delamaide, *The New Superregions of Europe* (New York: Plume, 1995), 139.

12. Jan de Vries, *The Economy of Europe in an Age of Crisis, 1600–1750* (Cambridge: Cambridge University Press, 1982), 108.

13. Delamaide, *New Superregions of Europe*, 138.

14. Robinson, *Encyclopédie du vin*, 436.

15. Ibid., 437.

16. Bottani, *Guide des pays du Ventoux*, 75.

17. Hubrecht Duijker, *Touring in Wine Country: The Rhone* (London: Mitchell Beazley, 1998), 114; Bottani, *Guide des pays du Ventoux*, 75.

18. Gwyn Campbell, "Domestic Demand and Export Imperatives for French and Australian Wines: A Historical Overview," in this volume.

19. Marie-Annick Carré, "Consommation de vin" in *Réussir Vigne* 67 (mai 2000), 2.

20. Rod Phillips, *A Short History of Wine* (London: Allen Lane, 2000), 152–59; Robinson, *Encyclopédie du vin*, 399.

21. Phillips, *Short History of Wine*, 173–75.

22. Johnson, *Story of Wine*, 342–47; Phillips, *Short History of Wine*, 267.

23. Gwyn Campbell and Nathalie Guibert, ed., "The Impact of Globalisation on the Wine Industry." Special issue, *British Food Journal* 108, no. 4 (2006).

24. Kathleen A. Brosnan, "'Vin d'Etat': Consumers, Land and the State in California's Napa Valley," in this volume.

25. Robert C. Ulin, "Writing about Wine: The Uses of Nature and History in the Wine Growing of Southwest France and America," in this volume.

26. Steve Stein, "Grape Wars: The Conflict between Quantity and Quality in the History of Argentine Wine," in this volume.

27. Linda Bramble, Carman Cullen, Joseph Kushner, and Gary Pickering, "The Development of the Wine Industry in the Province of Ontario, Canada," in this volume.

28. Marianne Ackerman, "Au rebours: Quebec's Emerging Indigenous Wine Industry," in this volume.

29. Gwyn Campbell, "Black Labour in the South African Wine Industry," in this volume.
30. Bertucchi, *Amphores*, 13, 53, 196–97.
31. Patric Choffrut, "Of Wine, Jews, and Provence," in this volume.
32. Brosnan, "'Vin d'Etat.'"
33. Bertucchi, *Amphores*, 200–201.
34. One of the most notable wine writers being Jancis Robinson; for a list of publications, see Jancis Robinson, "Fine Writing on Fine Wines," http://www.jancisrobinson.com/articles/books.
35. Julie Holbrook Tolley, "Women in the South Australian Wine Industry, 1836–2003," in this volume.
36. Campbell, "Black Labour."
37. Vicente Pinilla and María-Isabel Ayuda, "Market Dynamism and International Trade: Wine versus Fruit Exports and the Economic Development of Spain, 1850–1935," in this volume.
38. Rupert Tipples, "Wines of the Farthest Promised Land from Waipara, Canterbury, New Zealand," in this volume.
39. Campbell, "Black Labour."
40. Robert B. Anderson, Dianne W. Wingham, Robert J. Giberson, and Brian Gibson, "Indigenous Economic Development: A Tale of Two Wineries," in this volume.

# CHAPTER 2

## "VIN D'ETAT"

### CONSUMERS, LAND, AND THE STATE IN CALIFORNIA'S NAPA VALLEY

*Kathleen A. Brosnan*

A sommelier from a fine Chicago restaurant conducted introductory tastings at a local museum, always including good but reasonably priced wines in an effort to lure novices. Nonetheless, a few wine snobs still attended. One such oenophile raised his hand with a supposed query, but seemed more intent on revealing his sophisticated palate and wealthy wallet. He imperiously mentioned that he had purchased a case of "Chateau Something, 1985" and he wondered how long it should age. The sommelier gently chided him, suggesting that the trip from the store had done the trick. This anecdote is not intended to open a debate on the age of wines, but rather to reveal the stock that consumers place in the names of the wines they drink. There was something significant in the gentleman's conceit. "What's in a name?" When it comes to wine, "name" is everything, and the modern state dictates what appellation a wine bears.

## INTRODUCTION

The Napa Valley appellation has stood as a badge of craftsmanship to global consumers and offered a bond with a particular place. Napa County sits above San Francisco Bay, an hour north of the city. The

Mayacamas Mountains divide the county from the Pacific Ocean and Sonoma County to the west; the Vaca Mountains form the eastern border. Wedged between these mountains, carved prehistorically by the Napa River, and blessed with a temperate climate, bountiful sunshine, and cool evening breezes, the Napa Valley has long been a center of agriculture. The small valley begins at the foot of Mount St. Helena and moves thirty miles southwestward toward the marshy delta of the bay. Only one mile across at its northern end, the valley is just five miles at its widest. Such physical dimensions limited the amount of wine produced, and over time, led local vintners to emphasize the quality of wine.[1]

The Napa Valley appellation that captures this quality also reflects the power of the nation-state. As with other countries, a U.S. government agency approved the geographic designations for the Napa Valley and other winemaking regions. The government's imprimatur, however, extends beyond the state's encapsulation of the physicality of production. All economic activity, including the production of wine, generates both material goods and symbolic meanings. Commodities carry a price in the marketplace, but their producers and consumers also invest noneconomic values in them that vary from culture to culture and over time. Wine, for example, has had ceremonial significance in both Christianity and Judaism. At other times, poets evoked wine's romantic allure. Euripides suggested, "Where there is no wine, there is no love."[2]

Napa Valley vintners, as is explained in this article, have proven very effective in linking their vintages and the valley itself to the more positive cultural meanings associated with wine, and in many ways, the Napa Valley appellation now stands as the government's recognition of these values. This was not always the case. In the late nineteenth and early twentieth centuries, many Americans, particularly nativists involved in the temperance movement, had viewed wine with disdain because immigrants often preferred wine and because the fortified wines that dominated sales were high in alcohol. After the Repeal of Prohibition and World War II, however, fine dry wines emerged as status symbols. A core aesthetic of American capitalist culture, William Leach argues, offered a vision of the good life in which economic success provided access to cultural and social amenities, and material purchases brought consumers a sense of self-worth and their neighbors' recognition of their accomplishments.[3] Although the Napa Valley's share of the global wine market remained small, it emerged as the United States' premium leader in the postwar era and successfully sold the valley and its wines.

Like other entrepreneurs in the American West, Napa Valley vintners like to present themselves as a "collection of self-reliant individuals and local or occupational communities, tied together by a competitive market."[4] In truth, however, the industry, the consumer, and the state have all interacted to create Napa Valley's success and to contest the changing meanings of its wine over time. This essay examines the central role of the government, at both the national and local levels, in the history of the Napa Valley wine industry. Efforts to shape and control wine consumption—the late nineteenth-century California viticultural commission, federal Prohibition, the 1968 designation of the Napa Valley as an agricultural preserve, and the federal appellation system in the 1980s—also reveal the evolution and expansion of public authority in the United States. The United States adopted a less structured approach to viticulture than other countries, but given the enhanced capacities of the modern state, even this approach profoundly influenced change in Napa Valley vineyards.

James Scott contends that nation-states became modern when they attempted to reorganize disparate local activities, such as land tenure systems or viticultural customs, so as to make them more susceptible to government oversight and arguably more valuable in the marketplace. Across the globe, modern states enhanced their capacities beyond traditional powers of taxation and conscription. Governments regulated almost every aspect of life and applied schemes designed to rationalize the natural world. In doing so, states reshaped reality.[5] While this public authority has been shared with local governments within the federal system of the United States, it remained a transformative force. The most visible remnant of the U.S. government's efforts is the checkerboard pattern of the nation's landscape; the state imposed an artificial grid on the land to facilitate the distribution of the public domain. In a more pertinent example, the United States' appellation system has affected production options by limiting those areas from which grapes can be used in making wine, and by dictating the percentage of grapes necessary for varietal labeling. After World War II, historian Lizabeth Cohen argues, the American state pursued new activities designed to make its society a model for the world. According to policymakers, citizens lived in "a consumers' republic" committed to mass consumption and its supposed benefits: greater prosperity, egalitarianism, and political freedom. The state conflated citizen and consumer, and enforced policies designed to protect the rights of both.[6] The United States' appellation system is but one such policy: the government wanted to insure that bottle labels did not mislead consumers about the origin or content of the wines they drank.

Recognized by most critics and oenophiles as leaders in premium wine production in the United States, Napans eagerly embraced the federal appellation system. Napans had emerged as viticultural leaders in the late nineteenth century. In the mid-1800s, however, Napa County had trailed other California regions in wine production. California's first commercial wine ventures developed near Los Angeles in the 1830s. In the late 1840s and 1850s, when gold rush Argonauts overwhelmed the productive capacity of domestic winemakers, foreign imports flooded San Francisco. Attempting to secure a larger share of this trade, Californians turned over more land to grapes while looking overseas for better vines. Napa County was a late entrant in this trade. Non-Indians first settled in the valley in the 1830s and planted grapes mostly for domestic consumption, filling only four hundred acres by 1860. Wheat, cattle, and quicksilver mines were more ubiquitous and more profitable. The first commercial shipment from Napa in 1857 contained just six casks and six hundred bottles. In 1860, Los Angeles County held ten times as many vines as Napa County.[7]

Over the next twenty years, Napa County's viticultural landscape changed. Wine acreage increased nine-fold. The county soon possessed fifty-four wineries, including stone structures still visible today. More significantly, German-born men such as Charles Krug, Jacob Schram, and Jacob and Frederick Beringer; American George Belden Crane; and Frenchman Charles Carpy borrowed *Vitis vinifera* cuttings from nearby Sonoma and Santa Clara counties, and began to nurture European-style wines. A minority of such northern California's vintners had committed to the manufacture of fine wines, but faced difficulties in challenging national consumption patterns and global perceptions. First, there was a growing temperance movement at home. Those Americans who did imbibe were seventeen times more likely to drink beer. Consumers who drank wine rarely viewed California positively, if they thought of it at all. A lengthy 1862 treatise on wine-producing countries dedicated only one page to U.S. wines and made no mention of California.[8] In the

1870s, California's wine industry had experienced new growth. Shipments doubled to the East Coast to make up for the shortfall in more expensive imported wines caused by a national depression and decreased incomes, and by the *Phylloxera* that decimated French vineyards. Nonetheless, the reputation of California wines continued to suffer. Most of the state's vineyards contained Mission grapes, including many of the 3,600 acres in the Napa Valley in 1878. First carried to California by Franciscans in the 1700s and known for its musky flavors and aromas, the Mission grape was best suited for fortified dessert wines. Many wine producers also employed poor fermentation methods that further undermined quality. San Francisco wine merchants did little to promote the better vintages from Napa and the other northern counties.[9] Despite such setbacks, Napa Valley's renown spread gradually as its best vintners dedicated land to *V. vinifera*.

## The Board of State Viticultural Commissioners

In 1880, Napans stood on the precipice of a new era, just as the industry experienced its first significant public intervention. The California legislature passed "An Act for the Promotion of the Viticultural Industries," divided the state into seven wine districts, and appointed a representative of each district to a Board of State Viticultural Commissioners (BSVC). The legislature also ordered the University of California to provide instruction in viticulture. Reflecting general tenets of Progressivism, this law relied upon the expertise of industry participants and university officials to promote a vital economic activity. It assumed that commissioners, who served without compensation, worked for the greater good while simultaneously promoting their self-interests.[10] At the same time, American public authority in 1880 remained more limited and more decentralized than its European counterparts. The underfunded BSVC lacked the power to enforce policies for alcohol content, labeling, or quarantines.

Instead, the BSVC primarily focused on marketing and consumer habits, recognizing that despite improvements, Americans seemed hostile to domestic wines. The BSVC reported, "The County of Napa produces as much wine, and good wine too, as is imported into the United States from France."[11] Yet American restaurateurs and wine purveyors often replaced California labels with foreign ones. The BSVC partially attributed this problem to many growers' continued use of Mission grapes which "retard the popularity of this industry by producing wines unfit generally for anything except dessert use."[12] The agency tried to convince all growers to replant with *V. vinifera*, while simultaneously educating Americans about the benefits of wine in general and oenophiles about fine California wines in particular.[13] International expositions provided one showcase. The BSVC sent an exhibit to the New Orleans World's Fair in 1885 with pamphlets that discussed wine as part of a civilized cuisine and denigrated religious prohibitionists. The next year, the Napa County display for the North, Central and South American Exposition boasted, "The great product of this county, and almost the only increasing one, is wine and brandy."[14]

On other fronts, Eugene Hilgard of the University of California introduced better fermentation techniques and grape varieties that were adopted by Napa winemakers committed to quality vintages. For example, Gustave Niebaum, who made his fortune in San Francisco shipping and Alaskan furs, retired to life as a gentleman farmer in 1879. Zealous in his avocation, he offered reliable estate-bottled wines with a Napa Valley label. Another, H. W. Crabb, sold a national brand named "To Kalon" for his Napa Valley vineyard. At the 1889 Paris Exposition, Niebaum and Crabb received two of valley's eleven medals, and Napa County took almost half of the prizes awarded to U.S. wines.[15]

The BSVC's creation coincided with an unprecedented expansion of vineyards in Napa County. Wheat farms yielded to grapes. By 1890, vineyard acres reached eighteen thousand, and vintners produced 4,225,000 gallons, topping Napa County's nearest California competitor by more than 25 percent. A year earlier, William Bourn and his partners built Greystone, the world's largest winery, and took in grapes from Napa and nearby counties. The Viticultural Café featured Napa Valley wines. Established by the BSVC in the late 1880s, this café allowed San Francisco's residents and visitors to taste domestic wines, and in the board president's opinion, compelled local hotels, restaurants, and grocers to include those brands. The BSVC hoped to launch similar operations in Chicago and New York, but in the interim, sent Kate Field, a well-known lecturer, around the nation to stimulate demand and assuage temperance activists.[16]

These efforts to alter consumer behavior, however, fell short. Wine consumption declined in the 1890s, partly due to the nationwide depression. California's fine vintages continued to trail in worldwide perceptions. The BSVC complained that its wines were shunted into a cramped, undesirable location at the 1893 World's Columbian Exposition in Chicago in favor of European displays. Concessionaires there sold foreign wines and precluded Californians from even offering tastings. Exposition guides described continental wines in detail, but barely mentioned domestic ones.[17]

The BSVC's inability to alter consumption mirrored its overall ineffectiveness, as the *Phylloxera* crisis reveals. The BSVC hoped to halt in California the spread of the pest that had devastated European vineyards. Instead, the BSVC and Napa vintners created environmental conditions that contributed to the BSVC's demise and the vintners near ruination. Native to the Mississippi River Valley, *Phylloxera* traveled to France in the 1850s, and later arrived in California with *V. vinifera* cuttings from Europe. Hilgard found *Phylloxera* in the northern counties by the late 1860s. Drier summers had thwarted development of the winged form in California, and thus the louse moved more slowly than it had in Europe. The sluggish pace perhaps lulled the BSVC and local growers into complacency. The BSVC recommended inadequate cures, such as planting in sand or using bisulphide of carbon and potash. In the early 1880s, the BSVC's special *Phylloxera* committee noted, "There is no immediate danger of destruction of any vineyards not now seriously diseased."[18] Misreading experiments with *V. californica*, Hilgard and the BSVC insisted this native vine was resistant, despite French findings to the contrary.[19] They were wrong.

Napans extended questionable rootstocks and allowed *Phylloxera* to eventually thrive. The Napa District commissioner reported, "the full extent of the ravages during the past two years in the counties of Napa and Sonoma can scarcely be appreciated by those not familiar with the situation. Thousands of acres have been affected."[20] Indeed, by 1895, approximately 5,500 acres held bearing vines in Napa County, less than a third of those present five years earlier. By 1900, there were only 2,000 acres. Large and small wineries closed. Bourne had sold Greystone only three years after it opened. Even with lagging confidence in *V. californica*, Napans were uncertain about its replacement as the BSVC offered conflicting reports about different rootstocks. Not until the early 1900s did local vintners acknowledge successful French experiments with *V. rupestris* "St. George" and begin widespread replanting.[21]

In 1894, the legislature disbanded the BSVC because it had failed to change consumption patterns and had perhaps exacerbated the ongoing *Phylloxera* crisis. At the same time, the BSVC had offered no solutions for "Anaheim disease," although a solution for what is known today as Pierce's Disease still eludes growers. Caused by bacteria carried by a "grapevine hopper," this epidemic had obliterated thirty-five thousand acres in southern California.[22] In the late nineteenth and early twentieth centuries, state authority was growing, but was inconsistently applied. The nation-state created the land grant institution to aid agriculture, but Hilgard complained that university laboratories needed more money. Alternatively, the BSVC had no authority to enforce quarantines that might have thwarted or at least delayed *Phylloxera*, and it had limited funds for its promotional efforts. The BSVC initially called for an experimental vineyard; however, the legislature did not sponsor one until 1893—at Oakville in the Napa Valley—when the crises were beyond control.[23]

By 1920, Americans had become more accustomed to broad exercises of public authority, as the next state intervention in alcohol usage—Prohibition—revealed. In the first two decades of the twentieth century, Napa wine had enjoyed a gradual recovery after the *Phylloxera* crisis. In an extension of state power, the U.S. Department of Agriculture began to run the Oakville experimental vineyard. Local vintages, particularly those of noted vignerons such as Georges de Latour of Beaulieu Vineyards, revived the valley's reputation for dry wines. *Phylloxera* had eliminated many Mission grapes from the valley; by 1910, replantings filled sixteen thousand acres with *V. rupestris* "St. George" rootstocks and better grapes. Despite complaints about the low prices of the California Wine Association (CWA), local grape growers worked with this "wine trust." Created in the 1890s by vintners, merchants, and distributors that included prominent Napans such as Charles Carpy, the CWA dominated northern California production, and among other properties, controlled Greystone. Most replanting in Napa occurred in the upper valley near St. Helena. Orchards, fodder crops, dairy farms, and pasturage dominated the lower valley, while grapes disappeared from the Carneros region that straddles southern Napa and Sonoma counties just above the bay. San Francisco's Panama Pacific International Exposition gave Napa winemakers a last moment of glory in 1915.

Their display celebrated wine consumption as part of civilized society and family tradition, but a rising tide of temperance revealed that few Americans distinguished between wine and hard liquor. Anticipating greater federal restrictions, growers changed planting patterns again. By 1920, vineyard acres declined and the county's prune production outpaced grape cultivation.

## Prohibition and its Aftermath

In the late nineteenth and early twentieth centuries, some Progressives had tried to bring professionalism and expertise to bureaucracy with partnerships between government and businesses such as the BSVC. Other reformers pursued policies designed to mend society's ills, and frequently blamed individual alcohol abuse rather than the social constructions of industrial capitalism for those ills. Temperance gained support as alcohol use increased. Americans drank more beer and distilled spirits, but high-alcohol dessert wines were perceived as part of the problem with alcohol abuse. Prohibitionists rejected the idea of wine as part of a civilized cuisine. The United States' entry into World War I had allowed them to link abstinence and patriotism. Wine and beer received a two-year exemption to a wartime prohibition on using foodstuffs in alcohol production, but the future looked dim for Napa Valley's wine industry. In addition, in a xenophobic era, its large immigrant population, drawn heavily from Germany and Italy, did not enhance its image when vintners fought temperance.[24]

When the necessary number of states had ratified the Eighteenth Amendment to the U.S. Constitution in January 1919, beer and wine were among the banned items. Prohibition represented a "desire to restore an (imagined) American past,"[25] uncorrupted by industrialization, urbanization, and the ethnic immigration they seemingly spawned. A modern state acts autonomously, but is influenced by civil society. Here, state action reflected a minority religious view that took hold because U.S. state structures have been embedded in a constitutional system. The nation did not inherit a centralized preindustrial bureaucracy; Americans traditionally gave greater legitimacy to law and the Constitution.[26] As the state exercised more power, its actions invariably reordered relations between public authority and civil society, and between this society and its physical world. Prohibition had unintended consequences for society's consumption of alcohol and for the use of Napa's resources.

Under the Volstead Act that provided the terms for Prohibition's enforcement, most Napa wineries closed their doors.[27] Growers, however, discovered a twist. Shipping representatives from Chicago, New York, and other cities with large ethnic populations flooded the valley, demanding future shipments. A loophole in the law allowed families to make two hundred gallons of wine a year. Local growers could ship grapes for large profits in this home production market. The law also permitted wineries making sacramental wine and "medicinal" tonics to remain open. In the Napa Valley, for example, de Latour maintained Beaulieu's ties with the Catholic Church. High production figures at these wineries suggested widespread religious conversions, new health crises, or a more likely legal sidestepping with little fear of retribution. A local winery worker noted, "The churches don't use too much of that wine. Seventy-five tons could furnish all the churches in the United States. They found it leaked out somewhere. I don't know of any of the [open] wineries that didn't bootleg."[28] Diversified agriculture persisted, but many Napa Valley farmers responded to the new demand for grapes. Vineyard acreage increased more than 30 percent during the first five years of Prohibition. With the permission of revenue agents, de Latour planted new varietals every year. Beringers maintained its better vines by producing wine under bond to Beaulieu.[29] Most growers, however, turned vineyards over to thick-skinned varieties, such as the Alicante Bouschet or Green Hungarian, which traveled well, but were poorly suited to quality products. With the exception of Beaulieu, white wine grapes almost disappeared from the valley. Consumers preferred grapes with a heavy color and farmers chose those with high yields. At the time white grapes sold for about $10 a ton, and red grapes, especially Alicante, sold for $130, $140, or $150 a ton. Grape prices remained high for five years, and by then, more than 40 percent of the Napa Valley vineyards held Alicante, although some Zinfandel, Petite Sirah, and Carignane remained.[30] The bottom fell out again when supply outstripped demand. Some growers had anticipated these trends and returned to a more reliable crop—prunes.[31]

In the end, banning alcohol only whetted American appetites for it. Franklin Roosevelt made the Repeal of Prohibition central to his 1932 election, and a little more than a year later, it ended. Repeal revealed the full damage of the state's intervention. The Volstead Act lasted thirteen years; its effects were felt for decades. Napans reopened wineries in the waning months of 1933, but, with few exceptions, facilities had been stripped of most equipment. What remained was rusty, warped, or broken. Lacking experience, new industry entrants made wine under unsanitary conditions and stored it in infected cooperage. Most Napa Valley vineyards produced low-quality grapes that now contributed to California's surplus of young, poorly structured sweet wines. Given the excessive and substandard production, many new wineries closed by 1938. Leading local vintners released well-aged Cabernets, but these limited vintages suffered by association with the poorer products.[32] Prohibition also had affected consumer tastes. With Repeal, oenophiles who preferred fine dry wines again turned to Europe, while other Americans had learned to enjoy homemade wines with weak vinosity and coarse sweetness. As a San Francisco wine purveyor observed, "The people of America must be re-educated to an appreciation of fine wines."[33]

Some Napans prepared to improve local wine, spread the valley's reputation, and change consumer habits. In 1943, seven wineries—still privately owned and primarily family ventures—formed the Napa Valley Vintners Association (NVVA). They returned to the idea that quality must define their market niche, although bulk production was still essential to their financial survival. Linking symbolism and materiality, the NVVA erected signs promoting "bottled poetry," a description coined by Robert Louis Stevenson during a nineteenth-century visit. NVVA hoped to educate sophisticated customers in the finer aspects of wine, and in the 1950s hosted San Francisco conventioneers, such as the American Medical Association and the Western Conference of Bankers, who could regularly afford wine. Wineries wooed travel writers, created newsletters, and sent agents across the country offering blind tastings with comparable European products.[34]

In another partnership between the state and industry, Napa winemakers adopted ideas from viticulturists and enologists at the University of California–Davis regarding microclimates, grape varieties, cold fermentation, and stainless steel equipment.[35] With Repeal, the university eagerly returned to research on wine in support of the industry. A land-grant institution created under the provisions of the federal Morrill Act of 1862, the university proved one of the most significant agents of the state's intervention in agriculture.

Under the Morrill Act, the federal government granted the individual states large tracts of land to be sold for the support of institutions teaching mechanical and agricultural arts. The government hoped to nurture scientifically trained graduates who would productively harness the nation's natural resources. These agricultural modernists at the university worked within an associational state, based on cooperative planning between public actors and private economic groups rather than a rigid top-down state structure.[36]

The university's influence grew as Americans entered an unprecedented era of affluence. A rising demand for table wines in the 1950s and 1960s matched the expansion and greater wealth of the middle class. Traveling abroad, Americans discovered wine as a courtly aspect of daily life. The technical improvements and microclimatic cultivation that the university and industry jointly promoted had insured that tasty, stable wines were regularly available. In 1967, U.S. table wine sales exceeded dessert wine sales for the first time.[37] Nine years later, to observers' surprise, judges selected two Napa Valley vintages over French wines at a blind competition in Paris. Napa Valley did not replace France atop the global hierarchy, but the results suggested Napa's best products merited inclusion with the world's finest and solidified the valley's domestic leadership. A county supervisor noted, "We represent the only county in the United States which has within its boundaries an internationally recognized wine industry."[38]

## THE AGRICULTURAL PRESERVE

In the three decades following Repeal, while vintners had regained their competitive position, Napa County had remained home to diversified agriculture. Hillsides and the lower valley offered pasturage and fodder crops. Combined acres in prunes, walnuts, and pears exceeded those of grapes until the 1960s. Beef generated more gross receipts than grapes. In 1971, for the first time, grapes accounted for more than half of the county's agricultural output, and, in turn, land in vineyards reach a then high of 22,000 acres.[39] As the wine industry began to boom in the 1960s, however, a new threat loomed on the horizon. A trend toward greater urbanization had led to the loss of agricultural land across California. The problem was particularly acute in the San Francisco area where dramatic scenery, mild climates, and cultural amenities tempted suburban developers and dwellers. For example, forty miles south of San Francisco, the Santa Clara Valley once produced good wines and a third of the world's prunes. By the 1960s, tract houses and strip malls filled the region that became known as Silicon Valley, a moniker that captured all the perceived wrongs of rapid urbanization. Examining trends in 1966, Napa County planners anticipated similar growth and estimated the county's population would be 223 percent larger by the year 2000.[40] Such growth would choke the viticulture and rurality that many Napans championed.

Concern about the loss of agricultural lands prompted the California Land Conservation Act (1965), under which counties taxed farms at lower rates to offset the high prices offered by urban developers. Since farmers' participation was voluntary, many Napans found the law inadequate. The Napa County Planning Commission recommended regulations to create an "agricultural preserve" that would increase minimal zoning to twenty acres for building in unincorporated areas on the valley floor. Most vintners believed the preserve would halt a checkerboard pattern of sales that would be followed by total suburbanization. Other farmers were more willing to sell and joined developers and a few vineyard owners in opposition. In 1968, county supervisors unanimously agreed to create the preserve. They later incorporated adjacent hills into a second preserve.[41] This new government intrusion, albeit at a local level, revealed the growth of public authority in the United States. The county protected the wine industry and thwarted a competitive urban land market by restricting residents' private property rights. Napans, including those who were not in the industry but were concerned with conservation, readily acceded to this power.

As intended, the preserve stalled urban sprawl and population growth. With the new popularity of table wines and Napa's growing renown, the preserve gradually contributed to land scarcity on the valley floor. Even allowing for inflation, it helped boost property values substantially.[42] The preserve also sanctified winemaking at the cost of agricultural diversity. Grapes pushed the last fruit trees, cattle, and dairy cows beyond county borders. In 1966, after leaving his family at the Charles Krug Winery, Robert Mondavi had opened the first major Napa Valley operation since Repeal. At that time, there were seven privately held or family-owned facilities, one corporate operation (United Vintners bought Inglenook in 1964), and two cooperative wineries. With growing consumer interest in fine wine, many others soon followed Mondavi. The Napa name came to hold a certain cachet, and many hoped to capture its commensurately high prices. By 1980, another thirty-six wineries, both large and small, had entered Napa.[43]

## American Viticultural Areas

Mondavi and others had improved their wines and their market position through learning from their own experiences, incorporating the university's recommendations, and imitating certain European techniques, such as aging wine in small barrels. Borrowing from Europe again, they wanted their place—the Napa Valley—to be recognized by the nation-state, and consequently the world, as a distinctive viticultural region. The United States then lacked a regulatory scheme that distinguished premium wines or prohibited others from exploiting Napa's success through deceptive labels. In the mid-1970s, the Bureau of Alcohol, Tobacco, and Firearms (BATF) contemplated changes both to protect purchasers and to influence American and international consumers into accepting U.S. products as equal to European ones. The BATF first suggested each individual state establish physical boundaries for wine districts. Napa's vintners opposed this proposal, and instead sought continuing federal authority. The presidents of the NVVA and the Napa Valley Grape Growers Association testified that the BATF should retain control of wine labeling, arguing that the agency possessed the most knowledge and the greatest public authority to ensure that labels were uniform, honest, and legible. Implicit in their testimony was the idea that bulk growers from other areas could influence inadequately prepared state agencies to create viticultural districts with little meaning that would, in turn, dilute the importance of the Napa Valley appellation. Capturing the flavor of the debate, critic Nathan Chroman wrote, "If I were a California wine grape, I would love to call the Napa Valley my home . . . After all, aren't there plenty of cool breezes in the evening, sunshine during the day and nice people to tend to my every need? Throw in instant recognition and acclaim when I'm made into wine and life is truly beautiful."[44] Soon thereafter, the BATF amended its proposed regulations to maintain its jurisdiction. This new U.S. appellation system defined production boundaries and was not intended to convey statements of quality.[45] Nonetheless, in requesting federal jurisdiction, Napans recognized that the nation-state's imprimatur imposed material and symbolic value. A federal system implied uniform standards and reinforced a presumed hierarchy of domestic wine producers, even if this was not the stated purpose.

Napa winemakers sought another regulatory innovation to enhance their market position. By 1979, the *Wine Spectator* observed, "The Napa Valley is the spiritual center of winegrowing in America. It is the first place that people think of when talk about wine in America."[46] Proposed regulations initially called only for the continued use of geopolitical borders as functional appellations, such as "Napa County" or "Sonoma County." Again mimicking the French, Napans wanted other districts that reflected viticultural uniqueness within the valley, or what people perhaps now call *terroir*.[47] The BATF acceded. In addition to wines defined by political boundaries, the final regulations required that a minimum of 75 percent of grapes used in a wine must be grown in the region to earn an appellation of origin.[48] Grape growers from the valley floor and adjacent hills soon petitioned to establish "Napa Valley" as a federally approved American Viticultural Area (AVA), supposedly defined by the Napa River watershed. The petition caused controversy at the 1980 hearings because growers in eastern Napa County did not fall within the watershed.[49] The BATF had to decide whether to strictly define the "valley" and exclude 2,000 acres of county vineyards. Recognizing their dependence on those vines outside the watershed, vintners testified that the eastern portions should be included because they produced grapes with similar traits and had been used historically in valley wines. More significantly, the exclusion of those areas from the appellation would decrease the supply of qualified grapes and limit production. In 1981, the BATF approved the broader designation, concluding, as historian James Lapsely observes, that the idea of Napa Valley superceded the reality of the watershed.[50]

Quickly finding this Napa Valley appellation too broad to express the distinct microclimates and terrains that imprinted identifiable characteristics on their grapes, some Napa growers and vintners petitioned the BATF for recognition of sub-appellations.[51] The petition submitted to establish the viticultural district of Stags Leap as the third sub-appellation within the Napa Valley appellation reveals other federal agencies central to identifying AVAs. Stags Leap was the first AVA to be defined based on its natural conditions. The applicants for the proposed district of only 1,100 acres of vineyard land emphasized that it was set apart climatically from "the main Napa Valley floor because its unique configuration and orientation favor an inflow of cool air from San Pablo Bay during the growing season." Geologically, Stags Leap is characterized by igneous soils, particularly bale loam. While the designation of the AVA did not impose strict restrictions on the choice of grape varieties (the U.S. system remains less dictatorial than its European counterparts), the applicants emphasized the particular success enjoyed by Cabernet Sauvignon in the subregion.[52] A Cabernet from Stags Leap was one of the two winning Napa wines in Paris in 1976.

The Stags Leap Appellation Committee relied on federal agencies not immediately associated with viticulture for evidence to support the petition. The U.S. Geological Service (USGS) proved essential. Congress had created the USGS in 1879 in what Henry Adams called America's "first modern act of legislation" because it was based on the use of scientific data and encouraged economic enterprise. Congress gave the USGS the task of mapping public lands and classifying their geological structures and mineral resources. Its earliest directors believed that this state institution had to protect the national domain for the general welfare, but the agency's surveys have often fostered private, often inequitable development of the nation's resources. The USGS applied scientific methods to create cadastral maps that abstracted the earth into grids and provided the state with greater legibility of the landscape. Such maps, James Scott contends, facilitated boundary definitions, taxation, and commodification of the land.[53] The maps also helped winegrowers seeking AVA recognition. First, they provided a shorthand that permitted the quick identification and universal acceptance of district boundaries. Second, USGS surveys provided detailed information on rock formations and soil types. Stags Leap winegrowers used the A. H. Laude's Field Report on the Yountville Quadrangle in their application and drew on a 1978 report of the USGS Soil Conservation Service that disclosed different soil types in the proposed district. Finally, data from the U.S. Weather Service supported claims about unique weather patterns.[54]

The 1994 application for the St. Helena AVA, the tenth subappellation within Napa Valley, reveals the presence of the associational state. Deborah Elliott-Fisk, a viticultural geographer at the University of California–Davis, provided the "evidence relating the geographical features (climate, soil, elevation, physical features, etc.) that distinguish the viticultural features of the proposed area from surrounding areas," as required under federal regulations. Elliott-Fisk, who had worked on two other subappellation applications, drew on her research and that of other scholars to define the district's uniqueness: "The proposed St. Helena viticultural area . . . is marked by a uniform, steep gradient and significant river erosion. The bedrock geology is primarily volcanic, in contrast to the sedimentary soils to the south."[55] This research frequently utilized the reports of federal agencies. The state, through the BATF and in reliance on the expertise of these other state agents, sanctioned the new AVA.

## Expansion and its Consequences

Two government interventions—the agricultural preserve and the appellation system—had enhanced the value of Napa's fine wines. Eager to exploit these commodities, more newcomers entered the industry. By 1988, there were 164 wineries in the county. Twelve years later, almost 300 crowded the small valley and its hillsides.[56] The state, in association with the industry, had bolstered wine trade, but success came with environmental costs. By the year 2000, wine grapes accounted for almost 99 percent of the county's gross agricultural production. Nearly forty thousand county acres held grapes, more land than had been utilized in previous years with mixed agriculture. With little land available within the two preserves, new vignerons had turned to the higher hills that fell within expansive BATF borders for Napa Valley. For those eager to produce the "cult" vintages that reaped high prices and greater prestige, some research suggested that the quality of wine produced on these steep hills was superior. Deforestation often followed. In the 1970s, Napa County placed a moratorium on timber sales, hoping to slow growth. It did not. With great profits to be earned in grapes, newcomers simply burned timber they could not sell.[57]

Hillside operations grew larger in scope and reached more precipitous slopes. Expansion has been associated with problems within the watershed. In 1980, for example, heavy rains on a newly deforested hillside drove an avalanche of silt to the valley floor, wiping out other vineyards and blocking the main traffic artery. During an

October 1989 storm, sediment from a thirty-acre vineyard tumbled into the Bell Canyon reservoir, turning the drinking water red for the town of St. Helena. In 1987, the California Water Quality Board identified the Napa River as an "impaired" body with high sediment, nutrient, and pathogen levels.[58] Sediment and agricultural waste filled gravel beds, smothered fish eggs, and changed water temperature, visibility, and oxygen content. Diversions and road crossings, made necessary by the expansion of viticulture and tourism, hampered migration of steelhead trout, an endangered species. Napa avoided urban sprawl, but the explosion of vineyards put the valley at risk for a loss of biodiversity. The California Native Plant Society estimated that some 400 of 1,100 species indigenous to Napa County were threatened or endangered, including the Salt-marsh Harvest Mouse, the Northern Spotted Owl, and the California Red-legged Frog. Clearcutting threatened oak woodlands. Remaining trees competed with grapes for soil moisture. Oak regeneration became more difficult because fire suppression methods protected hillside vineyards that mingled with forests. [59]

The dedication of more acres to grapes generated huge profits, but also contributed to infestations. *Phylloxera* returned in the late 1980s and forced growers to replant more than 50 percent of the valley when they discovered that the AxR-1 rootstock was not resistant. Again, the state is visible. The university had heavily promoted this rootstock because of its adaptability to a variety of environmental conditions. In the regular expression of their authority, the county agricultural commissioner and University of California Cooperative Extension also staked out the valley to halt other pests. In lower and middle valley vineyards, for example, Napans had found the grape leaf skeletonizer, previously unknown to Napa. The glassy-winged sharpshooter, the vector for Pierce's Disease, remained an ongoing concern.[60] Monocultural production systems effectively "set the table" for pests to do what came naturally. Infestations and other environmental concerns prompted the mid-1990s creation of the Napa Sustainable Winegrowing Group (NSWG) by growers, vintners, and public officials interested in the Cooperative Extension's integrated pest management programs and protection of the watershed.[61] NSWG members, however, constituted a minority of Napa landowners. For some landowners, compliance with environmental regulations was at best an expensive inconvenience that could be turned into a commercial ploy. The American Society for Enology and

Viticulture, for example, catalogued the environment as a public relations issue. NSWG members, while often deeply concerned for the ecosystem, even acknowledged that sustainable agriculture was a "marketing advantage."[62]

## Conclusion

By 1980, Napans sought a specific state action—the creation of an appellation system—to help confirm an elite status in the global wine market. These were not the first public interventions. The University of California, an important agent of state power, weaves its way throughout this story. Even those agencies or state actions that failed to achieve their goals had profound impacts on Napa resources. The BSVC did not change national consumer habits, but it helped to prolong the use of nonresistant vines that allowed *Phylloxera* to wreak economic and ecological havoc in the 1890s. Prohibition was a more ambitious exercise by a nation-state whose authority was shaped by Progressivism and wartime mobilization. Prohibition contributed to a fluctuating demand for grapes that reordered valley farmlands in the 1920s and nearly destroyed the domestic wine industry, but it never stemmed the country's alcohol usage. The agricultural preserve and the appellation system highlight more expansive public powers and civil society's acceptance—indeed its recruitment—of them in the postwar era. State action protected the valley's viticultural leadership, but contributed to a loss of biodiversity and other ecological problems that the state and the industry have yet to resolve. Consumers and industry actors have defined the meaning of Napa wine, but the role of the state, even a less centralized U.S. state, can never be ignored.

## Abbreviations

HNVIR:    "History of Napa Valley, Interviews and
          Reminiscences of Long-Time Residents
          Collected by the Napa Valley Wine Library,"
          St. Helena Public Library, n.d.
NCDACR:   Napa County Department of
          Agriculture Crop Report

NVWLA:          Napa Valley Wine Library Association
RBSVC:         Report of the Board of State
               Viticultural Commissioners
SVC:           State Viticultural Commission

# NOTES

1. Anon, *History of Napa and Lake Counties, California* (San Francisco: Slocum, Bowen, 1881), 4–7.
2. Quotations found in Nina Wemyss, ed., *Soul of the Vine: Wine in Literature* (Oakville, CA: Robert Mondavi Winery, 1998).
3. William Leach, *Land of Desire: Merchants, Power and the Rise of a New American Culture* (New York: Vintage, 1994), 3–12; and Grant McCracken, *Culture and Consumption: New Approaches to the Symbolic Character of Consumer Goods and Activities* (Bloomington: Indiana University Press, 1988), 1–10, 121.
4. Theda Skocpol, *Protecting Soldiers and Mothers: the Political Origins of Social Policy in the United States* (Cambridge, MA: 1992), 42–43, quoted in Karen R. Merrill, "In Search of the 'Federal Presence' in the American West," *Western Historical Quarterly* 30 (Winter 1999): 454.
5. In the United States, Stephen Skowronek postulates that nation-state power developed in the nineteenth century in a patchwork pattern, dispersed among national agencies. Stephen Skowronek, *Building a New American State: the Expansion of National Administrative Capacities* (New York: Cambridge University Press, 1982), 290–92; and James C. Scott, *Seeing Like a State: How Certain Schemes to Improve the Human Condition Have Failed* (New Haven and London: Yale University Press, 1998), 1–8. See also Theda Skocpol, "Bringing the State Back In: Strategies of Analysis in Current Research," 3–28; Dietrich Rueschemeyer and Peter B. Evans, "The State and Economic Transformation: Toward an Analysis of the Conditions Underlying Effective Intervention," in *Bringing the State Back In*, eds. Peter B. Evans, Dietrich Rueschemeyer, and Theda Skocpol (New York: Cambridge University Press, 1985; 1993 repr.), 44–72.
6. Lizabeth Cohen, *A Consumers' Republic: the Politics of Mass Consumption in Postwar America* (New York: Alfred A. Knopf, 2003), 7–11, 403–7.
7. C. A. Menefee, *Historical and Descriptive Sketch Book of Napa, Sonoma, Lake and Mendocino* (Napa: Reporter, 1873), 128–34; Irving McKee, "Historic Napa County Wine-Growing," manuscript for the Wine Institute for the Wine Advisory Board, n.d., California

State Library; Charles Sullivan, *Napa Wine: A History from Mission Days to the Present* (San Francisco: Wine Appreciation Guild, 1994), 11–23, 399.

8. The European Mission grape, distinguished from *V. vinifera*, had been crossbred with "New World" vines; see Sullivan, *Napa Wine*, 9. See also *First Annual RBSVC* (San Francisco: Edward Bosqui, 1881), 61–62; Tom Gregory et al., *History of Solano and Napa Counties* (Los Angeles: Historic Record, 1912), 147–48; Charles Tovey, *Wine and Wine Countries: A Record and Manual for Wine Merchants and Wine Consumers* (London: Hamilton, Adams, 1862), 245; Mark Edward Lender and James Kirby Martin, *Drinking in America: A History* (New York: Free Press, 1982), 96.

9. McKee, "Historic Napa County Wine-Growing," 11; Sullivan, *Napa Wine*, 53–54; James Lapsley, *Bottled Poetry: Napa Winemaking from Prohibition to the Modern Era* (Berkeley: University of California Press, 1996), 205–9. The Napa District produced 297,670 gallons in 1870 and 2,460,000 in 1880. It included Solano and Costra counties, but most wine came from Napa; see *First Annual RBSVC*, 14.

10. Daniel T. Rodgers, *Atlantic Crossings: Social Politics in a Progressive Age* (Cambridge, MA: Belknap of Harvard University Press, 1998).

11. State Viticultural Commission, *First Report*, 62.

12. Ibid., 75.

13. Ibid., 185–88 (catalogue of available European vines).

14. Anon., *Catalogue of the Products of California Exhibited at the Southern Pacific Company at the North, Central and South American Exposition, New Orleans* (New Orleans: W. B. Stansbury, 1886), 98; see also *Viticulture and Viniculture in California, prepared specially for distribution at the New Orleans World's Fair, A.D. 1885* (Sacramento: State Printers, 1885), 7–23.

15. U.S. wines earned 28 medals in Paris compared to Australia (36); Portugal (289); and France (950). William P. Blake, ed., *Reports of the United States Commissioners to the Universal Exposition at Paris*, Vol. IV (Washington, DC: GPO, 1981), 726–32, quoted in Sullivan, *Napa Wine*, 98. See also "History of Gustave Ferdinand Niebaum (Nybom) by John Daniel," *HNVIR* Vol. I, 212–21; Eugene Hilgard, *University of California, Report of the Viticultural Work during the Seasons 1883–84 and 1884–85* (Sacramento: State Printers, 1886).

16. *Annual RBSVC for 1891–92* (Sacramento: State Printers, 1892), 8–9, 24; *Directory of the Grape Growers and Wine Makers of California* (Sacramento: State Printers, 1888), 26–31; *Napa County Land Register* (Napa: Hunt & Wood, 1885), 11; *Annual RBSVC for 1889–90* (Sacramento: State Printers, 1890), 7.

17. Ben C. Truman, *History of the World's Fair, being a Complete Description of the World's Columbian Exposition from Its Inception*

(Philadelphia: H. W. Kelley, 1893), 307–9; *RBSVC for 1893–94* (Sacramento: State Printers, 1894), 7–10; Lender and Martin, *Drinking in America*, 96.

18. *First Annual Report of the Chief Executive Viticultural Officer of the Board of State Viticultural Commissioners for the Year 1881* (Sacramento: State Printers, 1882), 173–74.

19. *First Annual RBSVC*, 89–92; *First Annual Report of the Chief Executive Viticultural Officer*; Hilgard, *Report of Viticultural Work, 1883–4 and 1884–5*, 207–10.

20. *RBSVC, 1891–92* (Sacramento: State Printers, 1892), 11–12.

21. *RBSVC, 1889–90* (Sacramento: State Printers, 1890), 22; Anon., *Principal Cellars: "Winehaven" on San Francisco Bay* (San Francisco: California Wine Association, 1909); *Directory of Grape Growers, Wine Makers and Distillers of California* (Sacramento: State Printers, 1891), 83–99.

22. *RBSVC for 1889–90*, 111–15; "Agroecosystems—Pierce's Disease," Texas A&M University System, Texas Agricultural Experiment Station, Agricultural and Research Center, http://beaumont.tamu.edu/research/Agroecosystems_default.htm.

23. *First Annual RBSVC*, 9; *RBSVC, 1891–92*, 8; *RBSVC, 1893–94* (Sacramento: State Printers, 1894), 26–27.

24. Sullivan, *Napa Wine*, 175–91, 399; Anon., *History of Solano and Napa Counties*, 148; Katherine M. Dowdell, interview by Irene Haynes, n.d., *HNVIR* Vol. I, 51; W. W. Lyman, interview by Lois Stone, n.d., *HNVIR* Vol. I, 161; George T. Mee and Thomas H. Mee, interview by Elizabeth Martini, August 16, 1964, *HNVIR* Vol. I, 186; Frank Pocai, interview by Irene Haynes, *HNVIR* Vol. II, 58–59; *Napa City & County Portfolio*, 104.

25. Morton Keller, "Taking Stock," in Morton Keller and R. Shep Melnick, eds., *Taking Stock: American Government in the Twentieth Century* (New York: Cambridge University Press, 1999), 2.

26. *Ibid.*; and Richard Hamm, *Shaping the Eighteenth Amendment: Temperance, Reform, Legal Culture, and the Polity, 1880–1920* (Chapel Hill: University of North Carolina Press, 1995), 171–73.

27. Frank E. Pocai, interview by Irene Haynes, January 9, 1975, *HNVIR* Vol. II, 64; Eugene B. Morosoli, interview by Gunther Detert, October 1979, *HNVIR* Vol. III, 104; Sullivan, *Napa Wine*, 197.

28. Steven Navone, interview by Irene Haynes and Elizabeth Martini, n.d., *HNVIR* Vol. II, 233–34.

29. Brother Basil, interview by Elizabeth Martini and Eleanor McCrea, n.d., *HNVIR* Vol. I, 25; Andre Tshelistcheff, interview by Richard G. Peterson, July 7, 1972, *HNVIR* Vol. II, 37–38; James Morgan Bray, "The Impact of Prohibition on Napa Valley Viticulture, 1921–1933," MLS thesis, California State University, San Jose, 1974, pp. 99–130.

30. Navone interview, 233; Maynard A. Amerine and Vernon L. Singleton, *Wine an Introduction*, 2nd ed. (Berkeley: University of California Press, 1972), 288, discussed in Lapsley, *Bottled Poetry*, 227.

31. *Acreage Estimates California Fruit and Nut, 1919–1953—by counties* (Sacramento: California Livestock and Crop Reporting Service, 1956); Sullivan, *Napa Wine*, 186–87, 400.

32. The slow exit of Alicante Bouschet and Green Hungarian is visible in grape acreage statistics; see *California Grape Acreage, 1978* (Sacramento: California Crop and Livestock Reporting Service, 1979), 8; see also Tshelistcheff interview, 7; Frank Pocai interview, 93; Lapsley, *Bottled Poetry*, 3–5; Sullivan, *Napa Wine*, 209.

33. Quotation from Paul Verdier, City of Paris department store, *San Francisco Chronicle*, October 11, 1933; see also Roy Raymond, Sr., interview by Robert Trinhero, n.d., *HNVIR* Vol. I, 242; Francis L. Gould, *My Life with Wine* (St. Helena: Francis Gould, 1972), 21; Sullivan, *Napa Wine*, 210.

34. "Napa Valley Vintners: The Early Years, 1943 to 1958," scrapbook, NVWL Press Release, May 18, 1994, NVWL; Porterfield, "Charles Krug and his Winery," 12; History of Napa County Viticulture and Wine Making by John Daniels, 23 November 1969, *HNVIR* Vol. I, 232–33, and Robert Mondavi, interview by Ina Hart and T. E. Wilde, December 29, 1978, *HNVIR* Vol. III, 200–8; Robert Louis Stevenson, *Silverado Squatters* (London: Chatto & Windus, 1883), 56.

35. Tchelistcheff interview, 7–9, 89–92; George Deuer, interview by Bernard Skoda, June 19, 1974, *HNVIR* Vol. II, 130; A. J. Winkler, interview by Ruth Teiser and Joann Leach Larkey, 1973, Regional Oral History Office, Bancroft Library, University of California, Berkeley, 16–34.

36. Regarding the Morrill Act, see Richard White, *"It's Your Misfortune and None of My Own": A New History of the American West* (Norman: University of Oklahoma Press, 1991), 145; Gray Brechin, *Imperial San Francisco: Urban Power, Earthly Ruin* (Berkeley: University of California Press, 2001), 281; Ed Weber, interview by Kathleen A. Brosnan, January 11, 2005, transcript in Brosnan's possession. Mr. Weber is Napa County's agent for the University of California Cooperative Extension. Regarding the associational state, see Jess Gilbert, "Agrarian Intellectuals in a Democratizing State: A Collective Biography of USDA Leaders and the Intended New Deal," in Catherine McNicol Stock and Robert D. Johnston, eds., *The Countryside in the Age of the Modern State: Political Histories of Rural America* (Ithaca: Cornell University Press, 2001), 215; and David E. Hamilton, "Building the Associative State: The Department of

Agriculture and American State-Building," *Agricultural History* 64 (1990): 207–18.

37. Lapsley, *Bottled Poetry*, 47–51, 137; "California Wine Outlook," Bank of America Report, San Francisco, September 1973, p. 6; and Paul Lukacs, *American Vintage: the Rise of American Wine* (Boston: Houghton Mifflin, 2000), 187.

38. John Teuter (Chair, Board of Supervisors, Napa County, Bureau of Alcohol, Tobacco and Firearms), testimony given in Meeting in the Matter of Proposed Regulatory Definitions of Appellation of Origin, San Francisco, November 13, 1979, transcript, NVWL 228; "Judgment of Paris," *Time*, June 7, 1976, 58; "Cabernet Sauvignon: An Assessment of Supply and Demand," *Grape Intelligence Report*, St. Helena, July 1989, pp. 1–2.

39. *NCDACR* (1967); *NCDACR* (1971); *Acreage Estimates of California Fruit and Nut Acreage, 1919–1953*; *California Fruit and Nut Acreage, 1971* (Sacramento: California Livestock and Crop Reporting Service, 1972), NVWL; Anne McLachlan, "The Wine Grape Industry of Napa, California, 1964–1979," Thesis, University of London, 1980, p. 2; and Irving Hoch and Nickolas Tryphonopoulos, "A Study of the Economy of Napa County, California," California Experiment Station, *Giannini Foundation Research Report* 303 (August 1969): 36. A prune farmer noted, "Some people even felt that the grapes were so worthwhile they even took out young and productive prune trees in order to raise grapes." Interview of Arthur Schmidt by Gunther Detert, 21 March 1981, *HNVIR* Vol. III, 149.

40. Napa County Planning Department, "Population Data of Napa County," Napa City-County Library, November 1966; "Draft Environmental Management Plan for San Francisco Bay Region," Vol. II, San Francisco, Association of Bay Area Governments, December 1977, p. 3; John J. Cuddy, *The Chapter in Your Life Entitled San Francisco and the California it Centers* (San Francisco: Californians, 1947), 48. In 1959, Santa Clara held some 73,000 acres of fruits and nuts; by 1992, only 1,900 remained, see *California Fruit and Nut Acreage* (Sacramento: California Livestock and Crop Reporting Service, 1959), 5; *California Fruit and Nut Acreage* (Sacramento: California Livestock and Crop Reporting Service, 1992), 10.

41. Volker Eisele, "Twenty-five Years of Farmland Protection in Napa County," in *California Farmland and Urban Pressure: Statewide and Regional Perceptions*, eds. Albert G. Medvitz, Alvin D. Sokolow, and Cathy Lemp (Davis: Agricultural Issues Center, Division of

Agricultural and Natural Resources, University of California, 1999), 103–23; and James B. Conaway, *Napa: An American Eden* (Boston: Houghton Mifflin, 1990), 82–92.

42. In 1967, land sold for five hundred to three thousand dollars per acre; in the 1990s, some prices per acre exceeded two hundred thousand dollars. See Hoch and Tryphonopoulos, "A Study of the Economy of Napa County," 14; James Conaway, *The Dark Side of Eden: New Money, Old Land, and the Battle for Napa Valley* (Boston: Houghton Mifflin, 2002), 1–6. County population teetered below 125,000 in 2000, substantially less than predicted in 1966. See "Projections and Planning Information, 2001 Updates for Napa County," (San Francisco: Employment Development Department, 2001), A–2.

43. Mondavi interview, 210–11; Sullivan, *Napa Wine*, 392–94.

44. Nathan Chroman, *Wine Review*, July 1975, pp. 1–2; see also Mondavi interview, 209; Jack L. Davies (President, NVVA), testimony (9-17), and W. Andrew Beckstoffer (President, Napa Valley Grape Growers Association), testimony (10-11) given before Rule Making Hearing of the BATF of the Department of the Treasury, San Francisco, April 13, 1976, transcripts, NVWL.

45. See Warren Moran, "The Wine Appellation as Territory in France and California," *Annals of the Association of American Geographers* 83 (1983): 700–7.

46. "California's Wineries," *Wine Spectator*, April 1979, p. 13.

47. Critics employ the term *terroir* to describe physical features—sun, soil, climate, water—that distinguish vineyards and their products. James E. Wilson, *Terroir: the Role of Geology, Climate and Culture in the Making of French Wines* (Berkeley: University of California Press, 1999), 22–56.

48. Lapsley, *Bottled Poetry*, 206.

49. Davies testimony, passim; and Beckstoffer testimony, passim.

50. Lapsley, *Bottled Poetry*, 207–9; Robert Mondavi, testimony given in Napa Valley Appellation Hearings for BATF of the Department of Treasury, Napa, CA, April 28, 1980, 42, NVWL.

51. Emmanuelle Vaudour emphasizes the need for spatial modeling and geographical information system data to more carefully catalogue characteristics of any particular locale; see Vaudour's "The Quality of Grapes and Wine in Relation to Geography: Notions of *Terroir* at Various Scales," *Journal of Wine Research* 13, no. 2 (2002): 117–41.

52. Stags Leap Appellation Committee (John Shafer, Chairman), "Petition to Establish the Viticultural Area of 'Stags Leap' under Title 27 Code of Federal Regulations, Part 9," submitted to the Director, BATF, April 13, 1987), Appellation File, NVWL, 1, 12.

53. John Opie, *Nature's Nation: An Environmental History of the United States* (Fort Worth: Harcourt Brace, 1998), 172–74; Scott, *Seeing Like A State*, 49–51.

54. Stags Leap Appellation Committee, "Petition," 1 (first quotation), 4 (second quotation), 43–52.

55. "Petition to Establish the St. Helena Viticultural Area in the County of Napa, California," submitted to the Director, BATF, March 9, 1994, 24—NVWL. The petition cited a number of scholarly publications by Elliott-Fisk as well.

56. Irene W. Haynes, "Napa Valley Wineries," Report prepared for the NVWL, 1988, NVWL; Conaway, *The Dark Side of Eden*, 26; "Petition to Establish St. Helena Viticultural Area."

57. The value of Napa's grapes exceeded $354 million by 2001, see *California Fruit and Nut Acreage*, 2001; "Napa River Watershed Task Force," Phase II, prepared for the Napa County Board of Supervisors, September 2000, p. 1; Stewart Smith, interview by Gunther Detert, March 9, 1985, *HNVIR* Vol. IV, 254.

58. "Napa River Watershed Task Force," 2, 4; Juliane Poirier Locke, *Vineyards in the Watershed: Sustainable Winegrowing in Napa County* (Napa: Napa Sustainable Winegrowing Group, 2002), 32–36.

59. Locke, *Vineyards in the Watershed*, 47, 51.

60. NCDACR (1999); George M. Schofield, "Cabernet Sauvignon: An Assessment of Supply and Demand," *Grape Intelligence Report*, St. Helena, August 1998, pp. 2–3.

61. *Integrated Pest Management: Field Handbook for Napa County* (Napa, CA: NSWG, 1997), 2.

62. American Society for Enology and Viticulture, "Environmental Issues: Compliance Overview," Sacramento, June 22, 1993, pp. 1–4, NVWL; Locke, *Vineyards in the Watershed*, 15.

# CHAPTER 3

## WRITING ABOUT WINE
### THE USES OF NATURE AND HISTORY IN THE WINE-GROWING REGIONS OF SOUTHWEST FRANCE AND AMERICA

*Robert C. Ulin*

It is often argued that quality wines come from vineyards that enjoy an especially favorable climate and soil. For example, in his 1980 book on Médoc wines, geographer René Pijassou[1] argues that the hierarchical ranking of Bordeaux wines in the influential 1855 classification was based on both improved technology in the vineyard, and wine cellar and natural conditions emanating both from a favorable microclimate and the *sous sol* or sub-soil. Pijassou claims that in contrast to most wine-growing estates of the nearby southwest French interior, Bordeaux vineyards benefit from their gravel, limestone, and clay soil, as well as a temperate climate produced by coastal proximity to the Gulf Stream and a system of rivers in the Garonne, Gironde, and Dordogne regions.[2]

More recently, James Wilson, in *Terroir: The Role of Geology, Climate and Culture in the Making of French Wines*, examines the *soul sol* (the deep soil through which plants absorb nutrients) of France's principal wine-growing regions from the perspective of geological formations that he believes account for qualitative differences between regions, as well as between vineyards within a particular region.[3] To ascertain geological formations, Wilson utilized the same seismic equipment that is commonly used in oil exploration. The equipment sends out sound waves and records the echoes to identify the bedrock. Prior to this technology, much discussion of the *sous sol* was a matter of speculation; however, Wilson's use of seismic technology allows scientists to both map vineyards without disturbing the vines and collect quality information.

Being commonly argued that the natural environment in California provides similar wine-growing conditions to Bordeaux, American scholars and wine experts place a commensurate emphasis on climate and soil. Even in the northwest part of the lower peninsula of Michigan, characterized by comparatively long and cold winters, Lake Michigan and the Traverse City Bay produce moderating climatic effects that enable wine growers to produce quality wines from grape varieties common in the cooler wine-growing regions of Europe.[4] One Michigan wine grower on the Old Mission Peninsula informed me that, following the advice of German oenologists, he moved around mounds of dirt in his vineyards in order to duplicate the growing conditions found in certain areas of Germany.[5] What is clear from all these sources is that we have invested a great deal in believing that climate and soil are indispensable to the production of quality wines. How, then, can one possibly challenge what appears to be the accepted wisdom of wine growers, oenologists, and a general public that follows the writings of scholars and wine critics?

In this essay, I assume the above challenge by arguing that the concept of "natural" has been used rhetorically and hegemonically to support the privileged position occupied by some wine growers, especially the proprietors of elite estates, and by large marketing firms and global corporations that have acquired elite estates. I argue that while climate and soil are factors in the production of "good wines," however subjective such a classification may be, the history of the wine-growing regions discussed here, and the hegemonic components of cultural representation, are likewise indispensable to understanding how some wines have assumed a super-ordinate position in the wine-growing hierarchy. What I am proposing, therefore, is a social science of wine making that hopefully will complement the science of the vine, while challenging reductionist and positivistic uses of "natural" that make historical processes and the consequences of human action appear as if they are simply given or unchanging.[6]

## THE USES OF "NATURAL"

The association of quality wines with superior natural conditions is by no means unique, as the human condition has generally often been regarded in natural terms at least since the Enlightenment, and arguably before. Anthropologists often look to the Enlightenment as pivotal to the creation of a "pre-academic" anthropological perspective. The Enlightenment thinkers argued against the determinations of tradition and the sense that life, natural and social, reflected a divine plan. For philosophers such as Jean-Jacques Rousseau and François-Marie Arouet de Voltaire the "authority of reason" replaced the "authority of tradition," in that humanity was viewed as an extension of the rational order of nature in what would come to be regarded as the "great chain of being."[7] For Enlightenment scholars, humanity possessed the potential to alter or change its social environments by exercising will in accordance with the laws of reason. Rousseau used the critical spirit of reason to challenge institutional inequities of eighteenth century French—and by extension European—society by highlighting the natural endowments of "primitive men" who remained closer to nature than their European counterparts. For Rousseau,[8] as would later be the case for Karl Marx, who likewise idealized the original condition of "man" through the primitive mode of production,[9] the fall of humanity, to borrow a religious trope, was attributable to private property, and thus societies without property remained as models of a lost and more just past.

While some Enlightenment thinkers invoked humanity's proximity to nature thematically to support a vision of critique and social justice, this vision would change in the nineteenth century without abandoning the importance of reason as an extension of natural law or the natural order. Although nineteenth-century theorists would embrace romanticism as a reaction to and rejection of reason, it could be argued that the Enlightenment emphasis on the original condition of humanity, and nineteenth-century views of progress were integrally related and mutually reinforcing. I think this is more apparent in social history than in the history of ideas, in that social history provides a context for what people believe and assert—the very sort of historical move that I hope to establish against the rhetorical uses of climate and soil in the wine-growing arena.

Nineteenth- and early twentieth-century scholars largely transformed the critical uses of Enlightenment reason and nature to support a view of human progress grounded in the natural conditions of human evolution. This is by now a story that is well known, so I will only sketch what are the important epistemological shifts. According to late, albeit diverse, nineteenth and early twentieth-century evolutionary theorists such as James Fraser, Edward Burnett Tylor and Lucien Lévy-Bruhl, indigenous peoples were thought to be closer to nature.[10] However, unlike Rousseau, they measured progress by how much distance had been placed between contemporaneous human communities, generally defined as "nation states" or "civilizations," and humanity's "state of nature" as represented in the nineteenth century by "primitive" or indigenous peoples. Such assumptions of progress were illustrative of a political agenda, as typified by European or North American colonialism. However, even nineteenth-century anthropologists intellectually formulated and reproduced dichotomies such as kinship and contract—traditional and modern—which came to distinguish the "indigenous other" from contemporary Europeans. Associating indigenous peoples with proximity to the state of nature established a civilizing or moral imperative for colonialism, while advancing Western culture as representative of the highest human endeavor. The anthropologist Johannes Fabian has referred to the process of categorizing others in the (dis)guise of science as closer to nature, while representing Europeans or Western culture more generally as superordinate, as the "denial of coevalness."[11] The denial of coevalness has nothing to do with empirical time or the relativism of time reckoning across cultures. Rather, it is an intellectual or strategic move, an act of technical reason, which claims that others who are not like us are non-contemporaneous. This is a strategy, as Edward Said likewise suggests, that contributes to the assertion by Western powers of political domination over non-Western others.[12]

Jean and John Comaroff have contended that Fabian's argument not only applies to indigenous peoples but also to Europeans, especially peasants, rural farmers, and workers, who lived in the shadows or peripheries of the market and the logic of exchange.[13] However, for our concerns here, that is, the wine-growing sector, it is the association of the natural with modern European state making and nationalism that becomes most interesting. Benedict Anderson has written about the making of the modern state and the cultivation of national sentiment as not only a political process involving government and law, but essentially as the outcome of an "imagined community."[14] The problem for virtually all theorists of the modern state is how people with local loyalties and identities come to identify with the nation state. For Anderson, national identities are forged from print capitalism, and the proliferation of literacy, in that newspapers, for example, allow residents of local communities to imagine others geographically widespread having a life just like their own. That is, the information shared through print media contributes to the formation of a common identity.

Anderson's views of nationalism as the imagined community are supported by Ernest Gellner, who emphasizes the historically transformative potentials of industrialization, and especially the increasing standardization of education.[15] Although both Anderson and Gellner perhaps gloss over the violence and contested identities that are part of the process of state craft and nationalism, and it is possible that their theories are eurocentric;[16] they nonetheless identify state making and nationalism as thoroughly historical and socio-cultural processes of modern times.

The above theory of imagined community and national sentiment that follows from such imagining is of interest because, from the perspective of nationalists and political parties with nationalist aspirations, nationalism is more about "blood" and "soil" than historical fashioning. This was most apparent in the Europe of the 1930s when German national socialists emphasized blood, a cultural theme that survives to this day, and the Italian fascists, not unlike the German national socialists, appealed to ties to the soil and motherland, women themselves being represented as closer to nature than men. What resonates here is the symbolic invoking of nature in multiple—not to mention material—forms to mask or conceal the social.

One may conclude that this is all very interesting and perhaps quite relevant to discussions of nationalism, but what does imagined communities, blood, and soil have to do with the history of the vine? As we know very well, the notion of *terroir* ("soil" and "region") among wine aficionados, growers, experts, and increasingly the general public, links quality wines with place, an association oftentimes with legal import, such as in France, to protect consumers from fraud and thus assure the authenticity of the wine. The idea that ensues from terroir is that grapes derive their special character from a particular soil and microclimate, and the taste of the end product—the wine—reflecting the distinctiveness of place. Terroir is especially important to the reputation of so-called quality wines because the intention on elite wine-growing estates is to vinify grapes that come from a single property rather than to mix grapes from multiple growers, and thus multiple terroirs. The connection of wine to place as an index of authenticity is therefore similar to the connection of a population bounded to soil as an index of their authentic national identity. In both cases, the connections to place are reputed to be "natural."

Let us consider an example from the nineteenth century, where the authenticity of grape plants merges with the authenticity of national identity. It is widely acknowledged that the *Phylloxera* blight of the last quarter of the nineteenth century had devastating consequences for French vineyards. For example, in the Dordogne between Bergerac and Périgueux to the north, approximately 75 percent of the vineyards were destroyed, while in the Gironde, the devastation was a lesser, but still significant, 40 percent. *Phylloxera* is caused by a plant louse or aphid-like insect that attacks and destroys the roots of some grape stocks. It is believed that *Phylloxera* was brought to France in the 1830s by elite growers who imported grape plants from America.[17] As Harry Paul notes, the *Phylloxera* blight of the 1870s, followed some ten years later by the odium, a powdery mildew residue on the leaves of the grape plant, led growers to turn to scientists for a solution to their vineyard woes.[18] Numerous remedies were proposed from the oenological centers at Bordeaux and Montpellier. With respect to *Phylloxera*, some suggestions included the use of pesticides, potentially risky if there are lasting residues, and the flooding of the vineyards to drown the insects. Even the celebrated French biologist Louis Pasteur became involved in suggesting the use of fungi to destroy the insects—but to no avail, as the *Phylloxera* endured.

The solution to *Phylloxera* that emerged, attributable to no single individual, was to graft fruit-bearing French *vinifera* vines with *Phylloxera*-resistant American rootstocks.[19] In 1887, The French Ministry of Agriculture sent a special delegation, led by Pierre Viala, a viticultural professor at Montpellier, to identify which American vines "thrived on chalky soil."[20] Contrary to what one may expect, the suitable vines were not found in California, but in the limestone hills of Texas where the American botanist Thomas Munson had been successfully experimenting with grape plants. Although Viala was strongly in favor of grafting to combat *Phylloxera*, he warned "against planting hybrid direct producers to replace the vines of French blood that produced famous wines: it would be antipatriotic to sacrifice the legitimate fame of a high-quality French product."[21] In my view, Viala's anthropomorphic comments are a rather spectacular example of naturalized culture.

Vilala's metaphorical association of French vines with French blood, although early by French standards—especially if we take Eugen Weber's account of the transformation of peasants into Frenchmen as authoritative,[22]—nevertheless approximates what Anderson refers to as the "imagined community." Viala's comment intends to stir strong sentiment for, and loyalty to, French as opposed to non-French vines. In fact, despite strong regional loyalty among French growers in general, the appeal to a vine as distinctively French probably resonated more fully than print capitalism in the last quarter of the nineteenth century, given that most peasants and farmers were illiterate. The appeal of *Vitis vinifera* as the French vine—as contrasted to the "otherness" of hybrids—provided a context within which growers from diverse regions could imagine their relation to other French growers and the challenges they faced, in spite of the fact that in some wine-growing areas such as Languedoc, hybrids were wide-spread.[23]

Moreover, one can hardly overlook the reference to "blood" at a time of French colonial expansion whereby the natural endowments of Europeans and progress distinguished the French from the colonized indigenous "other." In this case, we can see not only the anthropomorphizing of viticulture but also its cultural prefiguration as natural. The blood of nation-making is symbolically contiguous with the blood of the vine, thus obscuring what is historically fashioned by what is lawful or natural.

The above example shows the self-representation of French identity during a period when national identity was not yet self-evident. The various universal exhibitions of which the famous Bordeaux classification of 1855 is associated likewise contributed to the imagined community of the national patrimony, in that select French wines were exhibited as representative of French national culture.[24] The exhibiting of these regional wines would in itself be a mark of national consciousness making, but the fact that material culture was exhibited in relation to the material culture of other nations made the universal exhibition an especially symbolically charged display.

As suggested earlier, contemporary authors writing about French wine also contribute to the naturalization of identity. Consider, for example, Wilson's comments on the Alsatian wine-growing region. According to Wilson, Alsace is "Germanic in appearance (place, names, architecture), its unique dialect is from the barbarian Alemanni: its spirit and heart are from the Gauls."[25] Although Wilson goes on to elaborate on the geologic process as it contributes to soil composition in Alsatian vineyards, his references to the "barbarian Alemanni" and Gallic "spirit and heart" are highly romantic in rhetorical style,[26] thus ignoring how history contributes concretely to often multivocal and contested identities. His emphasis on the romantic trope of "spirit" contributes to the association of place and soil to naturalized regional, and, by extension, national sentiments. As we will see, the power of the text, in this case wine, scribed in natural terms becomes a considerable challenge to scholars committed to critical historical evaluation or deconstruction.

## WINE-GROWING HISTORY AS INVENTED

From the early 1980s through the early 1990s, I conducted field research among wine growers, notably those in cooperatives, in southwest France. My research commenced in 1984 in the Dordogne with two cooperatives located close to Bergerac. The Dordogne proved an excellent starting point because the growers in this region, like those of Languedoc, are often relegated to the margins of wine-growing history. With few exceptions,[27] histories of French wine-growing present us with a narrative of elites, presenting "history from above" as metonymic for the French nation state.[28] Even regional archives provide little direct material on local wine cooperatives, forcing me to reconstruct regional wine history from, following Jacques Derrida, the margins of history.[29] That is, it was necessary to look at what was excluded from the official texts, accounts, and documents about wine growing.

In addition, my wine-growing informants from the Monbazillac and Sigoulès cooperatives questioned why I had come to Bergerac when the much more celebrated vineyards of Bordeaux were so near by. However, my interest in history and belief that commodities have a historically fashioned social life[30] led me to explore how Bordeaux historically had come to occupy its privileged position in the Dordogne region.

Well into the twelfth century, the wines of Bergerac, some ninety kilometers east of Bordeaux, enjoyed the reputation of being superior to those of Bordeaux. Also until the close of the twelfth century, as Pijassou notes, the wine exported from the *Haut* Pays of southwest France, which includes Pèrigord, Agen, Toulouse, and Quercy, was considered to be of better quality, and thus more valued than that produced in Bordeaux.[31] This situation was reversed only as a consequence of the English occupation of the twelfth to fifteenth centuries when privileges were granted to Bordeaux growers, and Bordeaux merchants established a remarkable marketing structure with significant ties to northern Europe, especially England.[32]

Prior to the English Occupation, La Rochelle was the principal port through which southwest French wines were shipped to England. La Rochelle was more favorably located than Bordeaux, being directly on the Atlantic Coast and somewhat closer to northern European markets. As Henri and Bernard Enjallbert note, it possessed a far greater wine culture and commercial presence.[33] However, the defeat of the English at La Rochelle in 1224, and subsequent suppression of its commerce with England by Louis VIII, left the English little choice but to cultivate Bordeaux as their principal port even though access to the Atlantic was indirect via the Garonne River. Moreover, to reduce the likelihood of resistance to their rule, the English granted special commercial favors to Bordeaux merchants and wine growers. For example, wines from the interior were subject to higher taxation and not permitted to enter Bordeaux and its port until after December 1. These privileges led to the clearing of forests and the planting of vineyards around Bordeaux, and greatly augmented its wine export to England.[34] In sum, political rather than natural factors explain the ascendancy of Bordeaux wine growing and commerce.

While historical circumstances can provide alternative versions to the ascendancy of quality wines along "natural" lines, one must be careful not to identify history and historical process with essential facts. That is, the historical record is both inclusive and exclusive, so that what is included may appear to be unquestionable, the given, or the natural. Again, in Bordeaux wine-growing history, we find an example of what some scholars, following Eric Hobsbawm and Terence Ranger, would identify as the "invention of tradition."[35] Although Hobsbawm and Ranger ultimately maintain that there is a real history against which invented histories can be measured, they argue that the past is a social construction both with respect to human subjects that make their own history, and from the point of view of those who write about history.

The "process of invention" is well illustrated through the actions of southwest French elite growers during the seventeenth century. Elite growers in the Médoc region sought to distinguish their wines symbolically from those of the peasant masses in order to compete with Spanish, Portuguese, and Italian wines that flooded the French market. They augmented the quality of their wines by producing wines from lower yielding vine stocks, rather than seeking to duplicate the mass-produced wines coming from abroad. This was a highly successful strategy in that a market for quality wines (the "*grand crus*") was created in France and as far away as America to the west and Russia to the east. In the nineteenth century, proprietors of the *grands crus* elected to distinguish not only their wines, but themselves as well, by building their homes as small-scale replicas of the famous medieval chateaux, hoping to borrow symbolically from the cultural associations of a noble life as a means of distinguishing grower and wine from the mass of peasant producers. This is a point that I will return to later in discussing in the manner of Pierre Bourdieu, the social distinctions of taste, an issue in my view that is veiled by the assumptions of objective quality as associated with what we take to be natural.[36]

## THE AMERICAN STORY

The issues that follow from the examples that I have taken from southwest France are not entirely distinct from what one discovers in North America, when California is regarded as setting the standard of quality, based on superior climate and soil. However, American wine has a different history. There is no European aristocracy to symbolically replicate nor is there a tradition of peasant wines, as American homesteaders have always been capitalists cultivating grains rather than grape vines. Moreover, even to this day, Americans are somewhat more playful than French consumers in accepting a wide range of labels, albeit as tied to social class rather than any long-standing sense of aristocracy associated with French wines. That is, because American wine growers do not have to culturally embrace an aristocratic wine-growing past, they are considerably more able than their elite French counterparts to utilize humorous labels to successfully commercialize their wines.

In spite of associating California wines with an excellence that approximates, if not equals, Bordeaux, American wines of quality are relatively recent. The fact that grains were cultivated in large quantity in the American Midwest, and sugar cane in the Caribbean, is reflected in hard liquors distilled from fermented grains (e.g., rye, whiskey, etc.), and sugar cane (rum) being the alcohol beverage of choice. Moreover, as Paul Lukacs points out, American Prohibition and religious opposition to alcoholic beverages were more generally significant obstacles to transforming American consumption habits from hard liquor to quality wines.[37]

Moreover, of interest to our concerns here is the fact that the successful cultivation of American vineyards did not originate in California as one might imagine, but rather on the banks of the Ohio River outside of Cincinnati. While practically all American colonies had experimented with the European *vinifera* without success, it was the wealthy entrepreneur Nicholas Longworth who succeeded with the non-*vinifera* Catawba in the late 1820s. It was, as Lukacs notes, Longworth's goal to produce a dry table wine.[38] Longworth produced a wine popular with German immigrants by separating the skin of the Catawba from the clear juice. Longworth's efforts to produce a quality table wine succeeded well enough, until his death in 1863, that even though he had to contend with a temperance movement at home, his wines won recognition at international exhibitions abroad. Nonetheless, the combination of downy mildew, black rot, and the discovery by farmers that they could grow crops other than grapes more profitably put an end to wine growing in Cincinnati.

California wine production took off in the 1880s, where wine was presented as an antidote to whiskey.[39] In California, it was the creation of the California Wine Association (CWA), through the leadership of Percy Morgan, that "transformed forever California wine growing, taking it from a collection of small, mostly individual agricultural enterprises to a mercantile industry, from a local concern to a national and even international one."[40] Through the CWA, California wine was transformed from a non-distinct commodity, largely sold in bulk, to a product of distinction that would come to be associated with a consistent character and brand.

These commercial transformations that introduced California wines to national and international markets were accompanied by transformations in the vineyards. Unlike the growing region in proximity to Cincinnati and the American East more generally, the California vineyards, especially Napa, had a long, generally dry and hot growing season, and thus less problems with mildew. The European *vinifera* prospered in this climate, and thus California growers began to experiment with many quality grapes varieties, including Cabernet Sauvignon, Cabernet Franc, and Sauvignon Blanc. Moreover, the Napa Valley became home to numerous immigrants. Some, such as Charles Krug, had a family background in wine growing, and others, such as Gustave Niebaum, a Finnish sea captain who purchased Inglenook in 1880 from a fortune he had made in the Alaska fur trade, bought their way in. As Lukacs remarks, Niebaum had the capital to survive the vicissitudes of the market, and to hire experts to work the vineyards and vinify the wines.[41] Niebaum sought to emulate Bordeaux practices of associating wine with locale, and thus his corks bore the estate's name.

Although these early pioneers of California wines made prudent choices in terms of grape varieties and marketing, it is also argued that matching grapes with the right climate was paramount. André Tchelistcheff, for example, the French-trained wine maker at Beaulieu Vineyards, owned by Georges de Latour, was one of the first to notice that the Napa Valley contained several microclimates. The challenge was to match the right grape variety to a particular microclimate. According to Lukacs, change came largely through Tchelistcheff's guidance.[42] Cooler climate varieties such as Chardonnay and Pinot Noir were planted in the south, an area moderated by the San Pablo Bay, and warmer varieties such as Cabernet were planted in the north, an area noted for its high temperatures.

Although California wines improved immensely in the last twenty years of the nineteenth century, their rise to predominance in the United States and their acquisition of quality reputation worldwide is of relatively recent origin. Thus, Lukacs argues that the Paris tasting in 1976 was a turning point for American wines, as the highest rated wines in the blind tasting turned out to be from California.[43] While a single event may in fact exaggerate what is a longer process, Lukacs' point is that, although California produced quality wines from the end of the nineteenth century, it nearly took to the last quarter of the twentieth century for California and American wines to win recognition from important European juries.

There are a number of reasons for this besides possible European chauvinism. First, many American religious traditions considered that alcohol promoted anti-social and anti-rational behavior that brought those indulged closer to the baseness of nature and thus further from the ways of God. They thus promoted temperance, or abstinence from alcohol.[44] Second, because of a tradition of distilling from plentiful and diverse sources of grain, most American drinkers preferred spirits. This preference persisted well into the 1970s, when California wines came into their own. Moreover, American Prohibition in the 1920s forced many California growers, like the Gallo brothers and Cesare Mondavi, to close their saloons and simply sell their grapes in bulk. For example, Joe Gallo shipped seventeen freight cars of grapes to Chicago, where Gallo grapes had a good reputation for quality.[45]

The period following Prohibition did not advance the cause for quality American wines. The Gallo brothers became known for producing jug wines and highly fortified wines, sold at low cost in flasks, mainly to homeless men. Indeed, the notoriety of Gallo wine has only recently changed with the commercialization of estate bottled wines of higher quality. The point here is that although the potential for producing quality wines existed in California and was pursued by some wine growers, the objectives of some of the largest growers was to produce for a market that was anything but distinct.

The history of California wine reveals the dominion of large capital, and thus, in some senses, the importance of marketing that one finds in Bordeaux. As Lukacs relates, "Although there were plenty of New York, Missouri and other eastern wines available before Prohibition, California wine now dominated national production. To many people, it was becoming synonymous with American wine. And the specific California wines they knew likely came from the CWA.[46]

What is clear is that California wine making was controlled largely by entrepreneurs who had made their fortunes elsewhere and who had considerable capital to invest in building the wine industry. While small boutique vineyards have emerged much more recently—perhaps as a reaction among consumers to large, mass-produced wines—the presence of significant capital, as represented in United Vintners' purchase of Inglenook in 1964 and eventual sale to Heublein in 1968, continues to be pervasive.[47] What this means is that whatever benefits come from climate and soil, it is surely the history of marketing and the investment of large capital that allows some wine-growing areas and wine estates to rise to a position of dominance.

Marketing is also important to our understanding of Michigan wines. As noted earlier, Michigan's climate is not too harsh for wine growing. However, Michigan growers, and those who write about wine, turn to climate to explain why Michigan growers are beginning to produce quality wines, although generally of the genre one finds in the cooler climates of Europe. Moreover, it is often noted that Michigan as a peninsula state has a sandy soil, the very type of soil that is hostile to many agricultural pursuits exclusive of wine. Therefore, the potential to be just like California, that is in turn just like Europe, is based on reputedly natural growing conditions. In addition, many of the Michigan wineries employ European interns in the cellars, or the wine makers themselves have been trained in the principal oenological centers of Germany and France, thus reinforcing the actual and symbolic ties with European standards.

Nevertheless, Michigan growing conditions have been the subject of considerable controversy between growers and oenological experts. Prior to the development of quality wines in the last ten to fifteen years, Michigan was largely known, like much of the Great Lakes region, for the production of sweet wines and grapes utilized to make grape juice. However, oenologists at Michigan State's Agricultural School were convinced that Michigan wine growers could produce quality wines through introducing carefully selected hybrid plants. It was believed that hybrids were well suited to Michigan growing conditions and consequently grape varieties to be cultivated other than the Concord, typically used in making commercial juice. There is little doubt that, in the long run, the Michigan oenologists were successful in promoting hybrids, and thus in helping to change the consciousness among growers with respect to the commercial potentials of quality wines. It should be recognized, though, that the vicissitudes of the world market for cherries and apples—two other Michigan crops—has helped in promoting wine as a suitable commercial option.

Although Michigan has no equivalent of Pierre Viala to emphasize the nationalist and natural scripting of wine, Michigan does have its defender of the European vine. Ed O'Keefe, who is proprietor of Chateau Grand Traverse, argued that the European *vinifera* could prosper in Michigan's cooler climes. Rejecting advice from the Michigan State oenologues, O'Keefe experienced considerable success in cultivating *vinifera* varieties on his sizeable estate on the Old Mission peninsula. Some Michigan growers have taken note of O'Keefe's success and have followed suit, while others have planted their vineyards with a combination of *vinifera* and hybrids. What is apparent in Michigan, as in California, is the desire of growers to have their wines associated with particular locales. My Michigan informants would often remark that while they are surely committed to replicating the standards of quality associated with California and Europe, like California and European growers they also wish to convey that their wines are distinct in bearing the aroma and flavor that are particular to Michigan soils and climates. The notion of *terroir* is just as pervasive on the wine producing periphery as it is at the California and European centers.

## Terroir in Question

There is little doubt in the context of French wine-growing history that *terroir* has been used to counter fraud by guaranteeing the authenticity and origin of wine, and to establish quality by linking wine to a particular place and soil. *Terroir* is, moreover, an index of privilege, as few growers are able to consolidate their property into an area sufficiently large to be termed a "terroir." In a conversation with my Médoc informants, who are cooperative wine growers, they played symbolically on the notion of *terroir* in a manner that was both empowering and a source of resistance. Cooperative wines have long been regarded as non-distinct because they vinify the grapes that come from numerous estates or *terroirs*. It is believed among most wine experts that quality wines can only come from the grapes vinified from a single estate, although it is widely recognized that Napoleon's establishment of partible inheritance has meant that even the famous estates of the Médoc and Bordeaux are comprised of a variety of non-contiguous terrains. Furthermore, as noted earlier, in order to bottle wine with a chateau label a grower must show that the grapes come from a single estate—*terroir*. My informants, most of whom have widely dispersed properties, have turned this to their symbolic although not commercial advantage by arguing that their combined grapes really represent the true wines of their commune. The authenticity of grapes associated with the commune contests or at the very least gives new meaning to the notion of *terroir*.

Moreover, the sense that the true grapes come from the collective dissociates the notion of terroir or place of origin from what is natural, and thus foregrounds the identity of wine as socially produced or perhaps even politically constituted.

To truly understand the hierarchical ranking of wines and wine regions we must, as I have argued throughout, turn to the margins of history and raise questions concerning the subjectivity and cultural figuration of taste. If one accepts that quality wines are aged, and are produced from low yielding *vinifera* vines that are locally circumscribed, then it seems logically and perhaps even empirically verifiable, as Wilson argues for the Médoc, that "the secret of the quality vineyards is found in the internal composition and functioning of the gravel mounds."[48] I find no reason to doubt that Wilson did find consistencies in the geology or deep soil of quality vineyards that he explored through seismic techniques. However, the taste of so-called quality wines is not a natural endowment, but a function of educating the palate. That is, one acquires a taste for certain wines, and learns to discern quality as a consequence of accepted standards. It is the case that some consumers prefer dry wines to sweet, or young wines produced from higher yielding plants to the aged reds of Bordeaux. Moreover, although the *appellation contrôlée* legislation was created to ostensibly improve the quality of wines and protect against fraud, this legislation clearly defined wine as being a product of naturally fermented grapes. Consequently, the many wines produced from dried fruits by peasants were excluded. As Bourdieu has argued, the distinctions of taste are socially produced and tend to symbolically replicate relations of power.[49]

As we have seen, Bordeaux and California's rise to predominance was connected to historical factors and the superior marketing that was put into place. In the case of Bordeaux, it was privileges granted to English merchants that significantly elevated Bordeaux's commercial status, while in California the commercial history was tied to the CWA. My Michigan informants understand well the importance of marketing as they point out that the control of marketing by large distributors—those firms that ultimately are able to place wine on the shelves of supermarkets or the lists at local or chain restaurants—often favors wines that have a proven commercial record. Therefore, it is much harder for smaller wineries and certainly incipient wineries to succeed in commercializing their wines.

The fact that we attribute natural attributes to wine or look for natural conditions to account for quality is surely no surprise once we understand the uses of "natural," outside of the context of wine, to establish the foundations of privilege. After all, the cultural formulations of "natural" are the very social fundaments that engage our ranking of peoples, albeit ideologically and hegemonically. This is also true of wine. It has been my intention, therefore, not to dismiss climate and soil altogether—this would be frivolous. Rather I have sought to show the connections between the uses of the natural as a rhetorical device of politics and history that sets some wines apart from others, and that can even serve as icons of nationalism and the nation state. *Terroir*, in my estimation, needs to be refigured in accordance with the history of wine regions and the culturally mediated subjectivity of taste.

Lastly, it is important to critically re-evaluate *terroir* and the privileges that ensue from the hierarchical ranking of wine. This can be achieved through what I term the "social science of wine." The technical components and processes that inform the making of wine, while suitable for guiding the wine towards a desired taste—itself socially constructed—cannot adequately address the historical and cultural issues that are often concealed by our exclusive focus on the product and natural components such as climate and soil. This is surely a question of a different epistemological approach—one that links an appropriate way of knowing to its socially constituted object of knowledge.

## Notes

1. René Pijassou, *Le Médoc: Un grand vignoble de qualité*, 2 vols. (Paris: Tallandier, 1980).
2. Pijassou, Le Médoc, 1:214.
3. James E. Wilson, *Terroir: The Role of Geology, Climate and Culture in the Making of French Wines* (Berkeley: University of California Press, 1998), 189–91. Wilson argues that within a particular vineyard, qualitative differences in the soil can establish qualitative differences in grape plants that are just a few meters apart. The recognition of qualitative differences between plants that are separated by only meters has been used to explain the lesser reputation of Médoc cooperative growers, whose vineyards are in close proximity (row to row) from the elite estates.

4. When I have communicated to non-Michigan residents that I conduct research on Michigan wine growers, the response is generally one of surprise. Most individuals do not believe it is possible to cultivate vineyards in a climate as cold as Michigan. However, the early snowfall in late November generally provides insulation to the roots of the plants, and thus, protections against cold winters. Moreover, it is generally pointed out that the cold waters of Lake Michigan also prevent the plants from maturing too fast in the early spring when cold nights can be damaging.

5. The sun light and winds of a southern exposure are thought to be important to the growing cycle of some plant varieties.

6. I argue that a science that focuses on the technical components of wine growing and wine making cannot grasp the socio-historical and cultural processes that contribute to the distinction of wines. This argument is consistent with critiques that have been directed at the natural sciences more generally. See, for example, Thomas Kuhn, *The Structure of Scientific Revolutions* (Chicago: University of Chicago Press, 1962).

7. Arthur O. Lovejoy, *The Great Chain of Being: A Study of the History of an Idea* (New York: Harper and Row, 1960).

8. Jean-Jacques Rousseau, *The Social Contract and the Discourse on the Origin of Inequality* (New York: Simon and Schuster, 1964), 206–11.

9. Karl Marx, *Pre-Capitalist Economic Formations* (New York: International, 1964), 68–71.

10. James Fraser, *The New Golden Bough* (New York: Anchor Books, 1961), 20, 32–33; Edward Burnett Tylor, *Anthropology* (Ann Arbor: University of Michigan Press), 64–84; Lucien Lévy-Bruhl, *The "Soul" of the Primitive* (London: George Allen and Unwin, 1965), 12–42.

11. Johannes Fabian, *Time and the Other: How Anthropology Makes its Object* (New York: Columbia University Press, 1983), 31.

12. Edward Said, *Orientalism* (New York: Random House, 1978).

13. John Comaroff and Jean Comaroff, *Ethnography and the Historical Imagination* (Boulder, CO: Westview, 1992).

14. Benedict Anderson, *Imagined Communities* (London and New York: Verso, 1983).

15. Ernest Gellner, *Nations and Nationalism* (Ithaca, NY: Cornell University Press, 1983), 29–38.

16. See Partha Chatterjee, *Nationalist Thought and the Colonial World: A Derivative Discourse* (London: Zed, 1986).

17. See Philippe Roudié, *Vignobles et Vignerons du Bordelais, 1850–1980* (Paris: Editions du Centre National de la Recherche Scientifique, 1988), 154–67.

18. Harry Paul, *Science, Wine and the Vine in Modern France* (Cambridge: Cambridge University Press, 1996), 36–43.

19. Ibid., 89–98.

20. Wilson, *Terroir*, 48.

21. Paul, *Science, Wine and the Vine*, 27–28.

22. Eugen Weber, *Peasants into Frenchmen. The Modernization of Rural France, 1870–1914* (Stanford, CA: Stanford University Press, 1976).

23. One is reminded of Mary Douglas' structural argument whereby in crisis situations or liminal periods, the social body acts to protect its boundaries (see Mary Douglas, *Purity and Danger: An Analysis of Concepts of Pollution and Taboo* [London: Routledge and Kegan Paul, 1966], 99–103). Given the crisis precipitated by phylloxera during a period of late nineteenth century nation-state building, it is not surprising to find the close analogy between vines and the social body.

24. See Dewey Markham, *1855: A History of the Bordeaux Classification* (New York: John Wiley and Sons, 1998), 85–108.

25. Wilson, *Terroir*, 83.

26. See Hayden White, *Tropics of Discourse* (Baltimore: Johns Hopkins University Press, 1978).

27. See François Guichard, and Philippe Roudié, *Vins, vignerons et coopérateurs de Bordeaux et de Porto*, vol. 1 (Paris: CNRS, 1985).

28. For example, see Dion, *Histoire de la vigne*; Marcel Lachiver, *Vins, vignes et vignerons* (Paris: Fayard, 1988).

29. See Jacques Derrida, *Of Grammatology* (Baltimore: Johns Hopkins University Press, 1974).

30. See Arjun Appadurai, ed., *The Social Life of Things* (Cambridge: Cambridge University Press, 1986).

31. Pijassou, *Le Médoc*, 299.

32. Henri Enjalbert, "Comment naissent les grands crus: Bordeaux, Porto, Cognac," *Annales* 8 (1953): 315–28, 457–74; Robert C. Ulin, *Vintages and Traditions: An Ethnohistory of Southwest French Wine Cooperatives* (Washington DC: Smithsonian Institution Press, 1996), 39–62.

33. Henri Enjalbert and Bernard Enjalbert, *L'Histoire de la vigne et du vin* (Paris: Bordas S.A., 1987), 21–22.

34. Ulin, *Vintages and Traditions*, 87–91.

35. Eric Hobsbawm and Terrence Ranger, ed., *The Invention of Tradition* (Cambridge: Cambridge University Press, 1983), 1–14.

36. Pierre Bourdieu, *Distinction: A Social Critique of the Judgment of Taste* (Cambridge MA: Harvard University Press, 1984).

37. Paul Lukacs, *American Vintage: The Rise of American Wine* (Boston: Houghton Mifflin Company, 2000), 103.

38. Ibid., 24–26.

39. Ibid., 52.

40. Ibid., 53.

41. Ibid., 78–79.

42. Ibid., 123.
43. Ibid., 4.
44. My colleague, Fred Smith, shared with me a perspective with respect to his work on rum and slavery in Barbados that is remarkably similar to what I argue about the naturalization of wine. English colonists consumed gin as a beverage of distinction and left rum for the slaves, who were regarded as closer to nature. To this day, the English tend to avoid the rum shops that they believe precipitate anti-rational behavior.
45. Lukacs, *American Vintage*, 139.
46. Lukacs, *American Vintage*, 81–82.
47. Lukacs, *American Vintage*, 127.
48. Wilson, *Terroir*, 187.
49. Bourdieu, *Distinction*, 2.

# Chapter 4

# The Development and Economic Impact of the Wine Industry in Ontario, Canada

*Linda Bramble, Carman Cullen,
Joseph Kushner, and Gary Pickering*[1]

## Introduction

The Ontario wine region, like those of most other wine regions in North America, has experienced a sea change in terms of the quality, size, and economic impact of its wine industry. For most of the twentieth century, forces such as war, Prohibition, and consumer antagonism towards beverage alcohol militated against its growth, but in recent decades Ontario has experienced a wider and more revolutionary change than any other wine region in the North American jurisdiction.

This chapter first examines the origins of the Ontario wine industry and its development during the nineteenth century, and most of the twentieth century. In particular, it analyzes the impact of public policy on the wine industry and how the policy resulted in a state controlled system that brought the industry to a near standstill for several decades. Further, it examines the revolution experienced in the industry in recent decades as markets, consumer attitudes, and public policies underwent fundamental change. Ontario wineries now produce world-class wines and, with the growing acceptance of these wines both nationally and internationally, the recent growth in wine sales is expected to continue. This chapter also examines the economic impact of the Ontario wine industry, which currently provides direct employment for 6,350 people and for an additional 3,100 people in induced employment from the expenditures of its employees. This billion-dollar industry is also a significant contributor to government revenues, in the form of taxes and licenses.

## HISTORICAL DEVELOPMENT OF THE INDUSTRY

The development of the modern Ontario wine industry has been spectacular. In the course of three decades it grew from a small, low key industry dominated by mediocre wines to a high profile industry characterized by the production of premium wines. This section first examines the inhibitors to the growth of the industry, such as cumbersome regulations, high taxes, uneven quality and supply of grapes, scientific skepticism regarding the planting of high quality grapes, and the historical stigma associated with Canadian wines. It subsequently analyzes the factors underlying the rapid development of the industry. Finally, future challenges to the industry are discussed.

### Inhibitors to Growth

A major obstacle to the development of the Ontario wine industry was a highly regulated and highly taxed system. Many jurisdictions in North America became regulated after the anarchy experienced during Prohibition. Following the repeal of Prohibition, nineteen states in the United States enacted detailed legislation regulating the production, distribution, and sale of alcohol.[2] Similarly, the Liquor Control Board of Ontario (LCBO) was instituted in 1927 to regulate the Ontario wine industry. In order to solve the growing problem posed by unscrupulous entrepreneurs, whose wines were produced in unsanitary conditions and who at times used carcinogenic flavoring agents,[3] the LCBO encouraged the six largest wine companies that had existed prior to Prohibition to "acquire" the other fifty-seven companies. In addition, from 1927 to 1974 the Board placed a moratorium on the issuance of winery licenses—a measure unique in North America.

Another obstacle to growth in the industry was the inadequate supply of quality grapes. All New World wine-producing regions, except Canada and the U.S. Northeast (New York, Pennsylvania, Ohio, Virginia), knew they could grow premium *Vitis vinifera* varieties of grapes. For example, in the 1600s South Africa cultivated Chenin Blanc, as did Chile, which in the mid 1800s grew Cabernet Sauvignon. Further west, the Australians discovered the virtues of Riesling and Syrah. In the mid 1700s, Franciscan priests introduced *V. vinifera* grapes to California. The vines thrived because winter temperatures never fell too low, summer humidity never went too high, and fungal diseases posed no serious problems.

In Ontario, however, the winters were too cold for the more vulnerable *vinifera* plants to survive, and the summers too hot and humid to enable the grapes to resist an array of molds, bacteria, viruses, and pests, not the least being *Phylloxera*. Ontario winegrowers survived only by using hardier American and French hybrids. Although nearly half the world's vine species are native to North America, they proved to be poorly suited to making wine. Wines made from the species *V. labrusca, rotundifolia, riparia, aestivalis,* and *cordifolia* were not tasty. In fact, to most palates, they were wretched.

The first commercial wines of any success were produced from *V. labrusca* and *V. vinifera* (Niagara, Duchess, Isabella, Aurora) hybrids. However, such wines were characterized by a rank, musky, raw, "foxy" taste caused by the methyl anthranilate and O-amino acetothenone content of these species—a disagreeable flavor that could be masked only by diluting the wines with water, adding large amounts of sugar and flavorings, and sometimes, in order to re-fortify them, substantial quantities of alcohol. Indeed, from 1930 to 1950, the wine industry of Ontario was largely based on highly manipulated "ports" and "sherries." As a result of these poor wine-making practices, Ontario wines gained a notoriety that proved a major obstacle to overcome when its winegrowers subsequently adopted quality grapes and started to produce new, improved wines.

As noted, it was initially thought that *V. vinifera* grapes could not be grown in Ontario. The Vineland Horticultural Research Station, the only source of research and development available to Ontario growers, found only six of the fifty-seven thousand seedlings it evaluated in the period 1913 to 1938 to be "promising," and was unequivocal that *V. vinifera* could never be commercially grown in Ontario.[4] This lack of innovative research was a most devastating inhibitor to growth.

Government policies also presented difficulties. By the end of World War II, consumer tastes were shifting away from sweet, fortified wines to dry, table styles as soldiers coming home from Europe demanded better quality wines. The trend towards dry wines was maintained, but wineries had insufficient product to meet demand. Eventually, in 1973, the Province of Ontario passed the *Wine Content Act*, which allowed producers to use up to 75 percent of imported wine into a blend and still label it a "Product of Canada." However, federal restrictions against the import of new vines remained in place, so the *Wine Content Act* provided little motivation for growers to change, despite difficulty selling their grapes.

A further problem was the adversarial relationship between growers and vintners. The *Ontario Liquor Control Act* (1927), which placed a moratorium on new licenses and encouraged consolidation, led the number of wineries to fall from sixty-seven in 1927 to six by 1940. To correct the resulting imbalance in market power between small grape growers and the large wineries,[5] the Ontario Grape Growers Marketing Board, established in 1947, introduced a policy whereby prices were negotiated annually between the Wine Council of Ontario, a voluntary association of wineries, and the Marketing Board. This policy created an adversarial relationship between grape growers and wine producers.

Although the arrangement was better for growers because it permitted them to negotiate as a group, producers argued for flexible rather than fixed price arrangements. They needed that freedom because price reflected a combination of factors that varied geographically and over time. Their aim was to produce higher quality wines, and this could be achieved only through securing better locations, more appropriate clones, improved methods of vineyard management, higher brix levels, better physiological ripeness, and lower yields. To do so, however, was difficult since the growers were for all extents and purposes unionized to negotiate a price for their grapes, regardless of quality.

Unfortunately, the old adversarial system still characterizes the Ontario wine industry. In order to guarantee quality, vintners have had to invest millions of dollars in buying land and planting vineyards of their own, diverting money away from investment in capital improvements in the cellar, marketing, and promotion.[6] The net result is that, while there are growers of quality wine in Ontario, and vintners do work on individual incentive contracts with better quality growers, the overall structure of the industry continues to militate against harmonious relationships and improvements in quality.

## Contributors to Growth

Despite the unfavorable factors noted above, there are a number of positive factors promoting the growth of the Ontario wine industry. The first is the suspension of the moratorium on new licenses. In the 1930s, *Bright's Wines*, one of the larger wineries, hired a French scientist, Adehmar de Chaunac, to experiment with new clones and vines. De Chaunac worked for decades in very difficult economic circumstances, such as the Depression and the World War II ban on the importation of vines. After the war, de Chaunac imported several hundred vines, including better quality French hybrids, such as Baco Noir, Vidal, and Marechal Foch, and cool climate vines such as Riesling, Chardonnay, and Gamay Noir. By 1955, he had proved that Ontario could produce Chardonnay from 100 percent home-grown grapes.[7]

Although the larger growers required more evidence to convert to *V. vinifera* wines, a few single-minded and defiant, small, independent growers, and young European immigrants were prepared to take the risk and change the prevailing paradigm. Two of these, Donald Ziraldo, a local nurseryman, and Karl Kaiser, a young émigré from Austria and an amateur winemaker, believed they could commercially sell the wines they produced from Ziraldo's French hybrid grapes. In 1974 they successfully petitioned the government to revoke the forty-five-year moratorium on new licenses and grant them a license to manufacture wine. Within the year, they also received a retail license to sell wine.[8] Thus, 1975 may be considered the year that the modern wine industry of Ontario was founded.

Unlike the two largest wineries, Bright's and Andres, who by then had abandoned their vineyards, the new vignerons (see Table 4.1) became integrated grower-vintners. They believed that quality wines originated in the vineyard.[9] The grapes they planted were predominately *vinifera*, Riesling, Chardonnay, Cabernets, and Gamay.[10] Several others, such as John Marynissen and Charles Pillitteri, who had been growing tender fruit in Ontario for years, and who were amateur winemakers, also understood the potential of these varietals and opened wineries of their own.[12]

**Table 4.1** European-born wine producers in Ontario[11]

| Vintner | Winery | Country of Origin |
|---|---|---|
| Karl Kaiser | Inniskillin | Austria |
| Paul Bosc | Chateau des Charmes | France |
| Herman Weis | Vineland Estates | Germany |
| Klaus Reif | Reif Estates | Germany |
| Herbert Konzelmann | Konzelmann Estates | Germany |

Technology, defined in its widest sense, also made a significant contribution to the success of the industry. While many developing wine nations were able to rapidly exploit the commercial opportunities afforded by the new technologies (outlined below), Canada lagged behind, due in part to cultural inertia within the industry and the regulatory "baggage" previously referred to. An important distinction must be made between the availability of the technology and its actual implementation. While the differences between Old World and New World countries, with respect to the philosophy and use of modern technology, have become increasingly blurred over the last few years, this was not the case in the 1980s and much of the 1990s. As Australia, New Zealand, and many other New World nations could attest at the time, changes in winery technology were revolutionizing their industries.

These technological advances were, and largely still are, simple: the use of refrigeration to reduce and control juice and wine temperatures, particularly during fermentation; the application of simple processing procedures and products to maintain good winery hygiene and prevent spoilage of wines; and, new materials and designs for grape presses and fermentors that provide for greater control over the composition of the resultant wines, and therefore their quality. Taken collectively, these advances allow for the production of fruit-driven, intensely flavoured, largely earlier drinking wines with wide consumer appeal.

Although available for years, these technologies did not become widely used in Canada until the mid-1990s. Canada, being a traditional hybrid/juice industry, did not have the same interest in technological changes to wine making and wine-making equipment compared to other more specialized wine-producing nations. Furthermore, as wine making in Canada was relatively small-scale, there existed few suppliers of specialized wine-making equipment and often inadequate servicing of that equipment.[13] Only after the components were in place to provide the necessary motivation and infrastructure—such as the North American Free Trade Agreement (NAFTA), the Vintners Quality Alliance of Ontario (VQAO, more commonly known as VQA), and the Wine Assistance Program—was Canada able to utilise the "new" technologies.

The industry pioneers believed that they could grow the grapes to make better quality, premium table wines, but were unsure if they could sell the improved wines. The invidious stigma that accompanied the wines of the past had to be overcome, as was shown in the case of Donald Ziraldo: he secured French buyers for his premium wines, but they pulled out when he could not prove the provenance of his grapes.[14]

However, in order to satisfy both domestic and export markets, quality standards had to be established throughout the industry. This came about in the early 1980s, when under Ziraldo's leadership, the vintners, growers, journalists, and LCBO representatives formed the VQA, a voluntary organization that established an appellation system. The VQA became legislated into provincial law in 1989. [15]

The system geographically demarcated the top wine-growing areas in Ontario and set standards of production, which stipulated the varieties of grapes that would be allowed. These standards set it apart from other wine-growing regions in the Northeast United States, such as New York, Pennsylvania, Ohio, and Michigan which, unlike Ontario, do not require review by an independent tasting panel, or do not have regulations such as those stipulated in the production of Late Harvest and ice wine varieties.[16] Unlike the French *Appellation d'Origine Contr_lée* (AOC), the VQA does not regulate yield, harvest date, or training systems. However, the VQA has been the single most important factor in elevating consumer perception of the wines of Ontario, and generally in overcoming much of the negative stigma attached to Canadian wines.[17]

NAFTA jolted the industry into further collaboration and innovation. Coming into effect in 1989, NAFTA eliminated preferential treatment of Canadian wines in order to create a more level playing field for American wines.[18] However, the agreement frightened both growers and producers, who felt they could not compete with the Americans. The Wine Council of Ontario rose to the challenge in a number of ways: consumer access was improved by selling VQA wines directly to restaurants, thereby bypassing the 58 percent provincial tax; funding programs for capitalization, promotion, and marketing were started; and educational programs were established to promote training and development.[19]

Unlike the American Northeast, Ontario had large wineries, such as Vincor and Andres, that possessed the incentive and resources, as well as the ability to work collaboratively with smaller producers required to create an internationally competitive industry.[20] During free trade negotiations, the industry successfully lobbied the government for support, and via the Wine Assistance Program, Ontario agreed to subsidize the removal of Labrusca-based vines to enable growers to switch to *V. vinifera*.[21] However, the program was not entirely successful. Although some growers switched, many accepted the money offered, pulled up their vines, and did not replant, while those who had already taken the risk and planted *V. vinifera* vines received nothing.[22]

During the free trade negotiations, the government also gave wineries funds from the Agriculture International Marketing Strategy (AIMS) program to promote their wines and to invest in capital equipment.[23] At the same time, the LCBO adopted state-of-the-art retail practices, and began de-listing products that were not selling. The government also introduced educational programs for wineries.

Immigration has played a pivotal role in the adoption of the new technology. As was the case with many New World wine nations, immigrants from Europe brought their culture and knowledge of wine to Canada, thereby pioneering the development of the modern wine industry. Arguably, however, immigration from New World countries such as Australia, New Zealand, and South Africa during the 1990s, contributed most to the exponential growth in the quality of Canadian wines, as these trained winemakers and viticulturists brought with them an enhanced knowledge of "new" technologies that were subsequently modified and applied within the Canadian context.[24] The new technologies included the following: the use of specialized refrigeration systems to cool fermenting juice and preserve aroma and flavour concentrations; modern presses (for instance, the replacing of screw presses with membrane presses) that allow for gentle extraction of grape components; processing changes to minimize oxidation and microbial spoilage of wine; the use of higher quality oak barrels for maturing premium wines; and new enzyme and yeast preparations that allow for greater control over fermentation and over final wine flavor. [25] As more wineries developed during the 1990s, a critical mass was reached that made it attractive for winery equipment and material suppliers to service the Canadian industry. The relationship is now largely one of close collaboration and support.

An important technological change concerns ice wine production. Ice wine is the late harvest wine made from the juice of grapes that have been frozen on the vine and pressed while frozen. Due to the concentration of sugars, acids, and aroma compounds, the resulting wine is intensely aromatic and flavored, and characterized by a marked sweetness.[26] Canada possesses climatic and growing conditions conducive to dependable ice wine production, and is now the world's leading producer in terms of quantity and, arguably, quality. Its role as a flagship for the Canadian industry has been pivotal in promoting Canada's reputation internationally as a top producer of premium wine. However, to optimize and commercially exploit the unique growing conditions for ice wines, new winery technologies, such as press design, are of crucial importance. Extracting a profitable quantity of juice from rock-hard grapes and conforming to the stringent VQA quality production standards was difficult to accomplish with traditional presses. New, largely "home-grown" presses, which have now been introduced, have proved very successful.

On the viticultural front, the change from hybrid to *vinifera* grapes and the appropriate matching of vineyard site with grape variety were absolutely critical. The selection of clones and rootstocks, and particularly appropriate vineyard management practices, are ongoing technological considerations for the industry.

Many commentators argue that the further spread of new and appropriate viticultural and oenological technology is necessary to promote the Canadian wine industry. The role of formal grape and wine education in the development and application of technologies should also play a large role in improving quality and facilitating future growth. A number of tertiary institutions and programs have been established recently in Canada, and are just producing their first few crops of graduates, eager to apply the science and technology from their studies.

In addition, a number of vintners are experimenting with new winery technologies and products, such as micro-oxygenation, a new generation of wine-making enzymes, and Canadian oak for maturation of premium table wines. All of these show potential for improving quality or branding opportunities. The next few years will also show the results of current experimentation by industry pioneers with largely untried *vinifera* grapes, including Rhône and Italian varieties.[27] New designs in grape harvesters are currently on trial which should allow for machine harvesting of ice wine grapes, a development that is critical to servicing the recent large increase in grapes destined for ice wine production.[28]

The adoption of these new technologies should facilitate a steady improvement in the quality of Canadian wines. Wider adoption of irrigation technologies will also increase the possibilities for production in Canada's drier wine-growing regions. Production will always be limited by the short growing season, disease risk, and the susceptibility of vines to cold damage. Nevertheless, recent genomic research offers the potential to engineer *vinifera* vines with the necessary resilience to withstand a cold climate, as well as improved disease resistance, particularly important to the humid and wetter conditions affecting the Ontario wine industry.[29]

Wine tourism is another important factor that has contributed to the success of the industry. The Ontario wine region benefits from its proximity to affluent markets, such as the Greater Toronto Area, which had a population of over five million people, and American markets in western New York, Ohio, Michigan, and Pennsylvania. Moreover, the Niagara Region was already an established tourist destination, and therefore could be readily promoted as a wine tourism destination. As indicated later in this chapter, tourism is now a significant driver of economic activity in the Niagara Region.

Also, in common with other wine regions of the world, Niagara has post-secondary oenology and viticulture research and education facilities, specifically Brock University and Niagara College. In 1997, Brock University launched the Cool Climate Oenology and Viticulture Institute (CCOVI), which is the only research center in North America dedicated to the study of cool climate grape growing and wine making. Its Department of Biology runs several degree-granting programs in viticulture and oenology that prepare graduates for positions as viticulturists, winemakers, and sensory scientists in related fields of microbiology. Approximately 20 percent of the winemakers in Ontario are CCOVI graduates. Brock is also contemplating an MBA with a specialization in Wine and Spirits, the first of its kind in Canada. Niagara College offers diplomas in culinary arts, as well as field viticulture and wine retailing, thus providing the industry with highly trained personnel in wine sales and marketing.

## INDUSTRY CHALLENGES

There exist a number of challenges to the Ontario wine industry. The first of these is retail distribution. Wines can be sold in Ontario in only four ways: through winery retail outlets, restaurants, government-controlled (LCBO) retail stores, and private off-premise retail stores. In order to have a product sold by the LCBO, the supplier must provide a volume supply guarantee, and a marketing and sales promotion plan. Unfortunately, small producers and new entrants are often excluded from this channel of distribution because they cannot meet the volume requirements. The larger, established firms enjoy an additional advantage when placing their wines on the lists of local and chain restaurants because of brand-name recognition. Further, most of the 368 private retail stores are owned by the two largest companies (Vincor and Andres), which do not allow the sale of other brands.

Small wineries can only begin to compete when they have the resources to similarly engage in vertical integration of production and retailing, which in turn necessitates access to greater capital. One option is the use of electronic marketing, which allows the small winery to not only advertise its product at a very low cost, but also to sell the product directly to the consumer. As Gary Zucca, in a comparative analysis of California's regional wine associations, notes: "Although the regional associations almost, without exception have web sites, many wineries and vineyards still do not, and those that have sites, especially the smaller wineries, don't fully exploit the capabilities of the Internet. Potential customers out for a weekend drive now have the capability to access the Internet from their cars or cell phones, to find maps, and even to locate vineyards and tasting rooms with GPS positions."[30] Zucca's recommendation, that both wine associations and individual wineries sell wines and tickets to events, merits consideration by Ontario's wine industry.

A second major problem is international competition. Industry officials believe that the priority should be to boost wine sales to other Canadian provinces and to the United States. This, together with gaining increased access to the lucrative Asian ice wine market, is now a major challenge confronting the Ontario Industry as is the European market, which after years of negotiation allowed VQA wines to be sold in Europe.

Further, Canadian producers account for only 39 percent of domestic wine sales, one of the lowest percentages for domestic producers in wine-producing countries. The objective of Ontario wine producers is to achieve 50 percent penetration of the domestic market by 2010. Given that French, Australian, Italian, and Spanish producers account for at least 90 percent of their respective domestic markets, the 50 percent market share should be attainable. However, other countries are also looking to expand their markets, and in fact are successfully doing so by producing higher quality wines and adapting to changing consumer tastes. For example, New Zealand, although a small producer, has expanded its exports thirteen times since 1990. Australia and Chile are doing likewise.

To compete with the international firms in both domestic and international markets, Ontario producers must be both quality- and price-competitive. In the past, there have been several consolidations to gain economies of scale and marketing synergies. In addition, two large players from France, Boisset and Michele Picard, have recently made substantial investments in vineyards and wineries in Niagara. The challenge for the future is for the small firms to compete successfully against the larger firms. To do so, the romantic mystique of the small wineries must be enhanced, and a wine tourism business built around them.

A related issue is that of unpredictable currency fluctuations. For example, a weakening of the U.S. dollar, as occurred in early 2006, makes Canadian wines less competitive in both Canada and the United States. On the positive side, inputs—including grapes from the United States—have become cheaper, much to the detriment of Canadian growers. However, on balance, the weaker U.S. dollar is disadvantageous to the Canadian industry.

Also, greater collaboration is required between growers and producers. Industry leaders believe that the present conflict between growers and wineries will be resolved. Both the growers and wineries agree that the present system is unworkable and that the future of the industry depends on collaboration, which, according to some officials, may require provincial intervention.

Land-use policies pose another difficulty to be resolved. Ontario has three appellations, the Niagara Peninsula being by far the largest. Approximately, one half of the land in Niagara (fifty-four thousand acres) is designated "agricultural," of which 50 percent is planted with grapes. The wineries contend that in order to meet rising demand, they require all the available land. Farmers, on the other hand, want to retain the freedom to sell their property to the highest bidder, regardless of how they would use the land. Land-use policy, although required to preserve farmland, continues to be contentious. Land-use policies were similarly controversial in California, where as Kathleen Brosnan points out, two state actions—the creation of an agricultural preserve and the establishment of an appellation system— were instrumental to the success of the Napa County wine industry.[31] However, with success, property prices increased beyond the reach of the type of entrepreneurial, small investor responsible for the success of the industry. Instead, "extremely wealthy individuals with little or no experience opened 'boutique' wineries, producing a limited stock of 'cult' Cabernets that often sold at exorbitant prices. At the same time, large outside corporations took hold of some of Napa's largest, most established operations."[32] The consequence was larger scale cultivation leading to deforestation of hillsides, which in turn resulted in diminished biodiversity and greater susceptibility to pest infestations. Wine tourism also contributed to environmental problems, such as traffic congestion, and associated pollution problems accentuated by the cars of non-Napa residents who formed a growing percentage of the wine industry workforce.

The Niagara Region, where demand rather than supply factors limit the potential for growth, is in no immediate danger of experiencing similar environmental problems. Since only a small percentage of suitable vineyard land is under cultivation, there is no need for deforestation. However, there is a danger, as land prices rise, that the area will similarly be inundated by extremely wealthy individuals with little or no experience of wine growing, or by large corporations, that in the Napa Valley, changed the nature of farming.

As noted, wine tourism presents another challenge. Winery profits from on-site retail outlets are 50 percent higher than from other distribution channels. Increasing winery tourism and traffic to onsite outlets is therefore a high priority. In this regard, a wine route has been introduced. The challenge is to beautify the route to enhance the visitor's experience. As previously mentioned, the Internet can be used, and in fact is beginning to be used, by several producers to spread a cohesive message regarding the romantic mystique of the vineyards.

## The Economic Impact of the Industry

The first vineyards in the province of Ontario were planted in the seventeenth century using native varieties. A century later, European varieties were introduced, and in 1886, the first commercial winery in Canada was opened on Pelee Island in Essex County. Over time, the grape industry shifted to the Niagara region, where it remains centered. The number of wineries steadily grew, except for the half century from 1927 to 1975, when the government placed a moratorium on new wineries. With one exception in 1929, this policy was maintained until 1975, when Inniskillin Wines was granted a license. Thereafter, wineries proliferated, and at present there are nearly 120 wineries in the province.[33]

In 1998, KPMG, an international accounting firm, was commissioned by the Wine Council of Ontario to assess the impact of the Ontario wine industry on the provincial economy. In this chapter we use a similar methodology to determine the economic impact of the industry. The KPMG study,[34] however, includes neither induced effects from the expenditures of the employees of the wineries, nor the contribution of the wine industry to tourism in Ontario. In this chapter, we include both, which enables us not only to evaluate the industry's contribution to the Ontario economy, but also to compare it with the impact of the wine industry in California as analyzed in the often-quoted work, *The Economic Impact of California Wine*.[35]

The Ontario wine industry consists of four components: Ontario grape growers, Ontario wineries, Ontario wine retail outlets, including the LCBO, and wine tourism. Wine education and research are also industry-related.

### Grape Growers

To determine the impact of grape growers, we include only employment and sales associated with wine production, and not employment and sales associated with grapes destined for purposes such as home consumption and the production of commercial juices. Employment in the industry consists of 519 owner-operator growers, and the equivalent of an additional 549 full time positions and

84 indirect jobs, that is, those employed by suppliers to the grape growers. [36] Wages and salaries for the full time and indirect jobs are $26 million. Their sales total $36.9 million[37]

Table 4.2 presents a comparison of grape growers in Ontario and California. Ontario's revenue per grower of $74,000 is much smaller than California's $363,000 per grower.[38] One explanation is the smaller farm acreage of 34 acres in Ontario compared to 180 acres in California. Although there are some small farms in California, the large growers have farms in excess of 1,000 acres, whereas in Ontario, the largest farm is 300 acres. What is noteworthy is that the sales per acre are virtually the same in both areas. [39]

**Table 4.2** Comparison of grape growers in Ontario and California, 2000[41]

| Category | Ontario ($CDN) | California ($U.S.) | California/Ontario |
|---|---|---|---|
| Number of growers | 500 | 4,400 | 8.8 |
| Sales | $36,900,000 | $1,598,613,654 | 43.3 |
| Sales per grower | $73,800 | $363,320 | 4.92 |
| Acres | 17,000 | 800,000 | 47.0 |
| Acres per grower | 34 | 180 | 5.3 |
| Sales per acre | $2,170 | $1,998 | 0.9 |

## Wineries

Despite several winery mergers, the number of wineries in Ontario increased from sixty in 1993 to ninety in 2000. Some of the wineries are now integrated, having retail outlets on site, as well as restaurants and hospitality suites. The wages and salaries for the 1,857 employees are $81 million and sales are $186 million.[40]

## Retailing of Wine

The growth in the number of wineries in Ontario has not been accompanied by a substantial increase in the number of outlets available for the retailing of their wine. There are 600 provincially owned LCBO outlets, which sell all types of liquor and spirits, including wine. In addition, there are 368 retail wine outlets in Ontario, but these are largely owned and operated by the two largest wine companies (Vincor and Andres), and tend to be located in shopping

malls, either in or around food stores. These non-government controlled wineries do not sell wine other than that made by the company that owns the store. The number of these non-LCBO retail
stores is controlled by the government, and no new licenses are
being granted; therefore, the retail distribution alternatives available
to small- and medium-sized wineries are limited. These smaller
wineries have retail outlets on site, and in four cases also have restaurants. Many also attempt to retail their wines through the LCBO. In
2000, they sold 41,795,548 liters of wine worth $3.27 million, and
employed 2,122 people, with wages and salaries of $47 million. [42]

## Wine Related Tourism

The number employed and the monetary effect of Ontario wine
tourism are difficult to determine because the Niagara Region is a
popular tourist destination due to sites such as the world famous
Niagara Falls, Casino Niagara, and historic Niagara-on-the-Lake, as
well as its vineyards. However, wine-related events are also a major
attraction: Niagara Falls Tourism estimates that 5 percent of the
fourteen million people to visit the Niagara Region in 1999 engaged
in wine tourism. That is, 700,000 tourists visited the region for wine
related events. The annual Grape and Wine Festival, one of Canada's
premier festivals, annually attracts over 100,000 people; out-of-town
visitors spent on average $402 during their festival stay, chiefly on
restaurant meals and accommodation.[43] Other wine-related events
include the Six Unforgettable Weeks of Summer, which attracts
100,000 to 125,000 visitors, and the Icewine Festival, which attracts
10,000 visitors.[44]

Visits to wineries and vineyards are also popular. Each year some
250,000 to 300,000 people visit large wineries, such as Hillebrand
Estates and Inniskillin Wines; 125,000 visit medium-sized wineries,
such as Cave Spring Cellars and Kittling Ridge; while smaller wineries, such as East Dell Estates and Henry of Pelham, attract between
18,000 and 50,000 visitors.[45]

To determine the total expenditures by tourists, the number of
wine-related visitors to the Niagara Region (700,000) is multiplied
by the average expenditure of a tourist. For those who visited the
Niagara Grape and Wine Festival, the amount of $402.50 may not
be typical of other wine related tourists. We can, however, determine

the average expenditure of a typical tourist to the Niagara Region. According to Niagara Falls Tourism, a total of fourteen million people visited the region and spent, according to the Canadian Tourism Research Institute, $1.9 billion, representing $92 per visitor. This compares to an average of $160 per visitor to the California wine regions. In this chapter, we average the expenditure of a typical visitor with a Grape and Wine Festival visitor, to obtain $247 per visitor, or total expenditures of $172,900,000. Not all the expenditure is for wages and salaries. In the hospitality industry in Ontario, the wage component is approximately 30 percent of total revenue, which results in a wage bill of $51,870,000. Tourism in Niagara employs 24,000 people, of whom some 1,200 (5 percent) work in wine-related tourism.[46]

Table 4.3 presents a comparison of these numbers with tourism in California. It is interesting to note that although the California grape-growing sector is approximately forty-three times greater in size/value than that of Ontario, the number of tourists is only fifteen times greater.[47] The total revenues multiple follows a similar pattern, as does the tourism wage bill. These results may be the effect of the successful marketing of wine-related events in Ontario, due in part to the industry's proximity to large urban populations, and in part to the area's other tourist attractions. In fact, Niagara Falls tourism reports that although 5 percent of visitors are attracted by wine-related events, another 2 percent participate in wine-related activities.

Table 4.3 Comparison of wine-related tourism in Ontario and California, 2000[49]

| Category | Ontario | California | California/Ontario |
|---|---|---|---|
| Number of tourists | 700,000 | 10,700,000 | 15.2 |
| Direct employment | 1,200 | 15,300 | 12.8 |
| Total wages | $51,870,000 | $217,535,000 | 4.2 |
| Total revenues | $172,900,000 | $1,200,000,000 | 6.9 |

## Research and Education

Both post-secondary institutions in the Niagara Region—Brock University and Niagara College—have viticulture programs. At Brock, the budget for viticulture is $758,000, and the number of employees is six, whereas at Niagara College the budget is approximately $150,000, and the viticulture staff complement is two. In total, the expenditures amount to $908,000, and the number of jobs is eight. The sixty-six students enrolled in these programs also contribute to the local economy. One half of these students are out of province. At both institutions, a typical student spends $8,036 on room and board. Thus the thirty-three out-of-province students spend a total of $265,000. Given an average wage of $40,000 in the Niagara Region, the expenditure translates into seven jobs.[48]

## Total Economic Impact

Table 4.4 summarizes the industry components. In terms of employment, the industry provides 6,346 jobs and expenditures of $724 million. The wine outlet component dominates industry sales (45 percent), and also has the largest number of employees (33 percent). The wineries sector, although smaller, is larger in terms of wages and salaries paid. Education and research is by far the smallest component in all categories. The totals presented in Table 4.4 represent employment and expenditure effects for the entire industry, but do not include the induced effects resulting from employee expenditures.

Table 4.4 Wine industry sales and employment, 2000 ($CDN)[51]

| Industry component | Expenditure in $000s (%) | Wages & Salaries in $000s (%) | Employment (%) |
| --- | --- | --- | --- |
| Growers | 36, 900 (5.1) | 26,000 (12.6) | 1,152 (18.2) |
| Wineries | 186,000 (25.7) | 81,000 (39.2) | 1,857 (29.3) |
| Wine outlets | 327,000 (45.2) | 47,000 (22.8) | 2,122 (33.4) |
| Winery tourism | 172,900 (23.9) | 51,870 (25.1) | 1,200 (18.9) |
| Education & research | 908 (1.3) | 543 (2.6) | 8 (0.1) |
| Viticulture students | 265 (0.4) | | 7 (0.5) |
| Total | 723,973 (100) | 206,413 (100) | 6,346 (100) |

To determine the overall economic impact of the industry, one must take into account additional jobs created as a result of expenditures by those employed in the industry. To do so, a multiplier is applied to the employment or expenditure numbers. Using a standard employment multiplier of 1.5, the overall employment impact is 9,500 jobs.[50] A similar multiplier of 1.5 is applied to expenditures resulting in an economic impact of $1,085,000,000. An alternative procedure would be to apply different multipliers to the various sectors, but the difference would be minimal.

The results may be somewhat high to the extent that many of the employees in the growing industry are from the Caribbean, whereby their incomes in part are a leakage to the Ontario economy. However, in terms of overall wages and salaries, the offshore worker effect would be small. It should be noted that the multiplier methodology used here yields slightly smaller total impact results than the input-output methodology (IMPLAN) used in the California study.

## Government Revenues

As a billion dollar industry, the wine industry is a significant contributor to government revenues, be it in the form of taxes or licenses. Table 4.5 categorizes the contribution to government revenues under three categories—federal, provincial, and local. As indicated in the table, the provincial government is by far the largest recipient of taxes and fees paid by the wine industry, obtaining 78 percent of total tax revenues from the industry. Although detailed data are not available, the revenues to the municipalities are minimal compared to the revenues to the federal and provincial governments. The property tax is approximately one hundred dollars per acre. It should also be noted that the municipal tax rate on vineyards is 25 percent of residential rates. This distribution of revenues and the low tax revenues on vineyards may very well be a reason for municipal governments not protecting vineyards from residential and commercial development, which yield much higher municipal revenues.

**Table 4.5** Government revenues from the wine industry, 2000 ($CDN)[52]

| Type | Total |
| --- | --- |
| Federal revenues | $22,900,000 |
| Goods & services tax excise | $20,300,000 |
| Provincial revenues | $38,400,000 |
| Provincial sales tax, license fees, and others | $114,900,000 |
| Municipal revenues | n.a. |
| Property taxes, license fees, and others | n.a. |
| Total | $196,500,000 |

A comparison of Ontario taxes collected with those in California indicates that the California wine industry pays five times that paid in Ontario, although its sales are thirty-three times as large as those of Ontario.

## Summary and Conclusions

The Ontario wine industry, although moribund for years, has recently experienced dramatic growth. According to industry officials, free trade with the United States was considered to have been the single most determinant of growth, closely followed by the formation of a Vintners Quality Assurance (VQA) program. The vision and entrepreneurial zeal of a few key participants was also a key determinant of the success of the industry.

Currently, the industry—directly and indirectly—employs 6,350 people, and another 3,100 in induced employment from the expenditures of its employees. The industry generates approximately $724 million in sales and another $360 million in induced sales. The challenges that continue to confront the industry are not insurmountable, and therefore, the industry remains poised for even greater success given the potential to increase domestic market share. However, increased foreign competition in an oversupplied world market will remain the industry's biggest challenge.

## Notes

1. Linda Bramble, Cool Climate and Oenology Institute; Carman Cullen, Department of Marketing, International Business & Strategy; Joseph Kushner, Department of Economics; Gary Pickering, Cool Climate and Oenology Institute; Brock University, St. Catharines, Ontario, Canada, L2S 2J8. E-mail addresses: lbramble@cogeco.ca; cwcullen@brocku.ca; kushner@brocku.ca; gpickeri@brocku.ca.
2. Prohibition ran from 1916–27 in Canada and from 1918–33 in the United States. Prior to 1927, there was little to no regulation of the beverage alcohol industry in Canada. During the eleven years of Prohibition, over fifty licenses to manufacture wine were distributed without the benefit of quality controls or government interference.
3. Tony Aspler, *Vintage Canada. The Complete Reference to Canadian Wines* (Toronto: McGraw-Hill Ryerson, 1999), 13–17.
4. Ibid., 18.
5. Lynn K. Mytelka and Haeli Goertzen, "Vision, Innovation and Identity: The Emergence of a Wine Cluster in the Niagara Peninsula," paper presented at the Innovations Systems Research Network conference, Niagara-on-the-Lake, November 12, 2003.

6. According to the Real Estate Board, land prices in Niagara sell for between $7,000 and $20,000, unplanted with vines; in some cases, land has sold for as high as $60,000.

7. Aspler, *Vintage Canada*, 22.

8. Ibid., 21–28.

9. Before 1990, a winery could locate in an urban center without a vineyard. Four wineries were located in the Greater Toronto Area: Vinoteca, Magnotta, Southbrook, and Cilento. They were grandfathered, but subsequent to 1990, as a condition of the Canada-U.S. Free Trade Agreement (1988), any new entrant had to have at least six acres of vines under their control on the same site as the winery.

10. Aspler, *Vintage Canada*, 21–28.

11. Aspler, *Vintage Canada*, 21-28.

12. Ibid., 21–28.

13. Rob Scapin, VP Operations, Vincor Inc., personal communication.

14. Donald Ziraldo, personal communication.

15. VQA Ontario (VQAO) was designated as Ontario's wine authority on June 20, 2000, under the Vintners Quality Alliance Act, 1999. See http://www.vqaontario.com/aboutVQA/vqaOverview.htm.

16. Personal communication with Laurie Macdonald, Regulator for the VQAO.

17. Duncan Gibson, Acting President, Wine Council of Ontario, personal communication.

18. Tony Aspler, *The Wine Atlas of Canada* (Random House: Canada, 2006), 20–21.

19. Information from participation in the development of the Wine Council of Ontario's educational programs.

20. John Peller, President of Andres (now called Andrew Peller Ltd.), personal communication.

21. G. J. Pickering, "Icewine? The Frozen Truth?" in *Proceedings of the Sixth International Cool Climate Symposium for Viticulture and Oenology* (Christchurch: New Zealand Society for Viticulture & Oenology, 2006), 84–99.

22. Leonard Pennachetti, grower and proprietor, Cave Spring Cellars, personal communication. Pennachetti planted Riesling grapes on his Beamsville farm in 1978.

23. http://www.fas.usda.gov/cmp/com-study/1996/canada.html.

24. Dr. Deebie Inglis, Professor, Biological Sciences / Cool Climate and Oenology Institute, Brock University, and commercial winegrower, personal communication.

25. G. J. Pickering, "Icewine? The Frozen Truth?" 84–99.

26. Ibid.

27. Vintners Quality Alliance Ontario Annual Report (2005); see http://www.vqaontario.com/.
28. Dr. Deebie Inglis, Professor, Biological Sciences / Cool Climate and Oenology Institute, Brock University, and commercial winegrower, personal communication.
29. A. B. Shaw, "Climate of the Niagara Region" in *Niagara's Changing Landscape*, ed. H. G. Gayler (Carleton University Press, Ottawa, 1994), 111–37.
30. Gary Zucca, "Marketing the Regional Wine Industry: A Comparative Analysis of California Regional Wine Associations," paper presented at Wine in the World: International Conference on the History of Wine, University of Avignon, France, March 2–4, 2004.
31. Kathleen Brosnan, "'Vin d'Etat': Consumers, Land and the State in California's Wine Industry," paper presented at Wine in the World: International Conference on the History of Wine, University of Avignon, France, March 2–4, 2004, pp. 1–40.
32. Ibid., 30–31.
33. For a detailed history of the industry, see Grape Growers of Ontario, http://www.grapegrowersofontario.com.
34. KPMG, *Study of the Ontario Economic Impact Content of Ontario Wines Versus Non-Ontario Wines and the Ontario Economic Impact of Changes in the Relative Market Share of Ontario-Produced Wines* (St. Catharines: Wine Council of Ontario, 2002).
35. The data that we use in this study is, for the most part, obtained from KPMG, including *Update: Economic Impact of the Ontario Wine Industry on the Economy of the Province of Ontario in 1999 Final Report* (St. Catharines: Wine Council of Ontario, 2000); and *Study of the Ontario Economic Impact Content of Ontario Wines Versus Non-Ontario Wines and the Ontario Economic Impact of Changes in the Relative Market Share of Ontario-Produced Wines* (St. Catharines: Wine Council of Ontario, 2002). KPMG collected data from the Wine Council of Ontario (WCO), the Liquor Control Board of Ontario (LCBO), the Ontario Ministry of Agriculture, Food, and Rural Affairs, a survey of the wineries, and personal and telephone interviews with various industry participants.
36. The Ontario Grape Growers Board indicates that in 2003, the number of Ontario grape growers increased to 530. See Grape Growers of Ontario, http://www.grapegrowersofontario.com.
37. KPMG, *Study of the Ontario Economic Impact*, 8–10.
38. MKF, *Economic Impact of California Wine* (St. Helena, CA: MKF Research, 2000), 19–20.
39. Ibid., Appendix 2.1, 2.2, and 2.3.
40. KPMG, *Update*, 10, and KPMG, *Study of the Ontario Economic Impact*, 10.

41. MKF, *Economic Impact of California Wine* (St. Helena, CA: MFK Research, 2000), 19–20, Appendix 2.1, 2.2, and 2.3; and KPMG, *Study of the Ontario Economic Impact Content of Ontario Wines Versus Non-Ontario Wines and the Ontario Economic Impact of Changes in the Relative Market Share of Ontario-Produced Wines* (St. Catharines: Wine Council of Ontario, 2002), v, 10.

42. KPMG, *Study of the Ontario Economic Impact*, 8–10.

43. The study was part of a larger research project by the Ontario government, which surveyed twenty-eight major festivals and events across the Province of Ontario. It is interesting to note that the $400 expenditure was considerably higher than for any other event outside of Toronto in the Province. See Niagara Grape & Wine, *2003 Marketing Report: Economic Impact Study* (St. Catharines, Ontario: Niagara Grape & Wine, 2003).

44. KPMG, *Update*, 24.

45. Ibid., 23.

46. Niagara Grape & Wine, *2003 Marketing Report*, 31.

47. MKF, *Economic Impact of California Wine*, 19–20; according to the MKF study, the full impact of the wine industry on the California economy is $33 billion compared to approximately $1 billion for the Ontario economy.

48. The data were obtained from discussions with officials from the respective registrar's offices. At Brock University, the Cool Climate Oenology and Viticulture Institute employs six individuals for a salary budget of $422,702. Expenditures of $757,967 include salaries, operating expenses, and research grants and contracts. At Niagara College, expenditures are approximately $150,000, of which $120,000 is for salaries for one full-time and five part-time employees.

49. Niagara Grape & Wine, *2003 Marketing Report: Economic Impact Study* (St. Catharines, Ontario: Niagara Grape & Wine, 2003), 31; and MKF, *Economic Impact of California Wine* (St. Helena, CA: MFK Research, 2000), 24.

50. The Ontario Ministry of Tourism and Recreation uses a multiplier of 1.7 to determine the impact of visitors to a special event such as a rowing championship. In New Zealand, the multipliers are estimated to be 2.07 for grape growers and 1.75 for winemaking. See H. R. Bigsby, M. Trought, R. Lambie, and K. Bicknell, "*An Economic Analysis of the Wine Industry in Marlborough*, A Report to Marlborough Winemakers" (unpublished report, Agriculture and Economics Research Unit, Lincoln University, 1988). Other studies use much higher multipliers. For example, a recent study commissioned by the Regional Municipality of Niagara-Planscape, "*Regional Agricultural Economic Impact Study*" (unpublished report, Thorold, Ontario: Regional Municipality of Niagara, June 6, 2003) concluded

that the agriculture industry generated $500 million in gross farm receipts translating into a total impact of $1.8 billion for the region, implying a multiplier of 3.5.

51. KPMG, *Study of the Ontario Economic Impact Content of Ontario Wines Versus Non-Ontario Wines and the Ontario Economic Impact of Changes in the Relative Market Share of Ontario-Produced Wines* (St. Catharines: Wine Council of Ontario, 2002), 8, 10.

52. KPMG, *Update: Economic Impact of the Ontario Wine Industry on the Economy of the Province of Ontario in 1999 Final Report* (St. Catharines: Wine Council of Ontario, 2000), 15.

# CHAPTER 5

## AU REBOURS
### QUEBEC'S EMERGING INDIGENOUS
### WINE INDUSTRY

*Marianne Ackerman*

### INTRODUCTION

The first mention of wine in Quebec dates from the journals of the French explorer Jacques Cartier, who in 1535 discovered wild grapes growing abundantly on an island at the mouth of the St. Lawrence River. Impressed by the vista of a sprawling, savage vineyard, he named the island *l'ile du Bacchus*, subsequently changed to *l'ile d'Orleans*. A few decades later, Jesuits missionaries, lacking altar wine, embarked on the toil of fermenting wild grapes.[1] In 1877, "Beaconsfield," the first commercial wine farm, was established at Pointe-Clare, and by the late 1880s an estimated one hundred acres of vines were under cultivation.[2] Nevertheless, most wine was, from the start, imported. In 1739, for example, New France imported the equivalent of 775,166 bottles from France and Spain, for an adult population of 24,260—the equivalent of thirty-two liters each per year.[3]

However, after the secession of New France to Britain in 1763, spirits overtook wine as the most popular drink; both trade with continental Europe and indigenous production decreased. In the late

1800s, a wave of unusually cold winters and disease all but completely destroyed vine cultivation. This affected wine production for decades. It has been estimated that in 1935, only five acres of vines survived across a territory several times larger than France.[4]

Quebecers' taste for wine increased steadily during the second half of the twentieth century as a result of their frequent travels to Europe, where wine production was popular. In addition, an influx of European immigrants, notably from Portugal, Greece, and Italy, instilled a tradition of homemade wine, although grapes were usually imported from the United States. Artisan wine production began to take off in the mid-1980s,[5] by which time both Quebec society and the global context of wine production and sale had undergone radical changes.

This chapter focuses on forces and events within Quebec which had—and continue to have—considerable impact, not only on the re-birth of an indigenous wine industry, but on the competitive efforts of other wine-producing countries to sell their wares in Quebec. The intention of this chapter is to shed light on the particular difficulties and the potential for native Quebec viticulture, and tangentially, to highlight some of the issues faced by French wine growers working in the Quebec market.

## PROHIBITION

At first glance, forbidding winters and a short growing season might seem to be the determining factors for viticulture in Quebec. Although the southern parts of the province along the St. Lawrence River are situated at approximately the same latitude as the northern limits of southern France, Quebec's climate is continental. The growing season in the southern regions averages 100 days, with some pockets of microclimate reaching 125 days.[6] However, political and social forces have proven even more of an obstacle to the industry than nature. In the late nineteenth century, zealous social reformers and clergy across North America began campaigning for prohibition, a bid to outlaw the consumption of alcohol. The movement had a lasting impact on the industry. It led to a virtual nationalization of the industry by provincial governments, which warped the structures of the spirits industry and shaped public attitudes toward drinking for many decades.[7]

In the 1980s, the greatest obstacle faced by the pioneers of indigenous production was not Canada's severe climate, but rather the state monopoly that for several decades shut them out of the market. But first, some background on prohibition. The term is used to describe a period in North American history when "reformers" sought to obliterate the consumption of alcohol by all but the captains of industry, who, preferably, should sip their port behind the closed doors of their libraries after the womenfolk had retired to drink tea. Prohibition was aimed mainly at the poor. Politicians and clergy alike blamed drink for poverty, disease, slums, and other signs of social decay that we now recognize as being the initial price of rapid industrialization and urbanization. But no matter how wrongheaded it may seem today—or to a European at any time—the campaign against liquor must not be mistaken for a simple manifestation of conservatism or Puritan religion. The temperance movement was part of a wave of social reforms which, beginning in the 1880s, were advocated—indeed fought for—by a diverse coalition of intellectual, political, and religious leaders. The resulting legislation included giving votes to women, tax and tariff reform, cooperatives, compulsory arbitration, and public ownership of crucial services.[8]

In Canada, this Late Victorian movement was dominated by Protestants, which may explain why Catholic Quebec more successfully resisted "going dry" than did the rest of Canada. In 1898, the federal government held a national referendum on prohibition. Quebec voted decisively, "No." However, Quebec leaders were swayed by the national mood. In 1919, after a referendum in Quebec, the provincial government decided on a partial ban—beer, wine, and cider would be acceptable, spirits not. In order to implement this unique distinction, the Quebec government put itself forward, setting up the *Commission des liqueurs de Québec* (CLQ), a state-run corporation charged with conducting the trade and ensuring quality control.[9]

In 1921, the CLQ spent five million dollars buying up the entire liquor stock held by independent grocers and importers. In the first year of operation, it opened sixty-four stores, sold fifteen million dollars worth of booze, and netted a four-million-dollar profit— quite a good beginning for state entrepreneurship. A year later, the CLQ started bottling wine and spirits. The first stores looked like confessionals, with counters behind a metal grid. Bottles were kept out of sight and wrapped in brown paper. Spirits were rationed; wine was not. Prohibition in the United States and English-speaking Canada created a golden age for the Quebec monopoly. In 1930, gross sales reached $27.5 million, dropping to less than half that figure after the United States abandoned prohibition in the mid-1930s. Meanwhile, several large fortunes had been made in Quebec— notably by the Seagram and Bronfman families—and of course much of that trade was patently illegal.[10]

By the 1960s, both the provincial and federal governments in Canada embarked on a wave of interventionism, which naturally required larger budgets. The state alcohol monopoly came under pressure from politicians, and began to get serious about profit. The 1967 World Fair in Montreal was an important catalyst for public tastes. That noisy summer in Quebec's Quiet Revolution saw millions of visitors arrive from all parts of the planet, and with them a smorgasbord of exciting food and drink. Montreal began to see itself as a cosmopolitan city, ready for a more European attitude to the consumption of alcohol.[11]

In the early 1970s, the CLQ was revamped and given a wider mandate under the name of *Societé des alcohols du Québec* (SAQ). The first self-service stores opened. Customers were actually able to pick a bottle off the shelf and read the label. The first permits were issued for the production and sale of Quebec wines, along with legislation authorizing that the local product could be topped up by 20 percent of imported wine. But the real entrepreneurial energy came from the SAQ itself. In the late 1970s, wine tankers, or tank ships, began arriving with massive amounts of raw imported wines, which were then bottled by the SAQ and sold either in SAQ outlets or specially authorized grocery stores. By 1987, the North American Free Trade Agreement came into force and the SAQ was compelled to phase out tax advantages enjoyed by wines bottled in Quebec. Nevertheless, that same year, the corporation's sales surpassed the billion-dollar mark, and sales have been rising steadily ever since.[12]

The prohibition movement's bid to restrict alcohol consumption has been roundly thwarted by the state monopoly. The provincial government earns a great deal of money from its monopoly on alcohol. Originally set up to *control* public consumption, the SAQ now boasts about its success in *increasing* public consumption. The state plays a sophisticated game of marketing and distribution, and plays aggressively. It is virtually impossible for an independent foreign winemaker to approach a private individual, store, or restaurant in

Quebec. They must go through the SAQ, and therefore compete behind the scenes with wines from around the world.

## PIONEERS

Into this context, enter a handful of entrepreneurs whose vision was to plant a few vines and live by the time-honored vocation of viticulteur. Today, Quebec has thirty-two commercial vineyards, covering some one hundred hectares of vines—double that under production in the late 1800s—concentrated in the Dunham-Bedford region of the Eastern Townships.[13] The first real pioneer was a professor, Joseph Vandal (1907–1994), agronomist and plant geneticist at the University of Laval in Quebec City. Vandal traveled throughout France, Canada, and the United States in search of hardy roots which could survive and prosper in the extremes of Quebec's environment. By the 1970s, he had forged a number of robust varieties, including Marechal Foch, Leon Millot, and Eona. Virtually every viteculteur who has gone into production since then has made use of Vandal's research.[14]

For historic reasons, France enjoys a special relationship with Quebec, so it is not surprising to find French expertise at the heart of the re-birth of viticulture in contemporary Quebec. The first and one of the most successful ventures to date is the Orpailleur Vineyard, located in Dunham, in the Eastern Townships, an area south of Montreal and close to the American border.[15] It was founded by two French viticulteurs, Hervé Durand and Charles-Henri de Coussergues, in association with two Quebecers, Frank Furtado and Pierre Rodrigue. While the French partners provided expertise, their Quebec associates brought passion and cash. Frank Furtado is a successful impresario, famous for launching an International Fireworks Festival in Montreal, Toronto, and Vancouver.[16] Pierre Rodrigue is an entertainment lawyer and vice president of the Group Archambault Inc., a vast music enterprise in Quebec.

Orpailleur's first vines were planted in 1982; the first harvest came in 1985, with fifteen thousand bottles of white wine, baptized "Orpailleur"—"*chercher d'o*"—by singer Gilles Vigneault. De Coussergues hails from the Gard,[17] and has a diploma in plant genealogy. He spent several years working on his family vineyards at Costières de Nîmes before emigrating to Quebec in his early twenties.

His partner, Durand, is also from the south of France. He has a diploma from the Faculty of Agriculture at the University of Dijon, and studied the economics of wine production in Montpellier. Durand also worked at his family vineyard, *Le Chateau des Tourelles*, a domain near Avignon that produces a million bottles annually. The vinificateur is Marc Grau, also from the Gard.

Remarkably, L'Orpailleur has managed to sustain vine growth throughout the low temperatures of winter by pioneering and perfecting methods of protecting the plants. Clearly, this is an ongoing ordeal. One method has been to cover the trunks with earth that must be laboriously scraped away each spring. Their principal varietals are *Seyval noir, Vidal, Marechal Foch, de Chaunac, Chancellor* and *Geisenheim*. To date they produce nine labels, including three whites, one red, one rosé, as well as ice wine, aperitif, and sparkling wine.[18]

A quick survey of other vineyards in Quebec indicates a strong presence of French talent. One journalist referred to them as "*des Francais tetus*" ("stubborn Frenchmen"): "Il faut l`être pour quitter les Costières de Nîmes ou la Champagne et aller se faire viticuleur dans un pays qui n'est pas un pays, mais l'hiver." ("One must be [stubborn] to leave the Nîmes region or Champagne to produce wine in a land which is not a country but winter.")[19] Most vineyards are situated in the eastern townships, although note should be taken of Victor Dietrich, an Alsatian (recently deceased), and his wife, Christiane Jooss, who together built one of the most acclaimed vineyards in Iberville, in the Richelieu Valley. The domain *Dietrich-Jooss* is known for their whites and rosé.

A great deal could be said about the agriculture of viticulture in Quebec, but this chapter rather focuses on the social and business issues, taking a cue from Orpailleur's de Coussergues, who has been quoted as saying that the hardest battle he has had to fight over the years has not been frost—it has been and continues to be commercialization. Again, we return to the power and glory of the SAQ. When Orpailleur started out in the mid-1980s, viticulteurs could only sell on site where grapes were grown and wines bottled. They had to virtually launch themselves into agro-tourism in order to reach clients: guided visits of the fields, *dégustations*, a parallel boutique, a restaurant, and group tours—a wide range of activities—all to sell a few thousand bottles of wine each year.[20]

The *Cep d'Argent*, for example, was founded near the town of Magog in 1985, with ten thousand vines of a French hybrid called "*Seyval blanc*." Twelve hectares of vine produce eighty-five thousand bottles of wine each year. They also have a boutique and two reception rooms with a capacity to serve four hundred meals a day, and welcome some fifty thousand visitors each year.[21] Each grower has had to take an active part in the wine growers' association, devoting many hours to attending meetings, writing letters, and devising a fierce strategy to lobby politicians and the public for changes in the liquor legislation. To survive, they have had to battle against the state monopoly all the way, but they have done so with considerable success.

In 1996, Quebec vignerons won the right to sell their wines to restaurants. The snag was that they had to use the SAQ's transport network to deliver their products. In 1994, during the Olympic Games, de Coussergues disregarded the law and delivered his own stock, an act of defiance that brought him before the *Régis des alcohols* (Alcohol Commission), and nearly cost him his permit. Fortunately, for several years the Association des Vignerons du Quebec had as their president Guy Tardif, a man who was not only co-owner of the Clos Saint-Denis Vineyard and a university professor, but a Péquiste (Québec Separatist) cabinet minister. With Tardif's clout behind the growers, the SAQ slowly began to make a place for local wines.

In 2002, Quebec viticulteurs finally won the right to have their wines sold in SAQ outlets, although their presence is small and never given priority amidst the vast selection of imported wines. A store specializing in *produits du terroir* (regional produce) has also opened at Montreal's Atwater Market. However, only a few types of wines are stocked, and growers claim they are lost amidst the plethora of other local alcohol products: apple and pear liqueurs, ice wines, and ciders.

## The Bottom Line

In terms of natural resources, Quebec has little in common with the world's established wine-producing regions. Nevertheless, its population of seven million has in recent decades demonstrated a steadily growing appetite and taste for wine, along with all that accompanies this ancient pleasure: a desire not only to enjoy fine wines, but to delve into the immense culture of the vine, and to engage in the prestigious activity of growing grapes and bottling an original, home-grown vintages.

Growers and fans alike are quick to point out that, as of yet, there are no Quebec wines of "grand cru" quality. The best are respectable everyday table wines with little international presence. In a community that has always appreciated its own arts and crafts over imports, Quebec-made wines are beginning to gain ground. If not a huge part of the market, they are at least becoming established in the public consciousness.

According to a 2003 CROP (Centre de recherché sur l'opinion public) survey, 51 percent of Quebecers polled had tasted a Quebec wine. Of those, 64 percent found it compared favorably to imported wines, in terms of both quality and price, 26 percent said that it did not, and 10 percent had no opinion. However, a 2005 study found that only 40 percent of Quebecers were aware that wine was produced locally, and only 25 percent could indicate Quebec's wine-growing region. At the same time, fewer than 20 percent of SAQ outlets sell (and thus advertise) Quebec wines.[22]

The media, ever in search of personalities, has found no shortage of colorful eccentrics, so virtually every man and woman to produce a bottle of Quebec wine has be interviewed and photographed. By contrast, French and other foreign winemakers are left to the mercy of the critics, Robert Parker being the most feared.

For anyone who has visited Quebec, locally produced wine normally will not be among the top culinary memories of their visit. A French tourist is more apt to remember a particularly bad bottle of generically labeled Côtes du Rhone that he or she purchased at a corner store for the outrageous sum of six or seven euros and ended up dumping down the sink. As this chapter has shown, this unpleasant experience can be traced to the aggressive commercial ethos of the SAQ, and possibly to the willingness of French and other wine-producing natives to water down their reputation by selling gut-rot to far-off markets. By all indications, Quebec wine producers have for the moment set modest goals: to produce a good-quality table wine, marketed locally, with flair. The success and indeed the energy of this nascent industry suggest that foreign producers should resist dumping inferior, low-price wine into Quebec. Locally produced wines can easily best low-quality French wine, and Quebecers have long demonstrated a fierce loyalty to and pride in anything that is done well by Quebecers.

In terms of consumption patterns, it has been demonstrated that Quebec and France are following diametrically opposite trends: the French are drinking less wine each year, consuming more beer and whiskey, but actually less liquor than fifty years ago. On the other hand, the consumption of spirits in Quebec is dropping steadily, whereas wine sales are rising. In 2004, Quebecers consumed 110 million liters of wine, worth CDN $1.13 billion, and consumption is growing at an annual rate of 10 percent. The bulk of this is imported into Quebec and of imported wines, some 56 percent are foreign AOC (*Appellation d'origine controllée*) quality wines. Call it the "embourgeoisment" (process of becoming bourgeois) of what was once a predominantly working-class and peasant society, for as Quebecers get richer, they travel more and acquire "champagne tastes"—notably for French red wines. [23]

Increasingly, quality is becoming a crucial issue, as is the relationship between quality and price. Quebec wines are far from having the equivalent of an AOC, such as has long been in place in Ontario and British Columbia. But in the summer of 2002, the *Association des vignerons du Québec* (AVQ [Quebec Association of Wine Farmers]) created the *Comité d'appreciation des vins du Québec* (CAVQ [Committee for the Appreciation of Quebec Wines]), which tests and rates all local wines. Their intention is to put a quality control system in place, forcing discipline and procedure on all growers. Recently, the SAQ has agreed to put an *oenologue-conseil* ("oenologist adviser") at the service of growers to help improve their product.[24]

For the time being, Quebec consumers seem open-minded, if a touch skeptical about the local product. At a recent dinner party in Montreal, I ask our gastronomically inclined host his opinion of Quebec vintages. He replied: "We've produced a darn good $10 bottle of white wine that sells for about $16." Currently, only 1.5 percent of wines consumed in Quebec are produced in the province.[25] With free trade legislation in place, the Quebec government is unable to favor a local industry, even if it might want to. This clearly puts tremendous pressure on small-scale operations that must compete with a tidal wave of international products.

Considering the obstacles and struggles of Quebec's pioneer viticulteurs, it is obvious that passion and sheer hard-headedness are behind the tremendous efforts being made to establish an indigenous wine industry. Looked at bluntly, there is no real reason for Quebec wines, no natural circumstances begging to be exploited, no fierce local or even national market demanding the product. Yet, in the absence of reason, artisan viticulture has emerged with a vigor that bodes well for future growth. Every summer, more people are tracking down hospitable vineyards in the picturesque Quebec countryside. The media relishes writing about the colorful characters devoted to this improbable sector of agriculture. As we speak, Quebecers continue to take a gamble on the future of wine in Quebec.

## NOTES

1. Robert Prévost, "Bachus sur nos bords," in *L'Histoire de l'Alcool au Québec, eds.* Robert Prévost, Suzanne Gagné, and Michel Phaneuf (Canada: Société des alcools du Québec, 1986), 16–17; Tony Aspler, *Vintage Canada* (Toronto: McGraw-Hill Ryerson, 1999), 5.

2. Prévost, "Bachus sur nos bords," 58.

3. "Association des Vignerons du Quebec," http://www.vignerons-du -quebec.com.

4. Georges Masson, *Vigne et vin au Canada—Manuel de vinification* (Niagara: Georges Masson, 1983), reported in "Quebec Vine," http://www.orpailleur.ca/english/english_site/histoiry_vine_quebec .html.

5. Jancis Robinson, ed., *Encyclopédie du vin* (Paris: Hachette, 1997), 196.

6. http://wine.appellationamerica.com/wine-region/Quebec.html.

7. See Reginald E. Hose, *Prohibition or Control? Canada's Experience With the Liquor Problem 1921–1927* (New York: Longmans, Green, 1928); Herbert Asbury, *The Great Illusion: An Informal History of Prohibition* (New York: Greenwood, 1968); John Kobler, *Ardent Spirits: The Rise and Fall of Prohibition* (New York: Putnam's Sons, 1973).

8. See Cyril D. Boyce, "Prohibition in Canada," *Annals of the American Academy of Political and Social Science* 109, Prohibition and Its Enforcement, (1923): 225–29; Evelyn Leighton Fanshawe, *Liquor Legislation in the United States and Canada* (London: Cassell, 1893); J. C. Furnas, *The Life and Times of the Late Demon Rum* (New York: G. P. Putnam's Sons, 1965); David M. Fahey, ed., *Collected Writings of Jessie Forsyth 1847–1937: The Good Templars and Temperance Reform on Three Continents* (New York: Edwin Mellen, 1988); Ian Tyrrell, *Woman's World Woman's Empire: The Woman's Christian*

*Temperance Union in International Perspective* (Chapel Hill: University of North Carolina Press, 1990); John J. Rumbarger, *Profits, Power and Prohibition: Alcohol Reform and the Industrialization of American, 1800–1930* (Albany: State University of New York, 1981); see also Lee J. Alston, Ruth Dupré, and Tomas Nonnenmacher, "The Prohibition of Cigarettes in the U.S. and Canada: Interest Groups, the Silent Majority and the Propensity to Regulate," 2000, http://www.hec.ca/iea/cahiers/2000/iea0002.pdf.

9. Suzanne Gagné, "La Commission des liqueurs de Québec (1921–1961)" in *L'Histoire de l'Alcool au Québec*, eds. Prévost, Gagné, and Phaneuf, 72–124; Reginald G. Smart and Alan C. Ogborne, *Northern Spirits: A Social History of Alcohol in Canada* (Toronto: Addiction Research Foundation, 1996); Cyril Boyce, "Prohibition in Canada," *Annals of the American Academy of Political and Social Science* (1923): 225–29; E. R. Forbes, "Prohibition and the Social Gospel in Nova Scotia," in *Challenging the Regional Stereotype: Essays on the 20th Century Maritimes*, ed. E. R. Forbes, (Fredericton, NB: Acadiensis, 1989), 13–40; Ernest Thomas, "Drinking, Drunkenness and Crime in Canada," *Social Welfare* 4 (January 1924): 74–79; W. R. Riddell, "The first Canadian war-time prohibition measure," *Canadian Historical Review* 2 (1920): 187–90; Ruth Spence, *Prohibition in Canada* (Toronto: Carswell, 1919); Quebec History, "Prohibition in Canada," originally published in *The Encyclopedia of Canada, Vol. V*, ed. W. Stewart Wallace, (Toronto: University Associates of Canada, 1948), 172–73, http://faculty.marianopolis.edu/c.belanger/quebechistory/encyclopedia/ProhibitioninCanada.htm; Gerald Hallowell, "Prohibition," *The Canadian Encyclopedia Historica*, http://www.thecanadianencyclopedia.com/index.cfm?PgNm=TCE&ArticleId=A0006515; see also Ruth Dupré and Désiré Vencatachellum, "Why did Canada Nationalize Liquor Sales in the 1920s? A Political Economy Model," paper presented at the International Society for New Institutional Economics 9th Annual Conference, Pompeu Fabra University, Barcelona, Spain, September 22–24, 2005.

10. Greg Marquis, "'Brewers and Distillers Paradise': American Views of Canadian Alcohol Policies, 1919 to 1935," *Canadian Review of American Studies* 34, no. 2 (2004): 135–66; Association Against the Prohibition Amendment (AAPA), *The Quebec System: A Study in Liquor Control* (Washington, DC: AAPA, c. 1928); AAPA, *Government Liquor Control in Canada* (Washington, DC: AAPA, 1930).

11. Prévost, Gagné, and Phaneuf, *L'Histoire de l'Alcool au Québec*, 134, 218–19; Michael Vaughan, "No Where Else Comes Close. Quebec's

Love of Wine is Evident at Passion Vin," *National Post*, January 13, 2007, TO19.

12. Henry Linnett, "Wineries? In Quebec? (Industry Overview)," *Wines & Vines*, January 11, 1994, http://www.encyclopedia.com/doc/1G1 -16474204.html; Björn Trolldal, "The Privatization of Wine Sales in Quebec in 1978 and 1983 to 1984," *Alcoholism: Clinical and Experimental Research* 29, no. 3 (2005): 410–16.

13. Jancis Robinson, ed., *Encyclopédie du vin* (Paris: Hachette, 1997), 196; Rodeny D'Abramo, "The Quebec Wine Industry-Sectoral Note," June 7, 2005, http://www.littlefatwino.com/quebecwine.html.

14. Henry Linnett, "Wines? In Quebec? (Industry Overview)," *Wines & Vines*, November 1, 1994, http://www.encyclopedia.com/doc/161 -16474204.html.

15. "L'Orpeilleur," http://www.orpailleur.ca/english/english_site/histoiry _vine_quebec.html.

16. See Christopher Kenneally, "Visiting Quebec's Wine Country," February 25, 2007, http://www.fabuloustravel.com/gourmet/travel/quebec wine/quebecwine.html.

17. "Birth of the L'Orpeilluer," http://www.orpailleur.ca/english/english _site/history_born.html.

18. André Dominé, *Le Vin* (Paris: éditions Places des Victoires, 2001), 794.

19. Yanick Villedieu, "Le Québec a le vin dans les voiles!" *L'actualité* 28, no. 15 (October 1, 2003): 60.

20. See André Dominé, *Le Vin* (Paris: éditions Places des Victoires, 2001), 795.

21. "Vignoble Le Cepd 'Argent," http://www.cepdargent.com/index.php ?lang=en; http://www.bluewine.com/search/en/index.asp?no_categories =210113&nom_cat=Quebec.

22. Rodeny D'Abramo, "The Quebec Wine Industry-Sectoral Note," June 7, 2005, http://www.littlefatwino.com/quebecwine.html.

23. Rodeny D'Abramo, "The Quebec Wine Industry-Sectoral Note," June 7, 2005, http://www.littlefatwino.com/quebecwine.html.

24. See the AVQ website: http://www.vignerons-du-quebec.com/

25. Rodeny D'Abramo, "The Quebec Wine Industry-Sectoral Note," June 7, 2005, http://www.littlefatwino.com/quebecwine.html.

# Chapter 6

# Grape Wars
## Quality in the History of
## Argentine Wine

*Steve Stein*

At the outset of the twenty-first century, Argentine wines have begun to command serious attention worldwide from the experts as well as from the wine-consuming public. The fact that Argentina is capable of producing superb wines should come as no surprise. Its diverse Andean wine regions have almost ideal conditions for production—excellent soils, a dry climate with substantial variations between daytime and nighttime temperatures and near absolute control over water. What is surprising is Argentina's long-term hesitance to produce the quality wines it is clearly capable of. Whether in the early stages of the industry's growth at the end of the nineteenth century or one hundred years later, quality wine production was hardly the norm: only in the 1990s did Argentine wines begin to realize their enormous potential.

Why then did it take so long to achieve significant production of quality wines? It certainly was not for a lack of attention to the concept; the word "quality" has always been present in the vocabulary of major producers, winery associations, and even the Argentine government. Nevertheless, from the earliest years, wineries faced a crucial dilemma: produce large quantities of mediocre wine or much

smaller quantities of good to excellent wine. Industry perceptions of
the nature and growth potential of the consumer market proved to
be the deciding factor. In addition, at specific times, other critical
variables have had particularly strong influences on the quantity-
quality equation. These include human and technological resources
and specific national and local government policies.

## THE EARLY YEARS

It is common to use the adjective "infant" when referring to the early
development of an industry. In terms of production and income,
adulthood came shockingly fast to the Argentine wine industry.
Between 1901 and 1915 alone, wine production increased by 90.4
percent, making Argentina the sixth largest producer in the world.
The growth of consumption during this period was equally dramatic.
By 1915 wine had become the country's third most important consumer good after bread and meat, accounting for 8.7 percent of average family food and drink expenditures. The key date for the
beginning of this remarkable growth is the year 1885 when the rail-
road arrived in Mendoza. This provided a connection between the
country's most important wine production area and its primary wine
market, Buenos Aires. The Argentine capital was the country's largest
and fast-growing urban population center, expanding between 1869
and 1910 from 177,000 to 1.2 million inhabitants.[1]

Just as the accessibility to this enormous market inevitably shaped
the economy of Mendoza—by 1914, out of all production in the
region, 76 percent was wine related[2]—the fact that the market
largely comprised immigrants from countries where wine was popu-
larly considered a necessary part of the daily diet (Italy and Spain)
represented a key factor in winery decisions concerning quantity versus quality. Although they came from countries with well-established
wine traditions, the largely poor, male immigrants of peasant background did not demand a high quality product. Rather, their main
concern was access to abundant, and above all, cheap wines.

Indeed, the great majority of the wine produced from the early
years of the industry to the late twentieth century exhibited characteristics that may not have pleased the more discriminating palates,
but certainly were appreciated by cost-conscious consumers and producers. These were wines that, according to Pedro Arata, president

of the National Commission on Wine Research, were "thick," "with lots of color," "high in alcohol content," and "cloudy,"[3] which made them perfect for dilution with water—a process that producers often referred to as "correction" or "straightening out."[4] Wholesale distributors and sale outlets found this to be a particularly effective strategy for increasing profits. Indeed, for the most part, people involved in sales preferred heavy, alcoholic wines, not to please the clientele but because these wines could stand a greater injection of water than more refined products. As a result, as Santiago Bottaro noted, "Wines are watered to impossible levels throughout the country."[5]

In short, the rapidly growing domestic demand for strong cheap wines that usually outstripped supply impacted tellingly on the types of wines produced. Under these conditions, according to Arata, "good wine fetched the same price as bad wine . . . the Mendoza and San Juan wineries . . . have only one purpose . . . produce *lots of* wine and above all *quickly*. . . . The need has been to sell large quantities without worrying about the quality of the product."[6]

Irrespective of their goals for wine production, the inaccessibility of appropriate technologies, in the case of small wineries, and the misuse by some larger wineries of whatever up-to-date equipment they owned, constituted another important limitation on quality wine production. Banking on the future growth of the industry, a few wineries began to import updated technology: filters, manual pumps, and grape presses in the mid-1880s, and in the subsequent decade, grape crushers, hydraulic presses, and pasteurizers. Indeed, the rapid technological progress of the largest establishments in Mendoza placed them only some fifteen years behind those of the major French wine regions. However, as geographer Rodolfo Richard-Jorba underlines, the goal of such modernization was "to process the greatest quantity of grapes possible and produce the wines as quickly as possible for distribution to the market."[7] The uses of technology concentrated on optimizing the production of a relatively undifferentiated commodity for a price- rather than quality-oriented mass market.

The lack of concern for quality resulted in some serious technological oversights. One was the failure to import modern means of refrigeration for use during fermentation. This was particularly critical in the Mendoza and San Juan regions where hot summer temperatures made for grapes with high sugar content and wines with overly low acidity. Furthermore, the most common method of fermentation consisted of placing the juice in either very large cement-lined tanks or in 100 to 250 hectoliter wooden tubs made of poplar and pine. Neither the tank nor the wooden tub method promoted uniform fermentation. Moreover, the tubs often imparted less than ideal flavors to the must.

There were some exceptions: several of the largest and wealthiest wineries used tubs constructed of European and American oak (*toneles*) for fermentation and short-term storage. However, almost none of them used these containers to age their red wines. In fact, not until 1929 did a winery apply for a loan to purchase wood barrels for aging. Even then, the request was prompted less by a desire to improve the quality of the wine by aging than as a response to an enormous contraction of demand at the beginning of the Great Depression. The stated purpose was to better preserve existing stocks of wine until such time as demand recovered. The same concerns prompted a 1930 decree providing government support to wineries to "age" their product; the decree was annulled in 1933 after economic conditions had improved.[8]

While winemakers in early twentieth-century Argentina had some degree of choice over the technology they used, they had less flexibility when it came to employing "appropriate" human resources. Most vineyard and winery workers were Southern European immigrants, largely from rural Italy and Spain, for whom the thriving agricultural sector of Mendoza, and to a lesser extent San Juan, acted as magnets. However, the overwhelming majority were unskilled agricultural workers with little or no experience in viticulture.[9] Their lack of grape-growing experience had particularly grievous consequences during the harvest. As Arata notes, "Women, children and men are employed at harvest time . . . although such people, of all ages and categories, cannot cut the bunches of grapes appropriately without mixing in leaves, vine shoots and dirt, etc., and without ruining the plants themselves. The harvester, as is natural, wants to harvest the largest possible quantity and therefore does his work carelessly. . . . This means that even the best grapes reach the fermentation tanks in terrible condition."[10] The low skills and concern for picking the maximum number of grapes, regardless of condition, inevitably impacted the quality of the end product.

These harvest practices reflect the largely conflictive structural relationship between vineyards and wineries. From the inception of the industry through the late twentieth century, most wineries had no direct control over the production of the grapes used for their wines. Typically, they purchased grapes from growers known as *viñateros*, who generally possessed small plots, little working capital, and, like those wineries that did have their own vineyards, relied for day-to-day care of vineyards and for planting and harvesting on still another group of workers called *contratistas*.

No one under such a system considered quality to be a top priority. For those involved in grape growing, a "good year" was defined as the production of a large number of grapes. The *viñateros* also tried to harvest early and sell quickly before the grapes began deteriorating on the vines. For their part, wineries sought primarily to pay grape producers the lowest possible price. They were only secondarily concerned with quality.[11]

Another actor that played an increasingly influential role in the wine quantity-quality dynamic was the Argentine State, at both the national and provincial levels. Its influence started early. Emilio Civit, the Governor of Mendoza Province in 1909, revealed the basic features of the government's relationship to the industry using terms such as "protect," "defend," "stimulate," and "take care of."[12] The willingness to protect and nurture the wine industry was clearly reflected in a series of laws that, amongst other things, offered substantial tax breaks to wineries to support the expansion of production, and imposed high tariff barriers on imported wines in order to discourage foreign competition. Argentine producers thus operated in an environment of government support and protection that presented little incentive to make better wines.[13]

Notwithstanding these developments, there were various institutions and individuals that assiduously attempted to promote the production of good and even excellent wines from the earliest stages of the industry. Ironically, one of these was the same state whose policies played such an important role in the development of a quantity-oriented model. It was the government in 1853, spurred by Domingo Faustino Sarmiento, one of Argentina's most illustrious politicians and a future president, which persuaded a French wine expert, Michel Aime Pouget, to travel to Argentina from Chile to take charge of the *Escuela Vitivinícola Nacional* (National Viticultural/Wine School) in Mendoza. Pouget crossed the Andes, bringing with him not only wine-making knowledge, but most importantly French grape stock that would quickly replace the existing vines of *Uva Criolla*. Introduced to the New World by Spanish missionaries from the Canary Islands, the *criolla* variety was dubbed: "A high-yielding, very rustic crop . . . that produces an alcoholic wine of a yellowish pink color and with a disagreeable smell and taste."[14] As a result of the state-supported efforts of Pouget and others, a substantial number of *Uva Criolla* vines were pulled up to make way for Malbec, Cabernet Sauvignon, Semilion, and other French varietals.

The dramatic growth in the early years of an industry dedicated to responding to explosive market demand led to the amassing of prodigious fortunes by the most successful Mendoza producers. Several of these actually championed the cause of high quality products, expressing the goal of pursuing wine making as an art as well as a business. Including the Arizu, Tomba, Gargantini, Giol, and Benegas wineries, they comprised family firms of mostly Italian and Spanish immigrant origin. These were among the establishments that built up-to-date facilities filled with imported machinery, and oak tubs and barrels for fermentation and storage. In the view of French traveler and wine expert Jules Huret, their impressive facilities more than rivaled some of Europe's best.[15]

Using France as their model, these wineries worked at improving grape varieties and producing better wines. For example, from his Trapiche Winery, Tiburcio Benegas formulated the recipes for what he called "Suitable Varieties," including "Imitation Bordeaux Wine" and "Imitation Burgundy Wine." Imitation Bordeaux consisted of 75 percent Malbec with 25 percent Cabernet Sauvignon, another kind of Cabernet (Franc?), plus some White Semillon. Imitation Burgundy comprised 25 percent Grey Pinot Noir, 25 percent Gamay, 50 percent Romano and Tressot, and a touch of Pinot Blanc or Gamay Blanc.[16]

Although some contemporary observers lauded the ability of this small number of quality pioneers to "compete favorably with good Bordeaux wines,"[17] many of the grandest establishments with the most impressive technological innovations appear to have been directed more at show than at substantially improving their wines. Thus, Arata, for example, considered their considerable expenditure on imported equipment to have been "an enormous waste. . . . Anyone who has visited the wineries of Mendoza will admire the luxury of the wine containers and sumptuousness of the buildings. . . . Money, lots of money has been spent to store in these containers that cost like gold, that are gold in terms of their value, the worst results of badly made wine."[18] He went on to comment that "with few exceptions, these factories (wineries) are the worst imaginable, badly built, run even worse and by people without technical knowledge who ignore the most rudimentary principles of hygiene and who make unspeakable products that are distributed to the public in an astounding quantity of *damajuanas*."[19] When all was said and done, the quality concerns of a few dedicated producers were drowned in largely mediocre wine for an expanding mass of consumers who demanded nothing more than a minimally palatable, abundant, low-priced, and often adulterated product. In a context in which quality distinctions seemed to have had little or no importance, some of those winemakers who risked the time and money to produce quality wines suffered financially as a result. Clearly, in the Argentina of the early twentieth century, the most modern and best-equipped wineries were not those that made the finest wines but those that produced the greatest amount of wine. Turn-of-the-century oenologist A. N. Galante's summary of the early development of the industry mirrored Arata's view and offered a compelling explanation: "The growth of viticulture was so rapid and absorbed such an enormous amount of real capital that in no way could oenology keep pace. In addition, given the form and goals of grape production, it was easy to have wine making established as a manufacturing activity and with almost assured success."[20]

## THE CRISIS OF GROWTH

The prioritization of quantity over quality continued to be the dominant strategy for most of the twentieth century as wine output expanded dramatically. The growth in production reflected rising demand as large-scale rural-urban migration from the 1930s swelled the population of Buenos Aires and Argentina's other major cities, the sites of the industry's strongest consumer base. In addition, succeeding governments, beginning with Juan Perón (1946–1955), encouraged the industry in a deliberate strategy to supply plentiful cheap wines to those expanding middle and lower class urban markets that constituted their major political constituencies.

A major feature of these developments was the virtual explosion in grape production. Between 1910 and 1930, the number of hectares increased by approximately two percent a year, rising in the

1940s and 1950s to around 3.5 percent per annum. The next two decades witnessed an even greater output. In the 1960s, growth in wine production averaged about 3.3 per cent per annum, while from 1972–73 alone, the total amount of land under grape production went up 10.5 percent, peaking in 1977 at 350,000 hectares.[21]

An even more revealing reflection of industry growth was the steady rise in the amount of wine produced per hectare. Thus, while the area of land under grapes rose from some 150,000 hectares to 330,000 hectares between 1943 and 1973, wine production virtually tripled from nine million to twenty-eight million hectoliters. By 1972, Argentina produced more grapes per hectare than any other major wine-producing country.[22]

A key component of this process was the introduction—or reintroduction—of more productive grapes. Reversing the process of the late nineteenth century when the Argentines progressively replaced low quality *Uvas Criollas* with French varieties such as Malbec and Semillon, grape growers in the 1960s and 1970s increasingly uprooted the French vines, some nearly a century old, and replaced them with the higher yielding *Uva Criolla* strain. By the end of the 1970s, the *Uva Criolla* had become, once again, after one hundred years, the dominant varietal. The area under *Uva Criolla* was six times greater than that under Pedro Jiménez, another relatively low quality wine grape that was its closest competitor, and fifteen times greater than the area under Malbec, the grape that later rose to signature status for the quality-driven developments of the post-1990 years. In an environment in which wine continued to be simply another low-priced commodity, the words of experienced winemaker and winery owner Enrique Tittarelli go directly to the core of the matter: "You paid the same for fine wine grapes as common wine grapes. Since you paid the same and the common wine grapes are heavier, it wasn't good business to cultivate fine wine grapes or to make fine wine."[23]

The wine made during this period for the so-called "Argentine taste" was a heavily colored alcoholic beverage bordering on 13 percent proof and somewhat oxidized in flavor because of exposure to air during and after fermentation. As in the early days of viticulture, many producers stabilized their wines with boiled must, producing a sweetish drink similar to poor quality sherry. In addition, given the continued practice of adding water to the mix, another widely utilized production "technique" was the addition of ethyl alcohol, ostensibly to restore overly diluted wines. Moreover, in the hottest summer months it was commonplace for consumers to attempt to "improve" wine flavor by adding ice and soda to both whites and reds. It would appear that Argentine wine expert Carlos Tizio is not far off in estimating that less than 5 percent of all wines made during this period had any pretension to quality.[24]

Whatever the taste or the quality, the industry continued to grow. By 1970, annual domestic wine consumption had reached 92 liters; the population of Greater Buenos Aires drank 114 liters per capita, placing it alongside Paris and Rome as the world's highest wine consuming cities. Banking on what appeared to be limitless market expansion, Argentine winemakers repeatedly overlooked any potential warning signals. Rather, they expressed a familiar concern: to ensure that production kept pace with the growth of consumption.[25]

Market expansion was not the only factor operating during these years, as the Argentine government promulgated a series of laws in the 1960s and 1970s that forcefully stimulated the massive production of cheap, poor quality wines. Ostensibly intended to encourage agricultural production in arid zones on the eastern edge of the traditional wine-producing areas, these laws provided massive tax incentives. Investors were able to deduct 100 percent of their total expenditures in new vineyards, agricultural machinery, delivery trucks, wells, irrigation equipment, fertilizers, fungicides and insecticides, winery buildings, and even houses for managers and workers and their families, plus an additional 70 percent from the amount of tax paid on profits resulting from these activities. At a time when the economy in general was suffering from considerable inflation, successive governments further encouraged wine industry growth through the provision by state-run banks of credit at extremely low, fixed interest rates. Indeed, until the mid-1970s large wine-making firms were the recipients of somewhere between 80 and 90 percent of all loans made by government banks.[26]

The impact of state actions was dramatic. Many new investors, primarily seeking significant tax breaks, were attracted to the wine industry. These investors had little commitment to, or knowledge of, making quality wine. Existing producers also seized the opportunities presented by these same tax breaks to expand their own facilities. Despite their sometimes generations-long background in the wine industry, the production strategies of traditional winemakers differed little from the new group of winery owners. Whatever their origins, all were protected by the continuation of high tariff barriers on imported wines from foreign competition that might have motivated some to work toward higher levels of quality. Excessive protection and strict currency regulations also made it extremely difficult to import the kind of up-to-date equipment necessary for quality production. Winemakers in the 1960s and 1970s continued to utilize not only the technologies but often the equipment that had been imported nearly one hundred years earlier.[27]

All this perpetuated the bad habits that characterized the industry as winemaker and winery owner Adriano Senentiner revealed in this characterization of the industry in the 1970s:

> Mistreatment of the grapes was a constant in the industry . . . there was a total lack of cleanliness in the transportation of the grapes . . . that were harvested in . . . temperatures of 38 to 40 degrees [centigrade] and then left in the truck under the hot sun and had reached temperatures of up to 35 degrees by the time they reached the winery . . . so that it could carry the largest possible quantity of grapes, we had the harvesters . . . stamp on the grapes that were already in the truck . . . in some cases . . . a truck had to wait twenty-four hours to unload. In this interim, there were musts that had already fermented, with all that an uncontrolled fermentation involves, where enzymes and bacteria are at work. . . . Then in the winery . . . they used a series of buckets to lift the grapes to crushers with helicoidal screws that mistreated the clusters and allowed for substantial occidation. They did not help things at all. Because of all of this, I conclude that the grapes were ruined.[28]

Another surviving legacy from the early years of the industry was the continued separation of most wineries from the vineyards that produced their grapes. Growers, who did not want to risk their crops by leaving them on the vine too long, regularly sold grapes before they adequately ripened to wineries concerned with assuring large supplies and low prices, regardless of quality. Divisions in the industry also extended to bottling and distribution. Most wine was bottled in Argentina's major cities, far from where it was produced. Like grape growers, the majority of bottlers and distributors were quite independent of the wineries. Many, in fact, continued the practice begun decades earlier of watering substantial quantities of wine in order to increase profits.[29]

Basic flaws in this equation began to appear at the end of the 1970s, as the very factors that led to the massive growth of the

Argentine wine industry helped precipitate the sector's most serious crisis in the 1980s. Just when wine production was reaching its all-time high, the domestic market, which had constituted the corner-stone of the industry from the outset, started to shrink radically when a severe economic recession cut deeply into the purchasing power of the population. At the same time, alternative beverages, specifically beer and soft drinks, were experiencing rapid market growth. As a result, annual per capita wine consumption fell from a peak of 92 liters in 1970, to 76 liters in 1980, to 39 liters in 1999.[30] This finally brought the realization that future growth and develop-ment would not be possible without profound and fundamental changes. Thus, the very crisis that threatened to destroy the industry ended up opening the path to the success stories that Argentine wines began to write in the 1990s and into the new millennium.

## EPILOGUE: THE WINE REVOLUTION

In 2003, some two decades after the low-point of the Argentina's wine crisis, the jocular comments of British wine critic Chris Orr tes-tify to the dramatic transformations of the quantity-quality equation in the industry: "The first time I tasted Argentine wine was around ten years ago. I spat it out immediately. . . . Ruined tablecloth, shocked guests, embarrassed wife . . . If there was a wine problem to be had, then Argentina's wine-makers had it. . . . The past decade . . . Argentina's vinous product has become exactly the opposite. . . . often worthy of high praise, wines from Mendoza are worth keeping in the mouth, rather than sprayed all over the hostess's fresh table linen."[31] In fact, Orr was a bit behind in his praise of Argentina's progress. As early as 2001, one Mendoza wine bested various inter-national icons at blind tastings in Great Britain and the United States. Consistently rated by top critics on a par with, or superior to, wines such as Chateau Latour, Chateau Haut Brion, and Opus One, a 1997 Mendoza Cabernet Sauvignon produced by Nicolás Catena Zapata was pronounced one of the top ten wines in the world. Moreover, by the end of the 1990s, forty to fifty other Argentine wineries were also producing top quality wines, thus helping to reverse the century-long legacy of quantity over quality.[32] Interestingly enough, nearly all of the innovations of the 1990s had been suggested by critics of the industry nearly since its inception. These recommen-dations included limiting grape and wine production; planting fine

wine grape varieties; vertical integration in order to avoid the dis-
junctures and conflicts between grape producers, wineries, and distributors; and pursuing export markets.[33]

The first obvious change concerned grape and wine production.
Given the enormous imbalance between the huge domestic supply
and rapidly declining demand during the 1980s recession, Argentine
winemakers had little choice but to cut back. At the same time, several of the industry leaders, including some of the century-old wineries as well as relative newcomers, began to work on export strategies
in order to promote medium to long-term growth. As a result,
Argentine fine wine exports jumped by 800 percent between 1990
and 2000 (from 55,000 hectoliters to 492,000 hectoliters). In the
first eight months of 2003 alone, Argentine wine exports increased
some 35 percent.[34] This export jump denoted a sharp increase in
quality to internationally competitive levels. It reflected an increasing shift in production from *vino común*, or table wine, to premium
wine. In the 1990s, the area planted with *vino común* grapes
decreased by 32 percent (from 109,000 to 74,000, hectares), and
that planted with premium grapes increased by 27 percent (from
93,000 to 118,000 hectares).[35]

The movement towards the production of quality wines, while
initially driven by the export market, was also increasingly influenced
by changes in domestic consumption. As lower income groups
shifted away from wine towards consumption of beer and soft
drinks, wealthier consumers began to demand higher quality wines,
both imported and domestic. In recent years, this has led—particularly in Buenos Aires and other major cities—to the development of
a new wine culture that considers quality wine to be an integral part
of a more expansive life style, not just a staple placed on the table
next to the bread and the meat. The change is reflected in the sud-
den appearance of upscale wine shops and wine bars, expansion of
supermarket shelf space dedicated to premium wines, proliferation
of wine appreciation courses and wine clubs, and the launching of
various glossy magazines dedicated to the presentation and discussion of fine wines.[36]

The economic reforms adopted since 1988 by the Carlos Menem
government also greatly promoted what is referred to in Argentina as
the "*reconversion*" of the industry towards the production of quality
wines. The two most significant measures were the sharp reduction in

import and export controls, and the stabilization of the national currency. Simultaneously, the industry received major infusions of funds, from both foreign and domestic investors, totaling 500 million dollars alone in the 1990s.[37] A stable, high-value currency and abundant capital enabled Argentine wineries, for the first time in over fifty years, to begin to import large volumes of new wine-making equipment. The near total renovation of some wineries, with the purchase of everything from French and American oak barrels to the latest Italian and French grape presses, constituted vital steps in the move to the production of quality wines.

Argentine wineries also began to hire international consultants to help upgrade their wines. In the 1990s, renowned experts such as Paul Hobbs and Michel Roland made extensive visits to Argentina. Similarly, increasing numbers of Argentine winemakers traveled to the wine-growing regions of countries such as France, California, and Australia to gain insights on how to improve their methods. These exchanges of information and experience resulted in the introduction of important technological innovations in Argentina.

Spurred on by the push for quality, Argentine producers also engaged in the vertical integration urged by critics for nearly a century. Recognizing that overall quality goals could be realized only through close coordination between grape cultivation and wine making, Argentine wineries began to seek out highly qualified agronomists to work in tandem with their progressively better-trained oenologists. These coordinated efforts made the shift away from traditional mass production practices possible.[38] As part of this process, many of the country's top wine producers are increasingly purchasing their own vineyards or instituting training courses for independent grape suppliers in order to ensure a renewable supply of premium grapes. They also pursue new levels of quality by experimenting with novel vine clones and applying new techniques, such as drip irrigation. Indeed, the changes in the Argentine wine industry over the last fifteen years have been sufficiently far reaching for critics to go beyond praising individual wines to predicting the ascendance of an entire industry: "Given the country's potential and its wealth of potential vineyard land, there is every reason to expect that Argentina will challenge California in the years ahead as the preeminent fine wine producer in the western hemisphere."[39]

## CONCLUSION

For over a century after the inception of the Argentine wine industry in the 1880s, its products were, for the most part, unremarkable at best and barely drinkable at worst. Yet over the past decade, a substantial number of the country's wines have gained international prominence, precisely for their excellent quality. This chapter has examined the diverse factors that have impacted on Argentine wine production during three key periods: the early years of industry development from 1885 through 1915; the period of explosive growth of grape and wine production from the 1950s to 1980; and the era of "reconversion" beginning in the 1990s and continuing to the present day. This reconversion has involved utilizing the expertise of winery owners and winemakers; the application of technology in vineyards and production facilities; the building of structural relationships between vineyards, wineries, and commercial outlets; regulatory frameworks on national and provincial levels; and a changing consumer market.

At certain moments, specific variables have been particularly influential in determining wine quality. In the early years, it was the pioneering entrepreneurs, largely of southern European immigrant stock, whose decisions marked the path of the emerging industry. In the mid-twentieth century, state-sponsored tax legislation, along with continued high protection of the industry, spurred wine production to higher volumes. But the single most important determinant throughout the development of the Argentine wine industry has been the consumer market. At the start, the arrival to Argentina of enormous numbers of immigrants coming from largely peasant wine-drinking traditions spurred demand for cheap wine to accompany their meals. From the 1950s through the 1970s, the growth of a mass consumer market with limited, if any, expectations of quality ensured the continued production of abundant undifferentiated wines. Only in the 1990s, when the domestic market contracted significantly, did some of the industry's key players initiate concerted efforts to markedly improve their wines. They realized then that export markets formed a necessary component of future development and that, to be competitive, they would have to make a radical departure from the low quality products of the past.

# NOTES

All interviews cited, unless otherwise indicated, were carried out by the author in Mendoza, Argentina.

1  Alejandro E. Bunge, *Informe sobre el problema vitivinícola* (Buenos Aires: Sociedad Vitivinícola de Mendoza, 1929), 1; José Francisco Martín, *Estado y empresas, relaciones inestables: Políticas estatales y conformación de una burguesía regional* (Mendoza: Editorial de la Universidad Nacional de Cuyo, 1992), 255, 258–59; Ana María Mateu, "De productores a comerciantes: Las estrategias de integración de una empresa vitivinícola mendocina, 1887–1921," Jornadas de Productores a Comerciantes Conference, Universidad Argentina de la Empresa, Buenos Aires, 2002, p. 2; James A. Baer, "Buenos Aires: Housing Reform and the Decline of the Liberal State in Argentina," in *Cities of Hope: People Protests and Progress in Urbanizing Latin America*, eds. Ronn F. Pineo and James A. Baer (Bolder, CO: Westview, 2001), 129.

2.  Mateu, "De productores a comerciantes," 2.

3.  Pedro Arata, *Investigación vinícola: Informes Presentados al Ministro de Agricultura por la Comisión Nacional* (Buenos Aires: Talleres de Publicaciones de la Oficina Meterológica Argentina, 1903), 136.

4.  Santiago E. Bottaro, "La industria vitivinícola entre nosotros," thesis, Buenos Aires, Facultad de Ciencias Económicas, 1917.

5.  Bottaro, *La industria vitivinícola*, n.p.; see also Arata, *Investigación vinícola*, 142; Benito Marianetti, *El racimo y su aventura* (Buenos Aires: Editorial Plantina, 1965), 52; Mateu, "De productores a comerciantes," 14; "Cambios tecnológicos y transformaciones económico-espaciales en la vitivinicultura de la Provincia de Mendoza (Argentina), 1870–2000," Universidad de Barcelona, *Scripta Nova, Revista electrónica de geografía y ciencias sociales* 69, no. 83, August 1, 2000, p. 7.

6.  Arata, *Investigación vinícola*, 202, 254.

7.  Richard-Jorba, *Cambios tecnológicos*, 6.

8.  On the application of technology in the early wine industry, see Eduardo Pérez Romagnoli, "Contribuciones para una geografía histórica de Mendoza: Industrias Inducidas por la Fabricación de Vino Entre 1880–1930," *Revista de Estudios Regionales*, no. 11, 1994, Mendoza, Universidad Nacional de Cuyo, esp. pp. 81–82; Arata, *Investigación vinícola*, 128–133; Antonio Manuel Favaro, *Financiación bancaria de la industria vitivinícola: Problemas, soluciones*

*y perspectivas presentes y futuras de esta industria* (Buenos Aires, 1967); Argentina, Junta Reguladora de Vinos, *Recopilación de leyes, decretos y disposiciones sobre la industria vitivinícola: 1888–1938* (Buenos Aires: Ministerio de Agricultura, 1938).

9. Ana María Mateu, "Mendoza, entre el orden y el progreso 1880–1918," in *Historia de Mendoza. Aspectos políticos, culturales y sociales,* eds. Arturo Roig and Pablo Lacoste (Mendoza: Editiorial Cavier Bleu, 2003), 5–6; Richard-Jorba, *Cambios tecnológicos,* 3.

10. Arata, *Investigación vinícola,* 106. See also Juan Bailet, *Informe sobre el estado de la clase obrera II* (Buenos Aires: Hyspamerica Ediciones, 1985), 885.

11. A. N. Galante, *Estudio Crítico Sobre La Cuestion Vitivinicola; Estudios y Prognosticos de Otros Tiempos* (Buenos Aires: Talleres Oraticos de Juan Perrotti, 1915), 53; see also Masse, *Informe sobre la clase obrera,* 881–82; Richard-Jorba, *Cambios tecnológicos,* 7, 16; Marianetti, *El racimo y su aventura,* 91–103.

12. Quoted in Mateu, "Mendoza, entre el orden y el progreso," 2.

13. Ana María Mateu, "Estado y vitivinicultura. Las políticas públicas de la transición. Mendoza. 1870–1900," in *Actas de las jornadas sobre elites, cuestión regional y estado nacional argentina y América Latina, siglo XIX y primeras décadas del XX,* eds. Daniel Campo and Marta Bonaudo (Tucumán, Argentina: Universidad Nacional de Tucumán, 2002), 15–16; Rodolfo Richard-Jorba, "Conformación espacial de la viticultura en la Provincia de Mendoza Y Estructura de las Explotaciones, 1881–1900," *Revista de Estudios Regionales,* no. 10, 1992, Universidad Nacional de Cuyo, p. 149; Arata, *Investigación vinícola,* 5.

14. Arata, *Investigación vinícola,* 122; see also idem. 5, 185.

15. Jules Huret, *La Argentina. Del Plata a la Cordillera de los Andes,* trans. E. Gomez Carrillo (Paris: Louis-Michaud, 1913), 232–33.

16. Fernando Vidal Buzzi, *Vino y pasión: La familia Benegas y el vino argentino* (Buenos Aires: Editorial El Ateneo, 2002), 60. On the development of this group, see Mateu, "De productores a comerciantes,"; Ana María Mateu, "Los caminos de construcción del cooperativismo vitivinícola en Mendoza. Argentina (1900–1920)," *Jornadas de Cooperativismo y asociacionismo agropecuario y pesquero en Europa y América Latina, siglos XIX y XX,* Tenerife, Spain, September 2001, p. 4; Rodolfo Richard-Jorba, "Inserción de la élite en el modelo socioeconómico vitivinícola de Mendoza, 1881–1900," *Revista de Estudios Regionales,* no. 12, 1994, Universidad Nacional de Cuyo, pp. 172–73; Buzzi, *Vino y pasión.*

17. Pierre Casenave, French wine consultant (1903), quoted in Buzzi, *Vino y passion,* 123.

18. Arata, *Investigación vinícola,* 202.

19. Arata, *Investigación vinícola*, 236.
20. A. N. Galante, *La industria vitivinícola argentina* (Buenos Aires: Talleres S. Ostwald, 1900), 94. Excellent summaries of the mass production ethos of the early industry are contained in Ana María Mateu, "La vitivinicultura mendocina: una opción dura y no demorada en la periferia de la periferia? (1870–1920)," *XVIII Jornadas de Historia Económica*, Mendoza, Argentina, 2002, pp. 12–16; Richard-Jorba, *Cambios tecnológicos*, 4–5.
21. Daniel Aspiazu and Eduardo Basualdo, *El complejo vitivinícola argentino en los noventa* (Santiago de Chile: CEPAL, 2000), 8; Asociación Vitvinícola Argentina (AVA), *Anuario vitivinícola argentina* (Mendoza: AVA, 1973), 203.
22. Aspiazu and Basualdo, *El complejo vitivinícola argentino en los noventa*, 11.
23. Enrique Tittarelli, interview, August 14, 2003; see also José Vega in AVA, *Anuario Vitivinícola Argentina 1973*, 31; Ricardo Augusto Podestá, "La intervención del Estado en la vitivinicultura," in *Crisis vitivinícola: Estudios y propuestas para su soluión*, eds. Eduardo Díaz Araujo, et al. (Mendoza: Editorial Idearium, 1982), 68–69; AVA, *Anuario Vitivinícola Argentina 1973*, 203; Carlos María Juanarena, *La vitivinicultura en la Argentina* (Buenos Aires: Tesis, Facultad de Ciencias Económicas, Universidad de Buenos Aires, 1974), 16; Instituto Nacional de Tecnología Agropecuaria (INTA), *Variedades que más se adapatan a la elaboración de vinos finos en la Argentina*, 2nd ed. (Mendoza: INTA, 1987), 3–4.
24. Carlos Tizio, interview, August 18, 2003. Sources on the "Argentine taste" include Pablo Minatelli (present vineyard manager of Bodegas Norton), interview, August 7, 2003; Luis Coria, interview, August 16, 2003; Paul Caraguel (French manager of Bodegas Chandon), interview, November 17, 1999, provided to the author by Bodegas Chandon. The continued watering of wines is discussed by Marianetti, *El racimo y su aventura*, 304–5. The addition of ethyl alcohol is reported by Adolfo González Arroyo (head of a wine producers organization), "Intervención del Estado en la Industria Vitivinicola: El Estado y Los Productores" in Diaz Araujo, *et al.*, *Crisis vitivinícola*, 90. On the addition of ice and soda, consult Juanarena, *La vitivinicultura en la Argentina*, passim.
25. Aldo Biondolillo, "Exportaciones vitivinícolas argentinas," in Diaz Araujo, et al., *Crisis vitivinícola*, 129. For information on wine production and consumption, see Mario Domingo Rodríguez, "El 'Gran Buenos Aires,' extraordinario consumidor de vino," AVA, *Anuario Vitivinícola Argentina 1973*, 38–40. See also AVA, *Anuario Vitivinícola Argentina 1973*, 204. Producers' confidence was not even cooled by periodic crises of overproduction.

26. On the content of these laws see Podestá, "Intervención del Estado," 64–65; Carlos Jorge Mangni Salmón, "La ley nacional de política vitivinícola, No. 18905," in *Crisis vitivinícola*, eds.Diaz Araujo, et al., p. 47. Luis Coria, interview, August 16, 2003. Coria, an expert on Argentine wine legislation, was also helpful for gaining an understanding of these laws. On credit incentives, consult Richard-Jorba, Cambios tecnológicos, 9; Jorge Tacchini, "Mercado vitivinícola," in *Crisis vitivinícola*, eds. Araujo, et al., p. 98.

27. Marianetti, *El racimo y su aventura*, 311; Paul Caraguel, interview, November 17, 1999; and Juanarena, *La vitivinicultura en la Argentina* all provide valuable information on technology in this era.

28. Adriano Senentiner, interview, August 5, 2004. Interviews with Roberto Arizu, August 13, 2003, and with Luis Coria, August 16, 2003, were particularly useful on the impact of the tax laws on the wine industry. See also Salmón, "Ley nacional de política vitivinícola, No. 18905," in *Crisis vitivinícola*, eds. Diaz Araujo, et al., pp. 45–47; Tacchini, "Mercado vitivinícola," 98; Basulto and Avendaño, *El complejo vitivinícola argentino en los noventa*, 39; Richard-Jorba, *Cambios tecnológicos*, 10.

29. Mónica Barrera de Oro, interview, August 18, 2003; Marianetti, *El racimo y su aventura*, 305.

30. Aspiazu and Basualdo, *El complejo vitivinícola argentina en los noventa*, 56.

31. Chris Orr, "Regional Accents: Mendoza," *Food and Travel*, September/October, 2003, pp. 107–8.

32. Details on the tastings in the UK and the US are reported by Bibendum on their Web site, http://www.bibendum-wine.co.uk. The best comprehensive study of the major changes of the 1990s is provided by Aspiazu and Basualdo, *El complejo vitivinícola argentina en los noventa*.

33. Podestá, "Intervención del Estado," 71–72, provides an excellent summary of these perennial critiques.

34. "Nuevos rumbos para los vinos argentinos," *Clarín.Com*, Buenos Aires, November 9, 2003.

35. Idem.

36. An excellent summary of these developments may be found in Georgina Elustondo, "Buenos Aires, Buenos vinos: hay más ventas, locales y cursos," *Clarín.Com*, Buenos Aires, November 16, 2003.

37. International capital has entered the industry in a variety of ways including substantial investments in traditional Argentine wineries (Bodega Flichman, near Sogrape), buying existing wineries (Norton, near Swarovsky), and establishing new wineries (Salentein).

38. The importance of vertical integration was emphasized in a discussion with Bodegas Catena Zapata staff, including Jeff Mausbach, José

Galante, Cecilia Rázquin and Leandro Juárez, August 13, 2003. (Vertical integration is hardly complete in the industry; nearly all of even the best wineries continue to source a portion of their grapes from independent growers.) Aurelio Stradella, interview of Valentín Bianchi, August 8, 2003; Carlos Catania (INTA), interview, August 15, 2003. Catania, as well as numerous winery people, stresses the significance of the trend toward agronomist/oenologist teamwork.

39. *Restaurant Wine*, Napa, CA, XIII.5, July/August, 2001, p. 9.

# CHAPTER 7

# THE HISTORY OF WOMEN IN THE SOUTH AUSTRALIAN WINE INDUSTRY, 1836–2003[1]

*Julie Holbrook Tolley*

The substantial contributions made by women to the development of the wine industry in the Barossa Valley and other regions of South Australia have not been fully acknowledged. The histories of women grape growers and wine makers, and of their accomplishments not only as leaders and innovators, but also as stoical and reliable wine workers, often seem to have been overshadowed in conventional accounts, such as Charles Gent's recent study of the Australian wine industry, and by the colorful exploits of legendary figures such as the Barons of the Barossa, those invariably male "impresarios of the grape."[2]

The ideology of the gendered division of labor, which has persisted from European settlement in Australia to the present day, has affected the entire rural economy of South Australia, including the wine-growing sector. Wine literature largely reflects the prevailing social construct of gender-determined workspaces and consistently underrates the role of women in the production of wine.[3] In 1950, the influential wine writer Walter James wrote that "Women are not worthy of the custody of wine,"[4] and sixteen years later Andre Simon declared "A vintner is a wine man, a man who makes or buys wine to sell."[5] Only in 1988, with the appearance of *Vineyard of the Empire: Early Barossa Vignerons 1842–1939* by Annely Aeuckens, Geoffrey Bishop, George Bell, Kate McDougall, and Gordon Young, does the historical imbalance start to be addressed, a process considerably advanced by Jeni Port's *Crushed by Women: Women and Wine* in 2000.

According to Margaret Alston, 90 percent of farms in Australia are family owned and operated,[6] and it is in this context that the role of women should be considered, since many farm housewives are expected to labor unpaid on family properties, in addition to their domestic duties and responsibilities. This chapter, which is based on historical documents as well as interviews I conducted, focuses on female participation in the grape-growing and wine-making enterprises of the Barossa Valley and other wine-producing regions of South Australia.

## GENDERED DIVISION OF LABOR

The ideology of gendered spaces was part of the cultural heritage of early Australian immigrants.[7] Patricia Grimshaw, Marilyn Lake, Ann McGrath, and Marian Quartly convincingly argue that in the rural sector this ideology prescribed that while men worked out of doors, at a distance from the house, taming the exterior space by clearing, plowing, and fencing, their wives were responsible for the upkeep of the house and its environs, and care of the children.[8] Men thus occupied the public space and women the private, domestic sphere. Nevertheless, in addition to their customary domestic tasks, rural women were expected to enter the public space whenever needed to undertake tasks associated with farm production such as harvesting, sowing seed, milking dairy animals, or pruning vines. However, such work was rarely acknowledged and usually unremunerated. In fact, women were instrumental in creating the foundations of the colonial economy of South Australia, helping to establish dwellings and farms, as well as maintaining the household and nurturing the family.[9]

Alston has suggested that early statistics did not record the numbers of farm wives who were engaged in agricultural labor because the economic necessities that induced farm wives to work on the family farm threatened to undermine the self-esteem of the male breadwinner and, by extension in a patriarchal society, to damage the colony's reputation. Consequently, in 1893, the South Australian government decided not to officially record the female contribution to the rural economy.[10]

As a result of the widespread practice of patrilineal inheritance, marriage has constituted the usual point of entry for women to farming. This has caused difficulties as economic theorists, farming organizations, and government bodies—working within the framework of the dominant gender ideology—failed to recognize the value of unpaid work, whether in the domestic context or on the farm itself. In consequence, such women were customarily deemed in official records, such as census statistics, to be dependents of their husbands.

In the colonial family, the demarcation of public and private space was an important determinant of gender identity. While it was the male prerogative to move freely beyond the confines of the house and garden, the household was designated as the woman's domain. Women were expected to ensure that the home was both cheerful and morally uplifting, serving as refuge for the male provider; yet for most women it was a place of almost ceaseless toil and hardship.[11] An entry for 1920 in the diary of Fanny Barbour, who lived on a farm at Berwick, near Melbourne, reflects the contrast between her pleasure at working in her garden and her dislike of boring and repetitive household chores: "Since the middle of August . . . there has been nothing to enter except the rain, and wind-and every day alike-get up in the morning at seven-skim the milk etc. Get breakfast. Wash up-clean out fireplaces-do the rooms etc get dinner-pouring all day-so iron or wash-or do something in the house-most monotonous."[12] The deleterious impact of such work on women's health was noted early by the medical profession. In an article entitled "The Injurious Effects of Close Confinement and Overwork" that appeared in a health journal in 1885, a doctor noted:

> The poor man, as he is called, is much better off in this colony than the poor man's wife. If she has a large family, as most poor women have, she has a hard time of it. Her day is a constant round of cooking, scrubbing, making, mending, with a child in arms or one in prospect, from the time she gets up to the time she goes to bed. . . . She probably does as much actual work, spends as much nervous and

muscular force as her husband, and her hours are nearly twice as long. . . . She has no leisure, but is always doing.[13]

## THE HOME PADDOCK

As noted, women's domestic responsibilities were not confined to the house; they also covered the suburban backyard or its rural equivalent, the home paddock. The traditional suburban house in Australia was built on a standard quarter-acre block that comprised a front garden, usually planted with decorative trees, shrubs, and flowers, and a side path or drive leading to the utility area at the back of the house, where there was a tool shed and clothes line. Until the mid-twentieth century, the suburban backyard often contained a few fruit trees and a grape vine, a vegetable garden, and a fowl house, all of which were related to food production for the household. Houses in the country were surrounded by a similar, though much larger, space.

The farm wife's tasks in the home paddock were varied. Typically they included milking cows, keeping poultry, caring for orphaned and sick animals, and gardening. Like the hand rearing of animals, gardening was an extension of the nurturing role of the housewife and mother. As well as vegetables, the garden often included a small orchard or vineyard within or adjacent to the home paddock, which could be part of the woman's responsibilities. An indication of the variety of tasks that confronted a country housewife, as well as the tedium of her daily routine and in some instances the physical demands made on her, is given in the reminiscences of Hazel Colwell, who grew up on a farm on Yorke Peninsula in South Australia:

> Mother really worked hard, she made bread, butter, jam and preserved fruit . . . [she] tried to learn to milk the cow but she just could not manage to get one drop. It was the only thing I know of that beat mother. . . . When a sheep was killed it was put in a huge calico bag and hung on the bough of a tree near the house. It was worked on a pulley system and when mother wanted meat she had to let the pulley down, cut off the piece of meat she wanted, then go and chop it up with a tom-a-hawk—women had to be very versatile on those early farms.[14]

Soula, one of my interviewees from the Riverland, a large grape-growing area along the Murray River, recalled the grind of working in her vineyard in the 1960s: "After picking grapes all day I would go home, chop the wood, light the stove, make the hot water, bath the kids, wash the clothes and cook, and when he [her husband] comes home at six o'clock everything is ready."[15]

## BEYOND THE HOME PADDOCK

On certain occasions, in vineyards as in other types of farm, the home paddock was notionally extended. At times of peak activity, the farm wife and sometimes the children were expected to participate in work such as grape picking and pruning. Subject to patriarchal approval, some women also worked as casual laborers in vineyards belonging to neighbors.

Female participation in off-farm work on family grape-growing properties was most frequent in the period before the vineyards became productive. It usually takes at least three years for newly-planted vines to bear a substantial crop, and during this period, as is clear from the interviews carried out in South Australia, grape farmers frequently had to find alternative sources of income. For example, Fiona, who with her husband grew vines on their fruit block in the Riverland in the late 1940s, and Leanne, who lives and works on a family vineyard in the Barossa, both undertook paid work to supplement the family income while awaiting their first crops.[16] However, during the initial stages of vineyard development in the post-World War II soldier settlement scheme in the Riverland, grape growers found that the amount of time that men or women could spend in off-farm work was limited by the labor requirements of the vineyard. Stella Holliday, one of the contributors to Judith Weir's compilation of reminiscences about the soldier settlement at Cooltong, near Renmark in the Riverland, writes of the heavy workload entailed in clearing and preparing the block, digging irrigation channels, trimming roots, and planting the vines.[17] Indeed, the South Australian government recognized the physical effort and heavy time commitment required to establish vines by granting ex-servicemen and their wives a living allowance until such time as their properties started to return an income.[18]

## Photographs as Historical Evidence

The deconstruction of visual sources such as photographs can be just as useful as the analysis of written texts in providing information about the working lives of women. However, as Jay Ruby underlines, the methodology of analyzing photographs requires a knowledge of photographic history, a comparison of available negatives, researching the photographic objective of the photographer and the relationship with the subject, and how the photograph might have been used by third parties.[19] This is followed through by other researchers. For instance, Marianne Hirsch probes what photographs reveal about familial bonds, and the social and economic functions of the family, through analyzing where the subjects sit or stand in relation to each other, and the clothing they are wearing.[20]

In his turn, Terry Barrett concentrates on details such as the specific time of the day and the season that the photograph was taken, and the significance of the particular vantage point chosen by the photographer for the shot.[21] For Barrett, the deconstruction of a photograph begins with the identification of its subject matter, technical attributes, and form.[22] The subject matter may include people and objects, their location, the nature of the event being recorded, and the season and time of day. The composition and arrangement of the contents, as well as the viewpoint of the photograph, can also assist in analysis, as can technical information such as the kind and size of the camera and film.

Certainly a close examination and textual analysis of photographs taken in wine-producing regions such as the Barossa Valley and Riverland reveals hidden or forgotten details of women's activities, and indicates a long history of female participation in the wine industry.

There exist few photographs recording women's daily activities and their working lives within their homes. Although this was in part due to the difficulties of using relatively unsophisticated nineteenth-century camera technology in interiors with natural or limited light, photographs of women at work in the house were still rare well into the twentieth century when artificial lighting was commonly used. Moreover, women were seldom depicted working outside in the home paddock. The early photographers, usually men, evidently avoided recording women's everyday activities. As males, they possibly found difficulty relating to women's tasks, or found them too ordinary, unworthy of photographic documentation. While early photographs often show men dressed in working clothes, posing at an outdoor work site as if interrupted while actually working, women usually seem to be depicted in their most elegant clothing, as if they, as well as the men photographing them, wanted a conventionally feminine image to be presented, rather than one of a working woman.

As noted, the deconstruction of photographs involves problems of interpretation, notably concerning the relationships between the photographer, the subject, and the viewer.[23] A photograph dated 1911, which is included in Meredith Arnold's extensive collection of historical photographs of the locality, was taken at Waikerie in the Riverland by a farmer, Keith Dunstan senior. It shows a young man and woman wearing work clothes, standing in a newly cleared and ploughed plot of land.[24] Arnold identifies the subjects as "Mr. Keith Dunstan and his sister," and the photograph was probably taken to record a significant historical event for the family—the first planting of vines on the block of land that had been purchased the previous year. It is curious that Miss Dunstan's name is not included in the caption, but it seems to reflect a prevailing male attitude that women are not important in the context of land cultivation. The siblings are placed several yards apart, and while Mr. Keith Dunstan stands nonchalantly with his left hand on his hip, Miss Dunstan has her arms folded, staring at the camera, as if in defiance. This creates an atmosphere of disharmony, and I sense that her father who is taking the photograph does not approve of her working attire, and perhaps even disapproves of her participation in the work. Certainly, the image of Miss Dunstan is very unusual: rather than striking a conventionally feminine pose, she stands in the middle of the plot of ground on which she has evidently been working, wearing men's trousers and what appears to be a man's hat, which was highly uncommon for 1911. *Lasseter's Catalogue*, published in Sydney, also in 1911, contains no advertisements for trousers in the extensive women's clothing section, and none of the women's hats advertised resemble the simple and practical hat worn by Miss Dunstan.[25] By contrast, female canning factory workers photographed in 1915 are all clothed in dresses or skirts and blouses; female Red Cross workers photographed in 1916 are all dressed in long skirts and voluminous, long-sleeved blouses; and in a photograph taken in 1922, two female cooks pose in long skirts and aprons. The attire of these women conforms to the social conventions of the early twentieth century.[26]

Another photograph taken in 1909 at New Residence, near Pyap on the River Murray, shows a farmhouse and surrounding land belonging to the Freundt family.[27] The perspective of the photograph is very unusual, showing a very high viewpoint. Mark Freundt, the present owner of the property, whose grandfather and grandmother are shown in the photograph, has suggested that it was probably taken from the roof of the shearing sheds, which have since been demolished.[28] Considering the bulk and weight of photographic equipment at the time, this would have been a very difficult and hazardous feat. The shot gives an extensive view that not only shows how the home paddock is fenced off from the farm paddocks, but also—as was no doubt intended—suggests the impressive size of the property.

The photograph of the Freundt property reflects the prevailing gender ideology of the time in clearly showing the demarcation between the female and male domains. The layout of the buildings and structures within the home paddock can be clearly seen, including a cellar built separately from the farmhouse, a little smoke-house, and several pens for animals and poultry. The house stands in the center of the home paddock, the woman's domain, which is surrounded by a post and wire fence, and a neat picket fence separates the front garden from the larger utility area at the rear of the house. Mrs. Freundt poses on the back verandah, lifting up a baby to be seen in the photograph. She stands very much at the center of her domain, which includes the cellar, used to store meat and dairy products, and the animal pens. The impression that she has just emerged from the kitchen, which is reinforced by the smoke rising from the chimney, reflects an ordered domesticity.

Beyond the fence that encloses the home paddock lies the male domain, which extends beyond the limits of the photograph. Close to the fence, two men wearing work clothes with bowyangs[29] below their knees tend three teams of horses and two carts. One cart has the characteristic sloping sides of a German wagon, appropriate on a farm belonging to one of several German families in this village. In the background, also close to the fence, graze a small herd of dairy cows, which would have been milked by Mrs. Freundt.

Equally culturally revealing are three photographs taken at the Riverland village settlements of Ramco, Holder, and Gillen in 1894, the year that the settlements were established. According to Arnold, the local historian, the Ramco photograph was taken within a month of the founding of the village, after an acrimonious split from the nearby Waikerie settlement.[30] All three photographs show groups of men posing for the camera. No women are present,[31] despite the fact that women were amongst the first settlers.[32] Indeed, a Parliamentary Report in October 1895 indicates that Ramco had four married women and one single woman; Holder had forty-two married women and two single women; and Gillen had twenty-five married women.[33]

In the Ramco photograph, the nine men stand in front of a group of tents, some holding tools, as if they had been interrupted while working.[34] Distinctive features of this photograph, which illustrates Hirsch's assertion that photographs capture a specific cultural moment that gives a sense of identity and place, are the distance between the men and their defensive poses; most stand with either their arms folded or their hands in their pockets.[35]

The men photographed at Holder, in contrast to those at Ramco, stand close together in a cohesive group. They hold digging tools, having evidently been working together to grub mallee roots.[36]

Yet another photograph taken in 1897 documents the cultivation of the home paddock of a household at Murtho, a village settlement in the Riverland, where Jemima Birks and her husband, Richard, lived with their six children in a substantial home surrounded by fruit trees and vines.[37] Both stand within the home paddock in a patch of cultivated ground, possibly a vegetable garden. Jemima is shown facing the camera, and her husband, nearer to the camera, holds a long-handled hoe. Behind Jemima are four rows of trellised vines, planted a few yards from the house. It is uncommon for a woman to be shown in such an early photograph in her workplace dressed in her working clothes, but Jemima is wearing a pinafore, holds a plain straw hat, and has evidently been working in the garden. She stands beside an orange tree and holds her right hand up to touch a fruit. As she looks towards the camera, I can imagine her saying, "This is what I do. This is where I work. This is my space." It is likely that cultivating the vegetables, tending the vines, and harvesting grapes and fruit would have been part of her responsibilities within the home paddock, although Richard evidently did the heavier digging and cultivating work.

Surviving photographs from the early German settlements in the Barossa Valley, one of the oldest wine regions in South Australia, provide even more explicit evidence about female labor in the vineyards. The German settlers had small plots of vines for their own use, but the planting of the first commercial vineyard in the valley has been attributed to Johann Gramp who bought land at Jacob's Creek near Rowland Flat.[38] He planted his first vines in 1847, and made his first wine in 1850.[39] His holdings were gradually expanded to form the Orlando Winery.[40] A photograph of the Gramp family and helpers at the 1898 vintage shows a group of people in working clothes, posing formally in front of a horse and cart filled with grapes. It is evident from the stains on their hands and their clothing that the women and girls have been picking grapes. There is a young boy who kneels next to a metal bucket, whose job has been to carry buckets filled with grapes to the cart.[41]

A similar photograph taken in 1911 in the Hueppauff Vineyard at Bethany, the first settlement in the valley, shows family members during the vintage. The four women depicted have been picking grapes from the trellised vines, and a boy has been carrying buckets. One man sits on the cart holding the reins, and another man, who has been loading grapes, stands nearby. Two small children play between the rows.[42] Another photograph, taken around 1920 at Rowland Flat Vineyards, shows four women picking grapes, a man carrying the buckets, and another man loading grapes into the cart.

These photographs demonstrate that women participated in farm work outside the home paddock, while fulfilling their substantive tasks of mothering and household management.

## Written Texts as Historical Evidence

Contemporary written texts, like photographs, are an important source of information about the contributions of women to the development of the South Australian wine industry. These written sources include public records, such as books, newspaper articles and official documents, and personal records such as diaries, reminiscences, and work journals.

One of the most valuable written sources is the column in the Adelaide *Register* written by Henry Jones, a journalist whose nom de plume was the "Old Colonist." He describes the progress made in grape growing and wine making fifteen years after the colony of South Australia was first settled.[43] Among the properties he visited was that of Johann Friedrich August Fiedler, a founder of the village now known as Bethany. The Old Colonist noted that the Fiedler

**Figure 7.1** Orlando Vineyard, Rowland Flat, ca. 1920[44]

Winery was well established by 1851 and producing large quantities of excellent wine.[45] By 1862, Fiedler had been granted a license to distill brandy, and when Johann ceded the business to his son, Alexander, the firm continued to produce wine and brandy.[46] When Alexander died in 1875 (his father was then nearly eighty years old), his wife, Johanne, took over the management of the winery and was granted a distiller's license in her own name.[47] This implies a long-standing involvement in the family winery by Johanne, who had evidently acquired sufficient skill and experience to successfully manage a vineyard, winery, and distillery.

Sophia bis Winckel similarly became a winery owner after her husband died. Her vineyard on the Gawler River was originally established by Dr. Richard Schomburgk, who named the property Büchsfelde. A former gardener and vine cultivator from Potsdam, near Berlin, he had a keen interest in establishing a wine-growing enterprise in his new home in Australia.[48] By 1853 he had planted ninety-three different cultivars using cuttings from the gardens of Potsdam, and he gradually earned a good reputation for his wine. Upon his appointment as Director of the Adelaide Botanic Gardens in 1865, Schomburgk sold his five-acre plot to his neighbor,

Friedrich bis Winckel.[49] George Loyau, editor of the local Gawler newspaper, *The Bunyip*, recalled that while dining at bis Winckel's home in 1879 he was served "some excellent wine [that] would take first place at any exhibition where good wines are appreciated."[50] When Friedrich died in 1879, his wife, Sophia, took over the property, which by this time included eight acres of vineyard containing sixty-eight grape varieties, and a five-acre orchard of fruit trees.[51] Her success in maintaining and managing such a large property demonstrated that Sophia, like Johanne Fiedler, had gained extensive experience in the family wine-making enterprise.

The Barossa Valley also attracted Irish and English settlers. One of the pioneers in the Rowland Flat district was a young woman, Ann Jacob, who arrived in South Australia in 1839 to join her brothers, William, an assistant to Colonel William Light, Surveyor General for South Australia, and John, a cattle dealer. Ann's diary and her *Reminiscences*, held in the State Library of South Australia,[52] relate that on the voyage out she visited the famous Constantia Vineyard,[53] which had been planted in Cape Town in 1684, and had an excellent reputation for good quality wines. Several grape growers in South Australia imported vine cuttings from Constantia in the late 1830s and early 1840s.[54] These growers included John Barton Hack, who owned substantial properties in the colony, and George Stevenson, editor of the *Register*. Both men lived in North Adelaide—then a small village—where Ann Jacob stayed for a few months on first arriving in South Australia, and it may be assumed that the young Englishwoman, who showed such an interest in Constantia and grape cultivation in general, would have been familiar with their vineyards. It is also likely that Ann read about early grape growing in South Australia in letters sent to England by her brother William, who owned several cottages in North Adelaide and, as a surveyor, traveled extensively in the colony, and would have observed the planting of early vineyards.[55] The frequency of references to wine and grape cultivation in Ann's diary shows that she had a vivid interest in viticulture.

In October 1839, Ann Jacob purchased five hundred acres at a price of £1 an acre at Rowland Flat, at the junction of Jacob's Creek and the North Para River[56] on land that had been surveyed by her brother, William, and Johann Menge, an eccentric German mineralogist, who reported that the rolling hills and valley reminded him of the Rhone district and offered a good prospect for vine growing.[57]

Ann's property, which she called *Morooroo*, an Aboriginal word meaning big waterhole, was situated near Gramp's Vineyard in what is now recognized as a premier grape-growing district: "I brought £500 into the Colony and it was expended in purchasing 500 acres of land at *Morooroo*."[58] In previous accounts of the origins of this important property, it has been assumed that *Morooroo* was purchased, and a farm and vineyard established on it, by William and John, and not by their sister.[59] But the land grant, finalized in 1842, shows clearly—in Ann's own handwriting—that she was the purchaser.

On moving there, Ann slept in one room of a house that had been partly built, while her brother John and the workmen slept in a tent. Living conditions were difficult, "just better than camping out." Ann records cooking outside by an open fire, boiling salt beef and pork, and baking damper. For their Christmas Day meal in 1839 they had stewed parrot.[60]

Soon, thirty acres had been cleared and a mixed farm established, with cows, oats, barley, vines, and fruit trees. The main house was completed and several other buildings constructed, including three cottages for farm hands, and a large dairy in which Ann produced butter and large quantities of cheese that she exported to Mauritius.[61] An entry in her diary dated May 1, 1847, records that there was an "abundant crop" of grapes at *Morooroo*.[62] It is clear that Ann participated actively in the establishment and running of the farm and vineyard, as her brothers were frequently absent on business,[63] and her hitherto unacknowledged role in establishing the internationally famous Jacob's Creek label and vineyard should be recognized.

In 1850, Ann married Arthur Horrocks, and the couple moved to a property at Penwortham, near Clare.[64] The *Morooroo* property was signed over to William Jacobs. The homestead, which in 1851 was described by the Old Colonist as possessing "a considerable extent of orchard and vineyard,"[65] is currently owned by Orlando Winery, and the old walls of the original cellar have been incorporated into the nearby Grant Burge Winery.

Eliza Randall also made significant contributions to the establishment of vineyards in the region. Eliza arrived in South Australia with her husband David in 1845.[66] They took up two thousand acres at Mount Crawford in 1851, naming the property *Glen Para*. Eliza's diary reveals that she not only took care of the children and managed the household staff, but also took an active role in the running of the farm, which by 1862 possessed an orchard, extensive vineyard, and substantial two-story cellar.[67] In the early 1850s, Eliza wrote in her diary that she took "entire charge of the flower garden and orchard."[68] Moreover, as her husband was frequently occupied at a distance from the homestead, tending his large herds of dairy cows and beef cattle, Eliza possibly also helped manage the vineyard.

Further evidence of female management of vineyards is presented by the case of Elizabeth Nicholas, who in 1850 received her brother-in-law's share of a 480-acre property, *Gawler Park*, situated to the east of Angaston, that he had purchased in 1845 with her husband.[69] This transaction, recorded in the Land Titles Office, is puzzling, as the land would have passed to her husband. As a married woman, she would not, at that time, have been legally entitled to retain ownership of the property. Nevertheless, it can be assumed that Elizabeth would have been responsible for the "large garden with weeping willows and an extensive vineyard," described by the Old Colonist as being situated close to the house and inside the home paddock.[70]

## THE SITUATION TODAY

Women continue to be hidden contributors to the agriculture sector.[71] Although the Australian Bureau of Statistics has no data relating to the number of women currently employed in the wine industry in South Australia, women overall comprise about one third of Australia's agricultural workforce.[72] According to Alston, however, they continue to be subject to gender discrimination, holding less than 10 percent of positions as industry officials.[73]

While the public and private domains are not necessarily mutually exclusive, and farming women often work off the property, the ideology of a gendered division of labor persists in the typical Australian rural household. Women are still considered responsible for house care, the provision of meals, and child nurturing, and the movement of women out of the home paddock and beyond the front gate is, in societal terms, frowned upon. Indeed, should a farm housewife venture into public male space, perhaps to visit a friend or relative, even these days she might be expected by her husband to account for the time spent away.[74]

Haslam-McKenzie observed that the official undervaluation of women's part in the rural economy tends to be echoed in the attitudes of the women themselves. Thus, even when partners in a farming enterprise, they often refer to themselves as "helpers" of their husband farmers, rather than as "farmers" in their own right.[75] This attitude was reflected in the interviews I conducted with women who live and work on vineyards. Karen, despite being a partner with her husband in their vineyard, deferred to him as the guiding force of the enterprise and referred to herself as the "dogsbody."[76] Nevertheless, she labors at all of the tasks and is responsible for the day-to-day management of the vineyard, while her husband is occupied at a full-time job away from the property.[77]

In spite of the limitations imposed by societal conventions, farm women are, in practice and with patriarchal approval, increasingly involved in activities outside the house in order to supplement the family income.[78] It would seem that moving from the home paddock is considered acceptable if a woman can bring income into the family. However, by so doing, rural women are still "challenging normative values,"[79] which in turn can be a potential source of domestic conflict.[80]

Working off-farm may today be less frequent among women living on South Australian vineyards than in the rural sector as a whole: none of the women I interviewed on vineyards worked for wages away from the property. The income currently derived from family wine-growing enterprises, in South Australia at least, is evidently sufficient to maintain families.[81] This reflects a sustained period of prosperity for South Australian wine growers. This started for grape growers in the Cooltong area in the late 1940s, for instance, when there was a strong demand for specific varietals from the local distillery-wineries—Angove's Distillery and the Renmark Growers' Distillery.[82] Development was again stimulated in the 1970s by a dramatic swing away from fortified wines to white and red table wines, and this has been maintained since the early 1990s by a sustained expansion of domestic and overseas markets.[83]

## CONCLUSION

Women have always been involved in grape growing and wine making in the Barossa Valley, the Riverland, and other viticultural regions of South Australia. While the primary responsibility of women on family vineyards was considered to be tasks within the house and in the home paddock, they also made important contributions to the development and continuation of the grape-growing enterprise. A detailed analysis of primary sources, including photographs, diaries, newspapers, and government documents, shows that women also participated actively in work beyond the home paddock. Although never adequately recognized, and indeed often completely ignored by wine writers and historians, women's labor—whether paid or unpaid—has always been an integral part of the wine industry, as it has been of the rural economy as a whole.

## NOTES

1. This research project has been undertaken with the support of Australia's grape growers and wine makers through their investment body, the Grape and Wine Research and Development Corporation, with matching funds from the federal government.
2. Charles Gent, *Mixed Dozen: The Story of Australian Winemaking since 1788* (Sydney: Duffy & Snellgrove, 2003), vii.
3. For example, Gent, *Mixed Dozen*; John Beeston, "Yalumba goes global," *Australian Business Monthly*, February 1993, pp. 67–68; Robin Bradley, *The Small Wineries of Australia: A Guide to the Best Makers* (Melbourne: Macmillan, 1982); Len Evans, *Australia and New Zealand Complete Book of Wine* (Sydney: Hamlyn, 1973); James Halliday, *A History of the Australian Wine Industry 1949–1994* (Adelaide: Australian Wine and Brandy Corporation in association with Winetitles, 1994); André Simon, *The Wines, Vineyards and Vignerons of Australia* (Melbourne: Lansdowne, 1966).
4. Jeni Port, *Crushed by Women: Women and Wine* (Melbourne: Arcadia, 2000), x.
5. Simon, *Wines, Vineyards and Vignerons*, 55.
6. Margaret Alston, *Women on the Land: The Hidden Heart of Rural Australia* (Sydney: University of New South Wales Press, 1995), 1.
7. Patricia Grimshaw, Marilyn Lake, Ann McGrath, and Marian Quartly, *Creating a Nation* (Ringwood, Victoria: McPhee Gribble, 1994), 117.
8. Ibid., 120.
9. Ibid., 121.
10. Alston, *Women on the Land*, 3.
11. Kay Saunders and Raymond Evans, eds., *Gender Relations in Australia: Domination and Negotiation* (Sydney: Harcourt Brace, 1992), 180–81.

12. Katie Holmes, *Spaces in her Day: Australian Women's Diaries of the1920s and 1930s* (St. Leonards, NSW: Allen & Unwin, 1995), 54.

13. Margaret Allen, Mary Hutchison, and Alison Mackinnon, *Fresh Evidence, New Witnesses: Finding Women's History* (Netley: South Australian Government, 1989), 160.

14. Ibid., 167.

15. "Soula," interview, February 2003.

16. "Fiona," interview, February 2003; "Leanne," interview, May 2003.

17. Stella Holliday, "My memories of Cooltong," in Judith Weir, comp., *We Will Remember Cooltong* (Berri, South Australia: Cooltong Reunion Committee, 1995), 112.

18. David Mack, "History of Cooltong," in Weir, comp., *We Will Remember Cooltong*, 23.

19. Jay Ruby, ed., *Visual Anthropology* (London: Harwood Academic, 1990), 136.

20. Marianne Hirsch, *Family Frames: Photography, Narrative and Postmemory* (Cambridge, MA: Harvard University Press, 1997), 167.

21. Terry Michael Barrett, *Criticizing Photographs: An Introduction to Understanding Images* (Boston: McGraw Hill, 2000), 54.

22. Ibid., 15.

23. Richard Bolton, ed., *The Contest of Meaning: Critical Histories of Photography* (Cambridge, MA: MIT Press, 1989), 17.

24. Photograph appears in Meredith Arnold, ed. *Waikerie and District: A Pictorial History* (Waikerie, Australia: Waikerie and District Historical Society, 1989), 72.

25. Peter Hutton, ed., *Australia in the Good Old Days: Facsimile Pages from Lasseter's Commercial Review, no. 26, 1911* (Sydney: Paul Hamlyn, 1979), 146–49, 210–12.

26. Arnold, ed., *Waikerie and District*, 73, 79, 111.

27. Photograph appears in Margaret Munn, Bruce Tonkin, Janice Wachtel, and Nola Schulz, *Early Years of the South Australian Village Settlements: Kingston-on-Murray, Pyap, Moorook, New Residence, from 1894* (Berri, Australia: J. C. Irving, 1994), 29.

28. Mark Freundt, interview, February 2003.

29. Bowyangs were leather straps worn by laborers over their trousers and below the knees.

30. Photograph appears in Arnold, ed., *Waikerie and District*, 23. See also David Mack, *The Village Settlements on the River Murray in South Australia, 1894–1909: A Chronicle of Communal Life and Hardship* (Somerton, South Australia: D. B. Mack, 1994), 59.

31. Arnold, ed., *Waikerie and District*, 22–23.

32. Ibid., 247, 268.

33. Mack, *Village Settlements*, 10.

34. Photograph appears in Arnold, ed. *Waikerie and District*, 22.

35. Hirsch, *Family Frames*, 163.
36. Photograph appears in Arnold, ed., *Waikerie and District*, 22.
37. Mack, *Village Settlements*, 10.
38. Photograph appears in Annely Aeuckens et al., *Vineyard of the Empire: Early Barossa Vignerons 1842–1939* (Adelaide: Australian Industrial, 1988), 29.
39. *Adelaide Register*, July 15, 1927, p. 8.
40. Aeuckens et al., *Vineyard of the Empire*, 125.
41. Ibid., 149.
42. This is an unpublished photograph that is part of the author's collection.
43. In 1970, a number of these observations dating from November 1850 to March 1851 were collated into E. M. Yelland, ed. *Colonists, Copper and Corn in the Colony of South Australia, by Old Colonist* (Melbourne: Hawthorn, 1970).
44. This is an unpublished photograph that is part of the author's collection.
45. *Adelaide Register*, February 5, 1851, p. 9.
46. Reginald S. Munchenberg, F. W. Heinrich, Donald A. Proeve, Anne Hausler Ross, Geoffrey B. Saegenschnitter, Norris Ioannou, and Roger E. Teusner, *The Barossa, A Vision Realised: The Nineteenth Century Story* (Truro, South Australia: Barossa Jubilee 150 Management Committee, 1992), 16.
47. *South Australian Government Gazette*, September 7, 1875, p. 1684.
48. Aeuckens et al., *Vineyard of the Empire*, 27.
49. Katrina McDougall, *Winery Buildings in South Australia 1836–1936. Part 1. The Barossa Region* (Adelaide: University of Adelaide, Faculty of Architecture and Town Planning, 1980), 93.
50. George E. Loyau, *The Gawler Handbook: A Record of the Rise and Progress of that Important Town* (Adelaide: Goodfellow & Hele, 1880; Hampstead Gardens, South Australia: Austaprint, 1978), 96, citations are to the Austaprint edition.
51. Ibid., 97.
52. Ann's diary and her *Reminiscences* are part of the Public Records Group held in the archives of the State Library of South Australia, North Terrace, Adelaide, (SLSA) PRG 966/1.
53. Ibid.
54. Aeuckens et al., *Vineyard of the Empire*, 7.
55. Diary of William Jacob, at present held in a private family collection in Adelaide.
56. South Australian Land Titles Office (SALTO), General Registry Office, 39 Carrington Street, Adelaide, Old System Pkt. 21071.
57. Ioannou, *Barossa Journeys*, 14.

58. Public Records Group, State Library of South Australia, North Terrace, Adelaide, (SLSA) PRG 966/1.

59. For example, Aeuckens et al., *Vineyard of the Empire*, 38–39; Norris Ioannou, *Barossa Journeys: Into a Valley of Tradition* (Frenchs Forest, NSW: New Holland, 2000), 104; McDougall, *Winery Buildings*, 75; Munchenberg et al., *The Barossa*, 59.

60. Public Records Group, State Library of South Australia, North Terrace, Adelaide, (SLSA) PRG 966/1.

61. Ibid.

62. Ibid.

63. Ioannou, *Barossa Journeys*, 104.

64. Aeuckens et al., *Vineyard of the Empire*, 39.

65. *Adelaide Register*, February 5, 1851, p. 7.

66. Aeuckens et al., *Vineyard of the Empire*, 248.

67. Ebenezer Ward, *The Vineyards and Orchards of South Australia: A Descriptive Tour* (Adelaide: Advertiser and Chronicle Offices, 1862; Adelaide: Sullivan's Cove, 1979), 41, citations are to the Sullivan's Cove edition.

68. Eliza Randall, *Mrs. David Randall's Reminiscences*, ed. Geo C. Morphett (Adelaide: Pioneers' Association of South Australia, 1939), 9.

69. SALTO, vol. 67, fol. 218; and SALTO vol. 115, fol. 44.

70. *Adelaide Register*, February 8, 1851, p. 6.

71. Fiona Haslam-McKenzie, "Farm Women and the 'F' Word," in *Australian Rural Women Towards 2000: An Edited Collection of Papers on Women in Rural Australia as presented at the Rural Australia–Toward 2000 Conference July 1997*, ed. Margaret Alston (Wagga Wagga, NSW: Centre for Rural Social Research, Charles Sturt University, 1998), 25.

72. Ibid., 27.

73. Margaret Alston, "There are just no women out there: how the industry justifies the exclusion of women from agricultural leadership," *Rural Society* 8, no. 3 (1998): 197–208.

74. Grimshaw et al., *Creating a Nation*, 130.

75. Haslam-McKenzie, "Farm Women and the 'F' Word," 28.

76. A menial worker of low status.

77. "Karen," interview, February 2003.

78. Alston, *Women on the Land*, 17.

79. Grimshaw et al., *Creating a Nation*, 130.

80. Katrina Alford, "Colonial Women's Employment as seen by Nineteenth-Century Statisticians and Twentieth-Century Economic

Historians," Working paper 65, Canberra, Australian National University, 1986, p. 1.

81. "Leanne," interview, May 2003.
82. Tony Sheehan, "Cooltong and the Wine Industry," in *We Will Remember Cooltong*, comp. Weir, p. 112.
83. Ibid., 114.

# CHAPTER 8

# OF WINE, JEWS, AND PROVENCE

## Patric Choffrut

"There was something in this landscape, smiling although wild, that explained to me the spirit of the Southern Covenanters. . . . They dealt much more in blood, both given and taken; yet I find no obsession of the Evil One in their records. With a light conscience, they pursued their life in these rough times and circumstances."[1] In *Travels with a Donkey in the Cévennes*, Robert Louis Stevenson—better known as author of *Treasure Island* and *Dr.Jekyll and Mr.Hyde*—provides his readers with remarkable insights into the inner soul of a Presbyterian Scot visiting the last stronghold of another Protestant breed, the Huguenots of Languedoc. Both groups indeed fought, and died, for the same God—but the Southern Covenanters had a different *Weltanschauung* ("worldview"), possibly because they lived in a different setting, possibly because the sun is hotter there, the mountains produce chestnuts, and the valleys wine. Wine is part of the Mediterranean heritage, as is reflected in the languages of the region: "wine," in Hebrew, is *yain* (יין); in Greek, *oinos* (οινος); and in Latin, *vinum*—pronounced "winum."

## WINE AND JUDAISM

Wine has a very particular place in the conscience of the Jewish people. It was one of the three staples—*dagan* (grain), *tirosh* (new
wine), and *yizhar* (oil)—produced in *Eretz, Israel* before the Jews
were forced into Diaspora by Titus' conquest and the destruction of
the third Temple.[2] Claudia Roden writes that "wine presses, vats,
goblets, jugs, and amphorae" keep being discovered in excavations
of ancient sites.[3] The ancient Israelites would tread the grapes by
foot, and the result was probably very strong, considering the climate. Since it was not easy to keep the wine from turning sour, they
added spices, honey, or resin.[4] They also made sweet wines with
dried raisins; sparkling wines; and wines from fermented date, fig,
and pomegranate juices.

Scattered in the Diaspora, the Jews had to settle in other lands.
After the expulsion of the Jews from the lands belonging to the King
of France in 1349 CE, then from *Sfarad* (Spain) in 1492, Jews from
Southern France (*Serfat*) were relatively isolated from the rest of
their Jewish brothers in the Christian North (the Ashkenazic lands
stretching from Alsace to Eastern Europe) and the Christian South
(the Jewish ghettoes in Livorno and Rome). This does not mean,
however, that they were cut off from *Eretz Israel*. Men wrote and
spoke Hebrew, and in the rituals of the *Arba kehilot* (the four holy
communities of Avignon, Carpentras, Cavaillon, and L'Isle de
Venisse[5]), Jews used an impeccable Hebrew.

Moreover, the Jews in the Diaspora continued to make wine. The
*Encyclopedia Judaica* distinguishes ten kinds for wine in Talmudic
times,[6] which is the surest way to ascertain the importance of the
product. Indeed, wine was such an essential part of Jewish life—in
both religious and social functions—that the Rabbis even refused to
ban its consumption at the time of mourning the destruction of the
Temple, because such a decree would impose "unbearable hardship
on the public."[7] Of course, excess was not acceptable—a prayer
uttered in a state of drunkenness is considered "an abomination."[8]
But one is to drink four cups at the Passover *Seder*, two at weddings,
one at *Brit Milah* (circumcision). There is a tradition among some
communities where the child is given one drop of wine.[9] And
*Kiddush*[10] on Sabbaths and Festivals must be performed with
wine—not beer—as some dared suggest. It was also used to alleviate

anguish after a funeral: the mourners were to drink ten glasses of wine, to which were added four more.[11] This prescription has long fallen into oblivion.

## RELIGIOUS CEREMONIES

An interesting glimpse into the role of wine amongst the Jews of Southern France is afforded by a document recently discovered in the Rouen Archives. The document is written in Provençal by a Jewish convert to Christianity who was trying to lure his former brethren, if not over to the Holy Roman Church, at least away from the temptation of the "false prophet," Sabbetai Zevi,[12] who had many followers among the Sephardic communities, including in Provence. It was bad enough to deny Jesus the Christ, let alone support the wrong Messiah!

I gained access to one document, courtesy of M. Elie Nicolas of the Nouvelle Gallia Judaica research group. The text deals with the end of days, when the [real] Messiah will be back. Here, the writer, though now a Christian, strictly follows the Talmud: "at the end of days, wine will form an integral part of the banquet."[13] And the three staples—grain, new wine, and oil—are mentioned. Two are even written in Provençal-influenced Hebrew: "léen" for lehem (לחם), or "bread," and "iaïn" for *yain* (יין), or wine.

*Aqueou gran dieu qu'es eilamon*
*Vendra faire sa residance*
*Et nous dounara d'ourdounance*
*Nou comblen de benediction*
*Nou mandara la prouvisiou*
*Arralaren de bonei viandou*
*Nostei recoltou saran grandou*
*Pron d'oulivou, pron de raïn*
*Forceou léen, forceou iaïn*


This great God who is above
Will come down to dwell among us
And he will give us orders
Showering us with blessings

He will send us food
We shall slaughter good meat
We shall have large crops
Many olives, many grapes
Much léen, much iaïn[14]


Even though the *Arba kehilot* were about fifteen miles apart from each other in a sea of hostile non-Jews, the rituals of these four communities remained distinct from each other until unified in 1767![15] Except for the traditional prayers that are common throughout the Diaspora, the Provençal ritual, like the ritual of other Jewish communities, integrated distinctive elements—in this case, the liturgical prayers called *piyutim* (in Occitan, *òbras*[16]). Many of these prayers were written by renowned local rabbis such as Mardochée Astruc in L'Isle sur Sorgue; Jacob de Lunel, Mordekhai ben Jacob, Salomon Azoubi, David ben Joseph Carmi, Salom ben Moïse de Milhaud, and Jasse de Meyrargues in Carpentras; Gad ben Juda de Bedarride, in Cavaillon; and Joseph ben Abraham and Saul ben Joseph in Monteux.[17]

The three *piyutim* I was able to study[18] are from *Sefer HaKontrès*,[19] an abridged version of the *Sefer HaTamid*, "the Book of Constancy." They comprise alternative passages in Occitan and Hebrew, written in holy (i.e., Hebrew) characters (I leave the original Occitan in the translations, below). Some are mere translations, and some elaborations of the original pieces. *Piyutim* 1 and 2 were written to accompany a circumcision ceremony. *Piyut* 1 is a mere description of Abraham's circumcision and the announcement that Sarah was to bear a child, along with the prayer for the uniting of dispersed Jews in *Eretz Israel* at the end of time. *Piyut* 2, possibly written by Mardochée Ventura,[20] has three clear allusions to the role of wine in the ceremony, but stipulates the consumption of only one glass, instead of the customary two:

נעירה
רכובו על עבים
און ויירי פליין דוין
יסינה

Let us stay awake and sing
His carriage is in the clouds
*Un veire plen de vin* ("with a wine-filled glass")
In our right hands[21]

And further:

כום זה נקרא פגום
שי יא בגו דנגון
לא יקרב
פריניש די וין אב בראב
כום אחר נמלא

This glass, called *pagum*[22]
*Se i a begut dingun* ("If someone has drunk from it")
Will not get close to our lips
*Prenetz de vin au barrau* ("Get wine from the cask")
And let us fill another glass![23]

And finally:

לאנפאן קי אי שירקונשי
לשמונה
פיר קריני דיב שיאגיה נא
לילה ויומם
לא וירי אלא מאן
ברנה

*L'enfan que è circounci* ("The child who is circumcised")
on the eight (i.e. eighth day)
*Per cregne Dieu siégié na* ("May he be born to fear God")
Night and day
*Lou veïre a la man* ("with a glass in his hand")
In jubilation[24]

The third *piyut* is dedicated to *Purim* (the Festival of Esther).[25] We find the same allusions as in the other two *piyut*, as for example the divine clouds above[26] and especially the promise of the return to *Eretz Israel* at the coming of the Messiah: "*Quan nostre puple sera ramassa.*"[27] In *piyut* 3, wine is mentioned toward the end of the story, after Haman has been done away with:

קדשו היום עצרה

אי קי נישקון שי טינני פריפארה

שתוו ושכרו זמרו שורה

לאו ואאירי די וין א לא מאן

שתו עסיסים אחרי משמן

לאו מייב לא בריטקוה

ואשטרי קור ריפרשקוה

ידיכם שאו כום מורי

ורשא די וין אוב ואירי קי ביבראי

Celebrate the festival today
*E que chascun se tengue prépara* ("and let everyone get ready")
Drink yourself to intoxication, start a song
*Lou veïre de vin a la man* ("with a glass of wine in your hands")
Drink sweet wine after the fat (i.e. meat)
*Lou meou, la brescou* ("honey, the honeycomb")
*Vostre cor resfrescou* ("refresh your hearts")[28]
Raise up your glasses, my friends
*Versa de vin aou veïre que béourai* ("pour wine into the glass that I will drink from")[29]

Still, with all its strict adhesion to the ritual, the Jewish writer is not afraid of presenting in Provençal a contradictory version to the Hebrew formula "Gara la pepida" ("watch your thirst, don't drink too much!").

ואל וְיושא ודיו

יראג אל ודיפיפ

ותש ורכשו

*Lou vin es vidou* ("wine is life")
*Gare la pepidou* ("watch your thirst")[30]
Drink yourself to intoxication[31]

## FOOD AND DRINK

It was traditionally believed amongst Jews that wine contained vital calories and pharmaceutical benefits. The rabbis considered that wine taken in moderation induces appetite, "sustains and makes glad,"[32] and is beneficial to health: "Wine is the greatest of all medicines: where wine is lacking, drugs are necessary."[33] Interestingly enough, many centuries later, Louis Pasteur was to uphold the very same theory. Whoever buys their wine in the south of France is regularly reminded of Louis Pasteur's assertion: *"le vin est la plus saine des boissons"* ("wine is the healthiest of all beverages"), a quotation proudly displayed in every wine cooperative! Old wine was allegedly beneficial for intestinal disorders, so much so that "it was often diluted by a third with water"[34] in order to reduce its potency. But wine in general was also considered excellent for "opening the heart to reasoning,"[35] and an "inducement to the advancement of the young rabbis' calling."[36]

Traditional ideas of the benefits of wine remain in the Ashkenazic wined *matza kugels* (puddings), and the Italian *azzime dolci col vino* (sweet matzot—a brittle flat bread eaten with wine at Passover) that are still eaten during *Pessah* (Passover). I know of two recipes; both require fat (olive oil, or olive oil and goose fat) as well as *matza* flour and white wine. The one without sugar is the Roman recipe.[37] All the dishes with wine are reserved for *Pessah*, and sometimes *Purim*.[38] But, to be noted from Claudia Roden's masterpiece, a recipe from the Italian Piedmont—*Bruscadelle*—or toasted bread in red wine, which is eaten around Yom Kippur: "This is not so much a sweet as an old custom. In Piedmont they break the fast of Yom Kippur with slices of toasted brioche-type bread sprinkled lightly with sugar and cinnamon and left to soak in the local strong red wine until they are very soft and soggy."[39] The Jewish cuisine grew out of the need to adapt the rulings of *Kashrut*—the Jewish dietary laws—to the traditional cuisine of the place where the Jews were tolerated, while wine consumption habits were directly linked to vine growing. To my knowledge, there is no Provençal Jewish cookbook, but it might be safe to infer that Provençal Jewish dishes were very close to the local ones—which use very little meat, and singularly, very little pork, if any—and/or to the Piedmontese dishes. Wine recipes spread from southern France to neighbouring countries, with the exception of Italy, which is the only country where wined recipes are local, and not a mere copying of French cuisine.[40] For example, Jewish cookbooks mention *Cotognata* (quinces in wine) as an "*Antica ricetta italiana.*"[41]

There exist few texts about the consumption of wine among Jewish communities, but it would be a safe bet to say that Jewish behaviour depended on local mores and wine-making skills. The *Encyclopedia Judaica* notes that Mediterranean *Eretz Israel* produced wine, while Babylonia produced beer.[42] Later, the Jews in Germany and Eastern Europe took to drinking tea, mead, beer, or hard liquor, though they were better at selling these beverages to the Gentiles than at drinking them.[43] Every source stresses that intoxication is not tolerated by Jews, with the frowned upon exception of the rabbi who is often the butt of jokes for his tendency to indulge in strong liquor. Some authorities suggest that the traditional Jewish disinterest in wine is due to the poor quality of their kosher wines: because wine is to be drunk by everybody in the family over the age of thirteen, sweet wine is more popular among uneducated palates. Besides, sweet wine (from raisins or dried fruits[44]) is easier to make, and it keeps longer once the bottle has been uncorked.

Claudia Roden differentiates between the habits of Sephardic Jews—those living in North Africa where the French and other Christians introduced wine growing very early—and Jews living in the other Muslim regions, where "wine" is mostly liquor. She quotes a letter written from Alexandria in 1488 by the Italian Jew Obadiah of Bertinoro to his father in Italy, about the local celebration of the Sabbath:

> The following is the custom in all Muslim countries. They sit in a circle on the carpet, the cup bearer standing nearby. A small cloth is spread on the carpet and all kinds of fruit which are in season are brought and laid on it. The host now takes a glass of wine and pronounces the blessing of sanctification and empties the cup. The cup bearer then hands the cup to the whole company, always refilled, and each person empties it. Then the host eats two or three pieces of fruit and drinks a second glass and all the company says 'Health and life.' Whoever sits next to the host also takes some fruit, and the cup bearer fills a second glass for him . . . this is continued until each one has emptied six or seven glasses. . . . After all have drunk to their hearts' content, a large dish of meat is brought and each one stretches forth his hand and eats quickly, for they are not very big eaters. . . . A glass

of wine was drunk with each kind of food. Then followed raisin wine . . . then malmsey wine . . . and again native wine.[45]

הלבקנ חבש ינפ תארקל ידוד הכל ("Go, my loved one, towards your bride, Shabbat is coming, let us welcome her!") The description quoted by Roden might be somewhat exaggerated, but people in the Middle Ages would eat and drink profusely whenever they had the opportunity because there were times when they had nothing much on their plates. Thus, Sephardic Jews in wine-producing regions may well have seen no sin in downing wine while rejoicing in song at the prospect of the "coming of the Bride" in Synagogue at the opening of Shabbat (*lekha dodi*, לכה דודי).

The question here is whether Provençal Jews had a particular attitude toward wine, as opposed to the other Jews in the Diaspora, notably those who lived in lands with no tradition of wine growing. Roden notes:

> There was a strong ascetic streak in German Jews, and their lives were inclined to spirituality rather than sensual expression. Ethical writings from medieval times are full of encouragement towards frugality and self-restraint in eating—"the most animal of instincts." Rabbis expressed distaste at the way their French, Italian, and Spanish coreligionists enjoyed their meals and their glass of wine. In *Eat and Be Satisfied*, John Cooper quotes a thirteenth-century letter reprimanding the French Jews for "studying the Talmud with their stomachs full of meat, vegetables and wine" and another warning that "gross overeating is as dangerous to the body as a sword.[46]

## JEWS, GENTILES, AND WINE IN PROVENCE

Nevertheless, Jews in Provence had a tradition of both wine making and wine consumption. Generally in Europe—outside France and Germany, where they owned vineyards as early as the fourth century CE—Jews had to deal with Christian vintners, although these worked under rabbinical control. For example, Rashi, the famous Talmud commentator who lived in Troyes (Champagne) in the eleventh century,[47] was both a rabbi and a vintner.

In France, as Claudia Roden notes, Jews had famous orchards, possibly because vegetables and fruits were also used as medicines.[48]

Unfortunately, Roden does not say if she means France as it is today, or if these orchards were in Provence, which was not French until the late Middle Ages. Some Jews in southern Europe owned flour mills and vineyards. Others had to buy their grain and oil, but those with money, being barred from ownership of property, often ended up investing heavily enough in the business to control the market.

Jews in Europe also consumed wine. The Encyclopedia Judaica points out that the Jews in Spain were not shy about wine drinking: "Copious wine drinking by the upper Jewish social strata is also frequently mentioned in Jewish poetry in Spain."[49] As regards Provence, there are, alas, very few texts written by Provençal Jews in the local idiom that refer to wine, at least on the basis of the four sources that I was able to study. According to René Moulinas and Danièle and Carol Iancu—specialists of Provençal Judaism—any allusion to wine in the local ritual texts is strictly religious, and there is apparently no divergence from any other ritual, be it in Ashkenazic or Sefardic territories. Nevertheless, one can infer from a study of social history that the Jews of Provence did engage in wine making and wine drinking.

Indeed, Jews everywhere in southern France tried to produce wine because of its importance in their social and religious life. Wine is to abide by the rules of *kashrut* and has always been a spiritual element of Jewish life. Provençal Jews also adapted to the local traditions. As Danièle and Carol Iancu have shown in their remarkable book, *Les Juifs du Midi*, Christians and Jews both clashed and socialized. A spectacular example of animosity occurred in 1682 when the son of the Carpentras rabbi was abducted and baptized, never allowed to go back to his family. Again, in 1713, the Jews of Cavaillon were accused of ritual murder. In another case in 1757, an anti-Jewish riot almost occurred when a Christian fell into the well of the Carpentras ghetto.[50]

Nevertheless, there were constant social exchanges between Christians and Jews. This started with language, for both Jews and Christians in Provence spoke, and sometimes wrote, Provençal. The text discovered in the Archives in Rouen speaks for itself—anybody versed in the French language can notice the obvious influence, both in spelling and semantics, for such was the state of the Provençal language in the streets of the eighteenth century! People no longer knew how to write diphthongs, and the convert obviously hesitated on transcribing the "u" sound. He sometimes used the French "ou"—"*Aqueou*" instead of "*Aqueu*," and "*nous*" or "*prouvisiou*"— and sometimes kept the classic "o" of the Middle Ages in "*eilamon*" or "*benediction*." Jews in Provence certainly spoke Provençal—the Provençal of the times—from the perfectly classical Occitan of Crescas du Caylar (fourteenth century), to the heavily gallicized Comtadin Occitan of rabbis Mardochée Astruc or Jacob de Lunel (seventeenth and eighteenth centuries), and the anonymous rabbi-poet who wrote *piyut* 3.

Provençal also influenced Jewish names. Men had Hebrew names with the local pronunciation or translation: Ain (for "Haim," meaning "Life"), Benestruc ("Gad," the "lucky one"), Bendit ("Barukh," the "Blessed one"), Bonjour ("YomTov," Good Day, i.e., Holy Day), Cento ("Shem Tov," the Good Name, i.e., God), Abram and Aleotta ("Halafta"), Guerce ("Gershom"), Jacassay ("Yehoshua"), Milier ("Meir"), Mossé ("Moses"), Rubin ("Reuven"), Somié ("Samuel"). Women very often had Provençal names: Benvengude ("the one who came well," or "the one who is welcome"), Benestrugue ("the one who is lucky"), Blanquete ("the white one"), Douce ("the sweet one"), Juste ("the fair one"), Nerthe ("myrtle"), and Rousse ("the red-haired one").

Again, despite it being illegal, Christian nurses and servants lived with Jewish families, and many young Jewish men worked outside the ghetto. Jews played *boules* and *quilles* with non-Jews, danced to the same musical instruments (*galoubet* and *tambourin*).[51] The dietary rules being so stringent, the Jews could not eat or drink with Christians, but they certainly could invite Christians to their festivities, and it seems that many did. Bourgeois, nobles, and members of the lower classes often went to weddings, circumcisions, and even attended religious services! In 1784 a Christian innkeeper in Carpentras was finally allowed to serve Jews[52]—just before Jews were treated as citizens with equal rights.[53]

This social interchange continued to modern times. Dr. Bernard Ely, a physician and specialist of Provençal cuisine from Avignon, told me that in his youth, Provençal people were crazy about *matzot*, which they called *coudolles*.[54] They would travel far to buy a few at the few bakeries that would make them. However, he did not say anything about kosher wine.

## Popular Literary Traditions

Finally, it is interesting to see how wine is presented in two literary texts, written in Provençal, relating the story of Esther—a very popular tale especially among Provençal Jews.[55] The first passage, from Crescas du Caylar's "*Roman d'Ester*" comprises 447 lines, representing chapters 1, 2, and 9 of the *Megilla* (which has ten chapters).[56] It draws a medieval scene filled with castles, horses, many fair maidens, food, and much wine:

> 'Non vuelh qe a nostre celier
> Meta sarralhas botilier.
> Aitant cant nostra cort dura
> Cascu beva ses mezura.'

> Lo rei al cap de la semana;
> El ac dal vin la testa vana,
> En fon vera enrabiat,
> Tant fort se fon inubriat.

> I wish that to our wine cellar
> The butler should not put a padlock
> So long as our festivity lasts,
> Everybody should drink without limits.[57]

> The king got himself so intoxicated;
> His head was stunned by wine
> It made him truly enraged,
> He was so drunk.[58]

Crescas was a physician, so here are his medical remarks:

> Lo vin que begron fon aital
> Con cascun beu en son ostal,
> Qe non lor montet al cervel,
> Mais aiso mes vin novel;
> Galen lo dits:'De l'aiga mis
> Dal vin es caura que ieu m'ais.'

The wine they drank was similar
To the one that one drinks at home
So it would not make their heads turn,
And this is why he gave new wine;
So says Galen: "it pleases me
That wine be mixed with water."[59]

When the gentle folks had drunk too much, they lost all sense of decorum, and taunted each other as to the low conditions of their ancestors. Vashti says of her husband and King:

*Ben par qe trop aja begut,*
*Qe en aiso en sia vengut.*
*Mal sembla mon senher avi*
*Qe era tant bon e tant savi*
*Qe begra de vin per un bou*
*E el no o balanzera un ou.*

It does look like he has drunk too much,
That he should have come to this.
How little does he looks like my lord ancestor
For he was so good and so wise
That he was able to drink wine in a horn
And not stumble in any way[60]

And the courtiers tattle on her:

*Elz li van dir: 'Sénher, per ver*
*Ela nos a per fols tengus*
*E dis qu'el vin vos a mogut.*
*Paraulas dis folas e pegas,*
*Vostre paire gardet las egas.*

So they told him: 'Majesty in truth
She took us for fools
And says that the wine has moved you
She says crazy and heavy words;
Your father kept mares.[61]

The style and theme are quite different three centuries later in "La Tragediou de la Reyne Esther," written by Rabbis Mardochée Astruc (seventeenth century) and Jacob de Lunel (eighteenth century):

> *Madame, vous demande pardoun de la liberta,*
> *Sirou lou Rey, sa Majesta,*
> *M'a dit de vous lou veni dire,*
> *Sabe pas si lou fai per rire*
> *Ou si de vin es trop carga,*
> *M'a fa veni affatigua,*
> *Per vous announça la nouvelle*

> Madam, I beg your pardon for my frankness
> The king, His Majesty
> Has told me to go and tell you
> I do not know if he does so for fun
> Or if he is too loaded with wine
> He has made me come hastily
> For me to tell you the news[62]

Later, the two conspirators decide to poison the king:[63]

> *Yeou voli fare toun sentimente*
> *Voli dar din aques vino*
> *Oune bone medicine*
> *Que lou tourmentarate journe e gniotte*
> *Noun lou quitara que noun si morte*

> I want to do as you feel
> I will pour in this wine
> A good medicine
> That will torment him day and night
> And will not stop until he dies[64]

So Esther warns the King:

> *Vene d'apprendre soulamen*
> *Que dous gardes de la Veisselle*

*Vous voulien freta leis meisselles*
*D'un pouisoun rude et meichant*


I just found out
That two guards of the Palace
Wanted to rub your gums
With a strong and mean poison[65]

To reveal his villainy to her husband, Queen Esther invites Haman over for a meal:

*Haman, mangea et bevé s'en faire façoun,*
*Gousta un paou aqueou souesoun*


Haman, don't you fret, eat and drink,
How about tasting this saucisson?[66]

This sure was a far cry from the holy texts of the Jewish religion, but it was undeniably another aspect of the life of the Jews in Provence.

## NOTES

1. Robert Louis Stevenson, *Travels with a Donkey in the Cévennes* (London: Godfrey Cave Associates, 1980), 180–81.
2. Molly Lyons Bar-David and Yom Tov Lewinsky, "Food" in *Encyclopedia Judaica*, ed. Geoffrey Wigoder, CD-ROM, Judaica Multimedia, Jerusalem, 1996.
3. Claudia Roden, *The Book of Jewish Food, An Odyssey from Samarkand to New York* (New York: A. Knopf, 1999), 632.
4. I have personal memories of being offered "*vino nero*" (black wine) in the Sardinia of the 1970s. The wine was very strong (18 percent alc/vol) and untreated. It was like drinking pure unadulterated vinegar.
5. Today's L'Isle sur Sorgue.
6. Once deprived of their Temple, the Jews had to turn to their Rabbis for directions. It was decided to write down their various decisions, even if sometimes contradictory. These rulings are collectively and

improperly called "Oral Law," as opposed to the "Written Law," which is basically what the Christians call "The Old Testament." There were two groups of Talmud scholars: those who remained in Jerusalem (220–375 CE), and those who settled in Babylon (220–499 CE). See "Talmud" in *Dictionnaire de la civilisation juive*, eds. Jean-Christophe Attias and Esther Benbassa (Paris: Larousse, 1997), 281.

7. *Talmud*, Bava Batra (BB): real estate, possessions, inheritance, partnership, evidence, testimony, 60b.

8. *Talmud*, Eruvin (Er): rabbinical decrees regarding the Sabbath; extension of Sabbath boundaries), 64a.

9. Roden, *Book of Jewish Food*, 631.

10. The prayer marking the "entrance" of Shabbat.

11. *Talmud*, Ketubot (Ket): marriage contracts, and financial obligations; the mutual rights and duties of husband wife, 8b. This particular tradition has been discontinued.

12. Sabbetai Zevi was born in Smyrna in 1626 CE, and declared himself the Messiah in 1656. Despair was such among the Jews that many ardently followed him. He was given the choice by the Ottoman authorities to convert to Islam or be executed. He died in Albania in 1676 as a Muslim. His followers developed a particular Muslim sect in the Ottoman Empire. His last Jewish supporters were to be found in 1924 in Saloniki from where they subsequently moved to mainland Turkey. For more information, see *Encyclopedia Judaica*; Jewish Heritage Online, http://www.jhom.com/personalities/gluckel/shabtai.htm; http://en.wikipedia.org/wiki/Sabbatai_Zevi.

13. *Talmud*, Berachot (Ber): blessings and prayers; liturgical rules, 34b.

14. Anon., "Bisarerie (Oddity), Poeme su la miserou dei Jusiou a l'experance de son Messiou" ("A Poem about the wretchedness of the Jews, waiting for their Messiah"), *Manuscript Montbret 1669* (616), Bibliothèque municipale de Rouen; courtesy of M. Elie Nicolas, Nouvelle Gallia Judaica research group, CNRS, Université Paul Valéry, Montpellier, France.

15. Elie Crémieu, in Mordecai Karmi, *Seder HaTamid*, 2 vols, (Avignon, 1767).

16. Also spelled "obro," i.e., "pieces of work."

17. Danièle and Carol Iancu, *Les juifs du Midi, une histoire millénaire* (Avignon: Editions Barthélémy, 1995), 192–93.

18. I would like to thank Frédéric Vouland for providing me with copies of these rare documents.

19. "Sefer HaKontrès" in *Chansons hébraïco-provençales des juifs comtadins, ed.* Ernest Sabatier (Nîmes: André Catélan, 1887); and, in S.

M. Dom Pedro II d'Alcantara, trans., *Poésies hébraïco-provençales du rituel israélite comtadin* (Avignon: Segun fre`res, 1891).

20. That is, as recently as the eighteenth century.

21. "Sefer HaKontrès," *Piyut* 2, vol. 6, pp. 9–10.

22. Deteriorated, unfit for drinking.

23. "Sefer HaKontrès," *Piyut* 2, v. 22.

24. "Sefer HaKontrès," *Piyut* 2, v. 37–42.

25. That is, it is a ritual piece to be used around Purim, the festival of Esther.

26. "Sefer HaKontrès," *Piyut* 3, line 64.

27. When are people is assembled together; see"Sefer HaKontrès," *Piyut* 3, line 128 passim.

28. "Sefer HaKontrès," *Piyut* 3, v. 100–6.

29. "Sefer HaKontrès," *Piyut* 3, v. 107–8.

30. Interestingly enough, Frederic Mistral quotes these verses under "PEPIDO, pipido, pupido, papido, perpito, perpitojo, pepio, pipio, pupido (rom., cat: pepida): Lou vin es vido/Garo la pepido, Chant populaire juif"; Frederic Mistral, *Lou Tresor dóu Felebrige*, vol. 2 (Aix-en-Provence: P. Rollet, 1998), 539.

31. "Sefer HaKontrès," *Piyut* 3, v. 114–16.

32. *Talmud*, Ber 35b.

33. *Talmud*, BB 58b; Anon., "Wine" in Wigoder, ed., *Encyclopedia Judaica*.

34. Roden, *Book of Jewish Food*, 632.

35. *Talmud*, BB 12b.

36. *Talmud*, BB 12b.

37. Giuliana Ascoli Vitali-Norsa, "azzime dolci col vino" in her *La cucina nella tradizione ebraica* (Florence: La Giuntina, 1998), 368.

38. The celebration of Queen Esther's success in preventing a massacre of the Jewish population. The tradition is that participants must drink to celebrate, and intoxication is expected.

39. "Bruscadelle," in Roden, *Book of Jewish Food*, 578.

40. For example, fruit compotes using wine white or red, or fish poached in white wine, which was very popular in Russia and Poland, and came from French chefs working for the upper classes of St. Petersburg.

41. Vitali-Norsa, *La cucina nella tradizione ebraica*, 253.

42. Anon., "Wine and Liquor Trade" in Wigoder, ed., *Encyclopedia Judaica*.

43. The Jewish innkeeper is a traditional character of many Yiddish tales.

44. Roden, *Book of Jewish Food*, 126; Moroccan Jews call this drink "mahia."

45. Roden, *Book of Jewish Food*, 633.

46. *German beginnings*," in Roden, *Book of Jewish Food*, 43.

47. Rabbi Shlomo ben Yitzhaki, 1040–1105 CE.
48. "The Development of Ashkenazic Style of Cooking," in Roden, *Book of Jewish Food*, 42.
49. Haim Hillel Ben Sasson, "Wine and Liquor Trade, Middle Ages (to 16th Century)," in Wigoder, ed., *Encyclopedia Judaica.*
50. Iancu, *Les juifs du Midi*, 206.
51. As for example, in "Sefer HaKontrès," Piyut 1, line 6: "Let us praise Almighty God," "*Desur tambourin e viouloun*" ("to the sound of tambourines and violins").
52. Iancu, *Les juifs du Midi*, 206.
53. I remember a bible once exhibited at the small "Musée Judéo-Comtadin" under the Synagogue in Cavaillon. Someone had written in poor French and a hesitant hand: "This bible belongs to X . . . Whoever steals it from me, he will be guilloutined [*sic*]."
54. From the Occitan *còdol*, meaning "round pebble."
55. Prof. Michèle Bitton once pointed out to me the very high number of Jewish Provençal women called "Esther."
56. Crescas du Caylar, "*Roman d'Ester*," from "Megilla," in Patric Choffrut, "Pourim en Provence," unpublished manuscript, University of Avignon Library.
57. *Megilla*, lines 105–8.
58. Ibid., lines 169–72.
   1 Ibid., lines 157–62.
   1 Ibid., lines 169–72.
59. Ibid., lines 157–62.
60. Ibid., lines 215–20.
61. Ibid., lines 234–38.
62. Rabbis Mardochée Astruc, *La Reine Esther* (Carpentras: Le Nombre D'Or, 1970), I.99–115. References are to act and lines.
63. The *Megillah* only speaks about "laying a violent hand on the King." The later commentators spoke of poison, in a liquid form. There is, however, no mention of wine; see Rafael Hiya Pontremoli, *Meam Loez*, trans. Albert Benveniste (Lagrasse: Ed. Verdier, 1997), 155.
64. Astruc, *La Reine Esther*, III.10–14.
65. Ibid., III.42–45.
66. Ibid., IV.751–52.

# CHAPTER 9

# DOMESTIC DEMAND AND
# EXPORT IMPERATIVES FOR FRENCH
# AND AUSTRALIAN WINES
## A HISTORICAL OVERVIEW

*Gwyn Campbell*

## INTRODUCTION

France is historically the world's top producer of a wide range of fine wines. Its Bordeaux wines have dominated British and other northern European markets since at least the founding of the Angevin empire in 1154. In 2006, it was still the world's largest producer of wine (4,636 million liters), followed by Italy (4,409 million liters), and Spain (4,280 million liters).[1] However, France's wine-growing sector is in crisis, and its position as a pre-eminent wine exporter is increasingly challenged by other wine-producing countries. One of its major competitors is Australia. The world's fastest growing economy behind Ireland in the 1990s, with an average growth rate of nearly 4 percent a year (4.3 percent in 1999).[2] Australia was not traditionally known as a wine producer. Nevertheless, by 2006 it was the world's seventh biggest producer of wine (1,019 million liters),[3] fiercely competing with France for top export markets. This chapter examines the historical trends in the domestic market for French and Australian wines, and the consequences in terms of export strategy, focusing upon their competition for the British market.

# FRANCE

## The Home Market

The first large domestic market for wine was generated after the French Revolution by the new urban classes and their fondness for restaurants.[4] Demand was augmented by industrialization, notably from the mid-nineteenth century, with increased urbanization and a large and growing market for cheaper wines in the northeast, the Paris basin, and major ports such as Le Havre, Nantes, and Marseilles. Moreover, per capita income grew significantly from 1830 to 1870, and again from about 1880, boosting demand for wine.[5]

Viticulture thus shared in the "Golden Age" of French farming from 1852 to 1882, when agricultural production generally increased 30.8 percent in volume and 80 percent in value[6]—a growth due less to technical improvements than to an increase in area under cultivation.[7] The area under vines increased 13 percent between 1852 and 1874, to reach 2.5 million hectares, while from 1850 to 1875 wine production grew more than 50 percent.[8]

However, due to poor transport facilities, only wine-growing areas close to the main urban markets of northern France—notably around Paris, the Moselle, and the Côtes d'Auvergne—initially benefited from increased demand.[9] Bordeaux maintained traditional maritime links to northern and export markets, but southern French vineyards were largely excluded. Thus, in the early nineteenth century, the Vaucluse annually produced only some 250,000 to 350,000 hectoliters of wine which, except for Châteauneuf-du-Pape, La Nerte, Sorgues, and Châteauneuf-de-Gadagne output, was inferior.[10]

Only with the construction of an efficient railway network from the mid-nineteenth century were southern French vineyards granted access to the larger domestic markets.[11] From 1870 to 1879, the average annual production of wine was 51.7 million hectoliters. Overall, this represented an average 71 percent increase over the period from 1850 to 1859, although the increase was 152 percent in the South, which represented 31.4 percent of French wine production.[12] By the early twentieth century, the railways had helped transform the Languedoc plains into a huge supply region for the markets of northern France. However, the Languedoc red wines were weak, and in order to augment their alcohol content and color, they were reinforced with wines from Algeria where, in consequence, viticulture experienced rapid development.[13]

## Restraints

Nevertheless, the domestic market for wine was limited due to a number of factors, notably demographic restraints, and more recently, to declining consumption.

### *Demography*

During the nineteenth century, rising productivity associated with the Agricultural and Industrial Revolutions—and the commercial boom associated with the rise of the international economy—overcame the Malthusian nightmare that had plagued pre-industrial economies and permitted unprecedented demographic expansion, notably in the West where, during the nineteenth century, the population of Europe doubled and the populations of Britain, Germany, and the United States increased fivefold.

However, France failed to share in this demographic explosion. Although it was, in 1800, on the brink of over-population, and up to 1830 experienced rapid population growth (0.55 percent),[14] it thereafter slowed: between 1816 and 1901, the population rose by

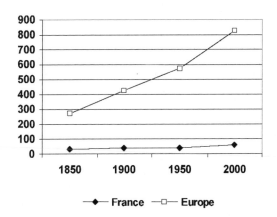

**Figure 9.1** Population: France and Europe, 1750–2000 (millions)[15]

only 8.4 million to 38.4 million. The population growth rate halved from 0.55 percent (1816–46) to 0.27 (1846–66), fell more slowly to 0.19 percent (1866–86), then dropped precipitously to 0.08 percent (1886–1901) before rising to 0.2 percent (1901–11).[16] This trend reflected a sharp fall in the birth rate, resulting from the widespread adoption of birth control, although with great regional variation, and an increase in the death rate from 1830, notably in infant mortality.[17]

Historians such as François Caron argue that weak demographic growth, alongside low per capita income, limited market demand and thus economic development.[18] Economists such as J. Marczewski and M. Lévy-Leboyer rather blame agriculture—which remained largely peasant and comparatively undeveloped until the post–World War II era—as responsible for slow economic growth.[19] Whatever the case, the population growth rate in France was largely stagnant until the post-1945 era. Even then, it remained well behind the rest of Europe: while the French population increased from 39 million in 1900 to 58.7 million by 2000, it constituted only 6.9 percent of the European population in 2000, compared to 9.2 percent in 1900 (and 13 percent in 1850).[20]

## Consumption

Historically, France had one of the world's highest rates of wine consumption. Annual per capita wine consumption grew slowly in the first half of the nineteenth century; between 1830 and 1840 it actually fell from 86 to 80 liters, rising thereafter to only 83 liters by

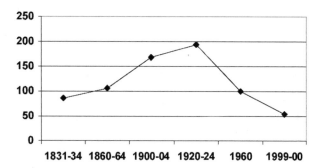

**Figure 9.2** France: Average annual per capita wine consumption, 1831–2000 (liters)[21]

1859. However, from 1860, it increased rapidly, reaching 136 liters in 1873, falling back to 93 liters in the middle of the 1880s depression (1885), rising dramatically to reach 168 liters by 1904, before falling again from 1909 to reach 128 liters by the eve of World War I.[22] Between 1919–21 and 1922–34, average per capita consumption rose from 148 to 194 liters,[23] but subsequently fell to 100 liters, and by 1999–2000 to 55 liters.[24]

By 2000, France was still the world's top consumer of wine (35.4 million hectoliters or 16 percent of the 221.4 million hectoliters consumed worldwide), just ahead of Italy (14 percent).[25] However, the trend is downwards: non–wine drinkers in France increased from 23 percent of the population in 1980 to 37 percent in 2000, while regular wine consumers fell from 47 to 24 percent of the population. Annual French wine consumption, which fell by 11.1 percent to four billion bottles between 2001 and 2005, is expected to fall behind both the United States and Italy by 2010. [26]

This reflects a growing preference for bottled water as a table drink (between 1987 and 2000 the table wine share of the domestic supermarket wine sales fell from 58 to 27 percent), a continued reluctance by French females to consume wine (men consume 75 percent plus of wine by volume), and falling wine consumption amongst younger age groups.[27]

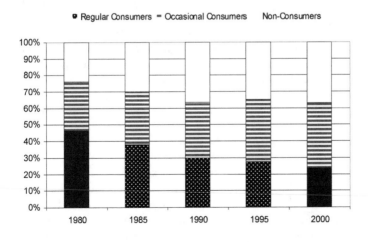

**Figure 9.3** France: Wine consumption, 1980–2000 (% of total population)[28]

Both private and public wine drinking have decreased significantly since the tightening up of controls and penalties on dangerous driving, notably with the introduction of speed cameras in October 2003 and the strict enforcement of a 0.5 blood/alcohol limit. Within a year, restaurant wine sales fell by 15 percent, forcing producers to consider reducing production of 750 milliliter wine bottles and promoting the sale of 375 milliliter bottles.[29]

## Australia

British settlers developed vineyards in Australia in the early nineteenth century, finding suitable climate and soils there. Wine production expanded rapidly in the second half of the nineteenth century, spreading from New South Wales to all other states, except Tasmania where natural conditions were unfavorable.[30] Currently, grape growing for fresh and dried fruit, and especially for wine making, is the largest fruit industry in Australia, practiced in all states and territories, in climates ranging from temperate to tropical.[31] The area under vine has expanded spectacularly over the last two decades—from 59 hectares in 1989–90 to 123 hectares in 1998–99, to 168,791 hectares in 2006—and is concentrated upon premium grapes and wines. Production is greatest in South Australia (notably the Barossa, Clare, Riverland, and Southern Districts, and Coonawarra), which produces just under 50 percent of the total, but irrigation schemes have led to wine production increasing in the other states,[32] notably in Victoria (Victoria, Great Western, and Sunraysia), New South Wales (Hunter, Riverina, and Sunraysia), and Western Australia (Swan Valley and Margaret River).[33]

### The Home Market

Due to the distance from external markets, Australian wine makers were until recently obliged to look to the domestic market for survival. Although Australia's population and population density was small compared to European countries, its population growth rate has compared favorably with other countries of new settlement. Moreover, it achieved a comparatively unsurpassed rate of urbanization. This, and the "All White" immigration policy practiced until

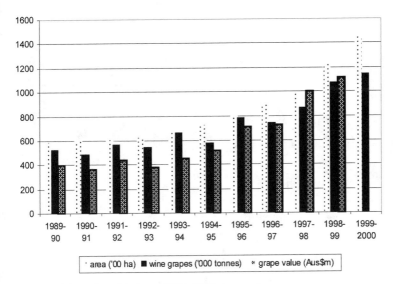

**Figure 9.4** Australian viticulture, 1989–2000: Area under grapes, production of wine grapes, and gross value of grape production[34]

the 1970s, meant it developed high urban concentrations of European populations, giving it the potential to develop a considerable home market for wine. However, most settlers were—until the post-1945 era—of British origin, and thus traditionally beer drinkers, only the minority of upper class British demonstrating an interest in wine.[35] This changed from World War II when an economic boom that lasted until the end of the 1960s—combined with mass immigration from southern Europe, notably Italy and Greece—created a population base with a preference for wine and the income to satisfy that preference.

Wine consumption was favored by the absence of taxes, traditionally imposed on beer and spirits, the most popular domestic alcoholic beverages. An excise tax of 50 cents per gallon of wine imposed in August 1970 proved so unpopular that it was removed in December 1972.[36] However, it was re-introduced as a wholesale sales tax (WST) of 10 percent in August 1984, and raised twice by 1998 to levels higher than those imposed in other major wine producing countries. The WST slowed the growth in domestic sales, notably of top quality wines.[37]

Despite this, Australian wine sales reached record levels in the late 1990s as the domestic market boomed from 1996, due to a

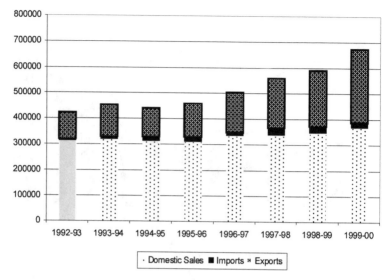

Figure 9.5  Australia: Wine trade, 1992–2000[38] ('000 liters)

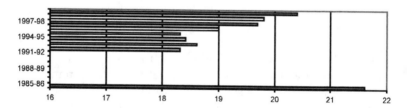

Figure 9.6  Australia: Per capita wine consumption, 1985–2000 (liters)[39]

combination of low interest rates, low inflation, and rising asset prices.[40] In 1998–99, domestic sales of Australian wines reached a record 348 million liters, up 3 percent on the previous year. Per capita wine consumption rose from an average of 3 liters in the late 1930s to a record 21.6 liters in 1985–86, after which it fell to just over 18 liters in the early 1990s, rose to about 20 liters by 2000, 26.8 liters in 2002–03, and 27.5 liters by 2003–04.[41] Traditionally, Riesling enjoyed pride of place on the domestic market, but during the 1990s, demand grew substantially for wines like Chardonnay and Cabernet Sauvignon.[42]

However, Australia is characterized by stagnant natural population growth common in most advanced economies. Moreover, the dropping of the "All White" immigration policy in the 1980s resulted—until the reapplication of immigration restrictions—in a significant influx of Asians who are not traditional wine consumers. All of this has countered factors agitating for increased domestic demand, such as rising income and the growing popularity of red wine amongst women.[43] Meanwhile, rapid expansion of vineyards has led to production surplus.

## The Domestic Market and the Imperative to Export

The failure in both countries of the domestic market to absorb wine production has led France and Australia to look increasingly to the export market. In 2000, wine was France's leading agricultural export and its eleventh most important export by value (at 3,809 million euros).[44] However, the growth in French wine exports has slowed, from 6.2 percent in 1978–87 to 1.5 percent in 1987–96.[45] In 1995, Bordeaux produced only 10 percent of French wine (worth $2.4 billion), but 50 percent of French wine exports,[46] and by 2000, Bordeaux's wine output was greater than that of Australia, and of Chile and South Africa combined.[47]

From 1999–2000, French wine exports fell 5.4 percent in value, from $4.86 billion to $4.6 billion. International sales declined an additional 4 percent between 2000 and 2002, when French wine sales remained buoyant in only two of their eight major foreign markets—Belgium and Japan. Given the decline in the domestic market, this has led to growing stocks of unsold wine. [48] Of notable significance is the decline in sales of Bordeaux, which has plunged into a crisis that has led to re-evaluation and a call for a diversification of French nonelite wines for export.[49] However, rising international competition also threatens jobs in an industry where the proportion of the French viticultural workforce engaged in exports increased between 1978 and 1995 from 17 percent to 25 percent. [50]

The relatively new Australian wines initially failed to establish a niche in international markets dominated by established producers, nonpremium wines suffering particularly as their low value to volume made it difficult for them to bear the cost of transport.[51] However, their international standing has radically improved since the 1960s. Between 1961–65 and 1966 alone, Australia moved from the fifteenth to ninth most important wine producer by volume, and from the fifteenth to sixth highest wine export earner.[52] The low

value of the Australian dollar and an aggressive publicity and promotion campaign led to further striking growth of Australian wine
exports in the late 1980s.[53]

In the 1990s, the world trade in wine doubled, reflecting a huge
surge in demand.[54] Increased Australian wine exports to Asia, combined with the extension of production into sub-tropical environments, were responsible for dramatic growth from 1995 to 1999,
when wine grape production almost doubled from 577,364 to
1,076,207 tons. By 1997, Australia was the world's fourteenth
largest producer of grapes, and ninth largest producer of wine by
volume.[55] In 1998–99, wine exports increased by 12 percent to
reach Aus. $1,068 million (216 million liters),[56] and in 1999–2000
to Aus. $1.4 billion,[57] resulting in an increase in the area under vine
to 146,000 hectares, the increase being particularly marked in South
Australia and New South Wales.[58] Also, in 1999–2000 the harvested
area of red grape varieties overtook that for white grapes for the first
time, reflecting both domestic and foreign demand.[59]

International demand for wine has been sustained, global consumption of wine steadily increasing. The European Union continues to be the world's largest wine market, accounting for 58 percent
of global consumption in 2005.[60] However, as worldwide overproduction of wine runs at about 25 percent annually, there is increasingly fierce producer competition for international markets.[61]

A critical foreign market is North America, where France's share
of the wine market dropped between 1997 and 2000 from 7 to 5
percent, while from 1995 to 2000 Australia tripled its wine sales to
take almost 3 percent of the market. By 2003, the volume and value
of Australian off-trade wine sales had surpassed those of France,[62]
and by 2005–06, North America constituted the second largest market for Australian wine, the United States absorbing $864.2 million
(204.9 million liters) and Canada $245.7 million (48.9 million
liters).[63] Other key markets are Southeast Asia, notably Singapore,[64]
East Asia—particularly China and Japan[65]—and Russia.[66]

Global competition in wine is fierce due to rising demand and the
fact that—compared to other alcoholic beverages—the market for
wine remains extremely fragmented, the top twenty-five labels
accounting for only 7 percent of global sales. Gallo's "E & J Wine
Cellars" is the largest label, though its sales are largely confined to
the U.S. market. By contrast, the top twenty-five beer and spirit
labels make up 30 percent and 18 percent of global sales of beer and
spirits, respectively.[67]

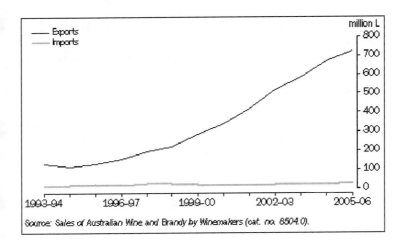

**Figure 9.7**  Australia: Wine and brandy exports, 1993/94–2005/06 by volume

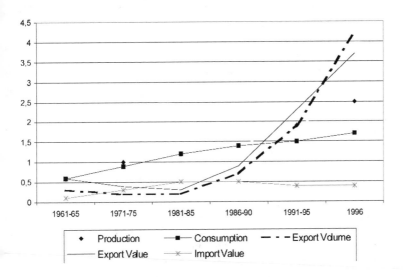

**Figure 9.8**  Australia's position in the world wine market, 1961–96 (%)[68]

# A Case Study: The British Market

Britain, the world's fourth largest consumer of wine by value, is a highly competitive market for wine, with about twenty-five different countries of supply. Per capita wine consumption in Britain rose from 2 liters in 1960 to 15 liters in 1997, and the trend continued with wine sales growing by 30 percent between 1998 and 2003.[69]

In 1997, British demand was overwhelmingly for still wines (88 percent by volume), with sparkling wines representing 8 percent of consumption and fortified wines 4 percent. Of still wines, whites dominated at 54 percent of the market, with reds at 43 percent and rosé at 3 percent. Nevertheless, the trend is turning rapidly in favor of red wine,[70] due to its reputedly cardiovascular health benefits, which have caused women—about half the consumer market and traditionally consumers of white wine—to change to red.[71] This has been reflected in a significant drop in sales of German wines.[72]

Other factors influencing the British wine consumer are previous acquaintance with the wine concerned, price, country, and occasion— some sixty percent of wine is consumed with a meal (mostly ordinary household meals) and 20 percent at parties.[73] The region and grape variety are of major concern only to a minority of wealthy consumers of prestige wines.[74] This has hit prestige outlets playing on the virtues of French traditional techniques and appellations. By the mid-1990s, 70 percent of wine purchases in Britain were from supermarkets—which offer a wide range of good quality wines, and trained staff advise customers specifically on wine choices—as opposed to 13 percent in specialist alcohol or wine retailers, and 6 percent in discount shops.[75]

## Competition for the British Market

Britain has for centuries been France's major wine export outlet. Currently, it also constitutes Australia's largest foreign market, absorbing 36.2 percent (261.5 million liters valued at $945.8 million) of its 2005–06 wine exports.[76] France is traditionally Britain's top supplier, in 1997, for example, representing one third of imported wine by volume and almost half in value.[77] Since excise taxes on wine in Britain are high, there is also considerable private import from France (e.g., rising from 85 million liters in 1993 to

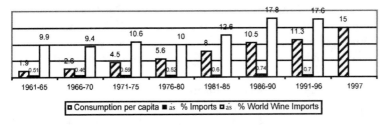

Figure 9.9  Britain: Importance of wine imports, 1961–97[80]

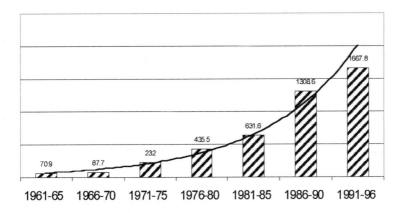

Figure 9.10  Britain: Value of wine imports, 1961–96 (U.S.$ billion)[81]

200 million in 1995), representing 10–15 percent of the market.[78] French wines also dominate the pub, club, and restaurant circuits.[79]

Nevertheless, French wine sales in Britain are falling. Since 1987, there has been a significant decline in sales of French sparkling wines.[82] The performance of AOC wines is more complex. Côtes du Rhône wines are selling well in Britain: their share of total French AOC wine sales to the UK grew from 11.3 percent in 1996 to 17.6 percent in 2003. However, British consumption of AOC wines in general has fallen, notably of wines from the Loire, Provence, the southwest, and from Languedoc-Rousillon.[83]

By contrast, in Britain, the market share of France's competitors is growing. This is notably the case of Australia. By 2000, the production of a limited range of nontraditional blends and an aggressive sales campaign led Australia to overtake France in the white wine market in Britain, where their middle range affordable wines have, despite the tendency towards reds, helped to create and enlarge a consumer market among women.[84] By 2005, Australia had surpassed France in the overall wine trade to shops, supermarkets, and restaurants.[85]

A number of factors account for the decline in the sale of French wines and the growing popularity of Australian wines in Britain. One factor is politics, such as anti-French feeling occasioned by French nuclear testing in the Pacific in 1996, and French boycotts of British beef over the issue of Mad Cow Disease.[86] Another factor is price policy: notably wide year-to-year price fluctuations and extravagant prices for low quality table wines that compare badly to lower priced good quality wines from the New World, especially from Australia, California, and Chile.[87] French AOC wines have also been troubled by problems of quality consistency.[88] In addition, French vintners are accused of using mystifyingly complex AOC labels.[89]

The pressure is on for France to follow Australia and the United States, which label their best wines according to the grape varieties they contain,[90] and which—alongside other wine-producing countries (New and Old World)—have increased their share of the British market.

Another advantage for Australia is that in sharp contrast to the French tradition of a multitude of family farms, the wine sector is become increasingly concentrated. In 1998–99, a total of 276 Australian wine businesses crushed fifty tons of grapes or more, but the top ten crushed 68 percent of these grapes and produced 70 percent of wine—the same proportion as in 1997–98.[91] By 1999–2000, the number of businesses crushing fifty tons or more of grapes remained the same—at 276—but the top nine were responsible for crushing 67 percent of the grapes and producing 68 percent of wine.[92] Currently, twenty companies alone account for 87 percent of all wine exports.[93]

Moreover, the present trend in what some term viticulture's "Big Bang" is for vertical integration, with big distributors buying up wine makers in order to ensure the output and price they desire. For example, in October 2000, the Melbourne-based Foster beer group took over the U.S. Napa Valley–based Beringer Blass Wine Estate for $1.9 billion, and in February 2001, Australia's Southcorp—owner of the Penfolds and Lindemans brands—bought Rosemount, a prestigious family-owned estate, for $725 million. R. Michel Mondavi, chairman

| Grapes crushed (tons) | No. of wine makers | Total grapes crushed (tons) | Wine produced ('000 liters) |
|---|---|---|---|
| 50–400 | 160 | 27,154 | 19,000 |
| 400–10,000 | 96 | 182,995 | 119,018 |
| 10,000–20,000 | 11 | 166,259 | 128,215 |
| Over 20,000 | 9 | 768,830 | 558,113 |
| Total | 276 | 1,145,238 | 824,354 |

**Figure 9.11**  Australia: Concentration of wine businesses, 1999–2000[94]

of Robert Mondavi, a U.S.-based company and the world's ninth largest wine maker (with an annual turnover in 2000 of more than $500 million) stated: "We've converted from being a cottage industry into a competitive consumer luxury-goods industry."[95]

France, with only one of the top ten largest wine companies in 2001 (Castel Frères),[96] and a largely fragmented rather than concentrated wine business, has reacted largely by emphasizing Gallic "tradition," as opposed to New World blandness, through high quality top price prestige appellations, produced largely according to strict AOC rules, and with allegiance to the sacred traditions of *terroir* (soil, climate, and position). Some estimates have put such vintages at 3 percent of production in Bordeaux where, for instance, St. Emilion Vintners has recently started taking on New World wines by launching aggressive advertising campaigns in key markets, such as London restaurants.[97]

However, France's traditional image as producer of the world's elite wines is being challenged, both by Old World producers such as Italy, and New World producers.[98] For instance, Australia is also increasing its exports of small-scale production, individual, artisanal wines, many of which are expensive.[99] Moreover, it has often been the French themselves who have encouraged the development of elite wines outside France. Two examples are the Rothschild joint ventures with Robert Mondavi in California and Gulisati Tagle in Chile, both resulting in local "grand cru" wines.[100] France has also formed joint ventures in China for the local production and sale of wines, thus detracting from French wine exports to potentially the largest future market for wine.[101]

Technology is also at the fore of global competition. Indeed, since the 1980s, a major debate has been raging about the wine production process, notably between France, which upholds the importance of tradition in wine making, and Australia, which has placed an emphasis on innovative techniques to promote the mass production of medium-range wines. This debate has carried over to marketing and sales, where France claims its large variety of wines to be of greater character and thus of more intrinsic value than the smaller range of generic New World wines.

Australia promotes new technology in production, and has a large viticulture R&D (Research and Development) program. National research organizations include the *Cooperative Research Centre for Viticulture*, the *Commonwealth Scientific and Industrial Research Organisation*, and the *Australian Wine Research Institute*. All states and a number of universities also participate in wine R&D.[102] Research focuses on grapevine variety improvement, pest and pathogen control, grape quality, resource and vineyard management, economic analysis and forecasting, and technology transfer.[103] For instance, in the 1990s, a large increase occurred in the number of vines grafted—mostly through mechanical bench methods—to rootstocks aimed to increase both salt and nematode tolerance and productivity.[104]

Australian viticulture is highly mechanized, and Australia is ranked amongst the top ten countries in terms of average grape yield (tons per hectare).[105] It aims to greatly boost production of medium-quality wines, aiming thus to enlarge the market. The use of stainless steel tanks, controlled fermentation, and nontraditional blends has brought accusations that they are reducing the taste range of wines, notably white wines.[106]

Other competitors have reacted quickly. For example, since the 1980s, Chile and Argentina have modernized their wine-marketing techniques (including vine training and irrigation) along the lines of Australia and California, while simultaneously keeping prices low.[107] And the need to compete is also gradually changing French production techniques. Thus, following the decision of Le Pin, and other right-bank Bordeaux wines, to ally California techniques to the region, there is a growing tendency towards tradition being replaced by high technology methods producing small-batch wines at moderate prices designed for cult appeal.[108] Moreover, "flying wine makers" are spreading Australian techniques abroad, helping to revolutionize production in most grape wine countries, including France.[109]

Yet another factor is "fraudulent practices." As noted, while New World producers concentrate upon wines made from single grape varieties, blends are the norm in France. This tempts French producers to break AOC rules by importing grape varieties from outside their wine region in order to modify a wine considered deficient in quality or alcohol content, or to enhance profits. For instance, in March 2001, the Bordeaux producer Marion was charged with fraud: one quarter of its wine stock—the equivalent of the product of their own 36.4 ha vineyard from the 1996, 1997, and 1999 vintages—comprised red wine blends that included other Burgundy appellations. Olivier Morice, their lawyer, acknowledged Marion's guilt, but argued that the practice was traditional and also prevalent in the face of competition from New World, and that the law should be changed to accommodate it. The response of the Burgundy Fine Wines Traders Union was that "Quality goes hand in hand with respect of the appellation rules. . . . It's out of question to shake the rock that's been the foundation of our success."[110]

## CONCLUSION

Both France and Australia are faced with the problem of small home markets relative to total domestic wine production. This has placed the emphasis for the future health of their respective viticulture sectors on production for export. Since the 1980s, France's traditionally dominant position in international markets has been increasingly eroded, notably by Australia, which has achieved great success with a combination of mass production of a restricted number of good quality varietals at reasonable prices, vertical and horizontal integration, and aggressive marketing. French wines suffer from their image of complicated varietals and labeling, variable quality, and high prices. It would seem that if France is to retain a leading position in the international wine market, it will need to develop a two-pronged strategy, on the one hand improving the dependability and integrity of tradition of elite wines, and on the other emulating Australia and other New World producers by adopting modern production, structural, and marketing techniques to compete in the widening market for reasonably priced, good quality, and simply labeled wines.

## NOTES

1. Jancis Robinson, *Encyclopédie du vin* (Paris: Hachette, 1997), 436; Australian Bureau of Statistics, "1329.0—Australian Wine and Grape Industry, 2006," http://www.abs.gov.au/AUSSTATS/abs@.nsf/mf/1329.0?Open Document.

2. U.S. Department of State, *FY 2001 Country Commercial Guide: Australia* (Washington, DC: U.S. Department of State, 2000), 9.

3. Australian Bureau of Statistics, "1329.0—Australian Wine and Grape Industry, 2006," http://www.abs.gov.au/AUSSTATS/abs@.nsf/mf/1329.0?OpenDocument.

4. Robinson, *Encyclopédie du vin*, 436.

5. François Caron, *An Economic History of Modern France* (London: Methuen, 1979), 12–13.

6. Alain Beltran and Pascal Griset, *La Croissance économique de la France 1815–1914* (Paris: Armand Colin, 1988), 51.

7. Beltran and Griset, *La Croissance économique de la France*, 51.

8. Ibid., 52.

9. Robinson, *Encyclopédie du vin*, 436.

10. Jacques Galas, "L'Agriculture" in *Histoire de Vaucluse*, eds. Jacques Galas, J. P. Locci, René Grosso, and Sylvestre Clap (Avignon: A Barthélemy, 1993), 25.

11. Robinson, *Encyclopédie du vin*, 436; Beltran and Griset, *Croissance économique de la France*, 49.

12. Beltran and Griset, *Croissance économique de la France*, 52.

13. Robinson, *Encyclopédie du vin*, 437.

14. Caron, *Economic History of Modern France*, 12–13.

15. Jean Fourastié, *L'économie française dans le monde* (Paris: Presses Universitaires de France), 22; Courrier International, *Le Monde en 2000*, December 1999, p. 98.

16. Ibid., 7–8.

17. Ibid., 8–9.

18. Caron, *Economic History of Modern France*, 5.

19. Ibid., 4–5.

20. Fourastié, *L'économie française*, 22; Courrier International, *Le Monde en 2000*, p. 98.

21. Nourrisson, *Le buveur*, 321; Carré, "Consommation de vin," 2.

22. Didier Nourrisson, *Le buveur du XIXe siècle* (Paris: Albin Michel, 1990), 25, 321.

23. Ibid., 321.

24. Nourrisson, *Le buveur*, 321; Marie-Annick Carré, "Consommation de vin," extract from *Réussir Vigne* 67 (May 2000): 2.

25. *Réussir Vigne* 69 bis (2001), 2; Carré, "Consommation de vin," 2.

26. BBC News/Business, "US' To Become Top Wine Consumer,'"
    http://news.bbc.co.uk/1/hi/business/6314325.stm.
27. *Réussir Vigne* 69 bis, 2; Christine Monceau, "La demande de produits
    agricoles et des IAA stimulée par les exportations: Le rôle majeur de
    la PAC," *Economie et Statistique* 329–30, (November 10, 1999): 125;
    Carré, "Consommation de vin," 2.
28. *Réussir Vigne* 69 bis, p. 2.
29. Frances Robinson, "French Government May Finally Bite Wine Tax
    Bullet," http://www.decanter.com/news/47590.html.
30. http://www.abs.gov.au/ausstats.
31. David Oag, "Grape Production in Australia," in *Grape Production in
    the Asia-Pacific Region*, eds. Minas K. Papademtriou and Frank J.
    Dent, (Bangkok: FAO, 2001), 20, in the web edition,
    http://www.fao.org/DOCREP/003/X6897E/x6897e04.htm.
32. Australian Bureau of Statistics, "1329.0—Australian Wine and Grape
    Industry, 2006"; Glyn Wittwer and Kym Anderson, *Tax Reform and
    the Australian Wine Industry* (Adelaide: University of Adelaide,
    1998), 2.
33. W. McLennan, *Year Book Australia, 1996* (Canberra: Australian
    Bureau of Statistics, 1996), 414.
34. McLennan, *Year Book Australia, 1996*, p. 415, http://www
    .abs.gov.au/ ausstats.
35. http://www.abs.gov.au/ausstats; Rod Phillips, *A Short History of
    Wine* (London: Allen Lane, 2000), 177–78, 263.
36. Wittwer and Anderson, *Tax Reform*, 3.
37. Ibid., 1, 3–4.
38. http://www.abs.gov.au/ausstats.
39. Australian Bureau of Statistics, "1329.0—Australian Wine and Grape
    Industry, 2006."
40. U.S. Department of State, *FY 2001 Country Commercial Guide:
    Australia*, 9.
41. Australian Bureau of Statistics, "1329.0—Australian Wine and Grape
    Industry, 2006."
42. Harvey Steiman, "The Wines of Australia," http://www.winespectator.com.
43. Carré, "Consommation de vin," 2.
44. Monceau, "La demande de produits agricoles," 125.
45. Ibid., 125.
46. Darrell Delamaide, *The New Superregions of Europe* (New York:
    Plume, 1995), 138.
47. Andrew Catchpole, "Chairman of the Bordeaux," *Telegraph Weekend*,
    November 17, 2001, p. 9.
48. William Echikson et al. "Wine War," *Business Week*, March 3, 2001,
    36–38.

49. UEBL: Belgium/Luxembourg, http://www.vins-rhone.com/uk/home.asp.
50. Monceau, "La demande de produits agricoles," 125.
51. Wittwer and Anderson, *Tax Reform*, 1.
52. Robert Osmond and Kim Anderson, *Trends and Cycles in the Australian Wine Industry, 1850–2000* (University of Adelaide: Centre for International Economic Studies, 1998), 84.
53. Wittwer and Anderson, *Tax Reform*, 1.
54. http://www.aboutwines.com/home/reference/regions/index.html.
55. Oag, "Grape Production in Australia," 1; Australian Bureau of Statistics, "1329.0—Australian Wine and Grape Industry, 2006."
56. http://www.abs.gov.au/ausstats/abs@.nsf/Lookup/.
57. http://www.abs.gov.au/ausstats/abs@.nsf/0/. The average price of wine produced in Australia rose 30 percent in the 1990s, while the average price of table wine exported rose by 46 percent—Australian Bureau of Statistics, "1329.0—Australian Wine and Grape Industry, 2006," http://www.abs.gov.au/AUSSTATS/abs@.nsf/mf/1329.0?Open Document.
58. "Record Year for Wine and Grapes in 2000," http://www.abs.gov.au/ausstats/abs@.nsf/0/.
59. http://www.abs.gov.au/ausstats/abs@.nsf/0/.
60. "Global Wine Consumption Increases," http://www.sommelierindia.com/blog/2006/07/global_wine_consumption_increa.html.
61. Sean Shesgreen, "Wet Dogs and Gushing Oranges, Winespeak for a New Millennium," *Chronicle of Higher Education* 49, no. 26 (March 21, 2003): B15, reprinted May 17, 2003, http://winebusiness.com/html/MonthlyArticle.cfm?aid=72638&issueid=72603).
62. Echikson *et al.*, "Wine War," 36–38.
63. Australian Bureau of Statistics, "1329.0—Australian Wine and Grape Industry, 2006."
64. *Le Moci* 1354, October 9, 1998, p. 53.
65. Echikson et al., "Wine War," 36.
66. Anon., "Impact Databank Releases Its 2000 Global Drinks Market Report," *Wine Spectator Online*, February 21, 2001, http://www.winespectator.com/Wine/Daily/News.
67. Ibid.
68. Osmond & Anderson, *Trends and Cycles*, 84.
69. Karine Nichterwitz, "The Role of Côtes du Rhône in the British Market," *Mémoire de Maîtrise* (Avignon: Université d'Avignon, 1999), 8, 11, 15.
70. Nichterwitz, "Role of Côtes du Rhône," 9.
71. Ibid., 8–9.
72. R. Usher, "Portugal's Grape Escape," *Time Magazine*, August 21, 2001, 63.

73. Nichterwitz, "Role of Côtes du Rhône," 12.
74. Ibid., 13–14.
75. Ibid., 12.
76. Australian Bureau of Statistics, "1329.0 - Australian Wine and Grape Industry, 2006."
77. Nichterwitz, "Role of Côtes du Rhône," 6.
78. Ibid., 7.
79. Ibid., 13.
80. Nicholas Berger, Kym Anderson, and Randy Stringer, *Trends in the World Wine Market, 1961 to 1996* (University of Adelaide: Centre for International Economic Studies, 1998), 187; Nichterwitz, "Role of Côtes du Rhône," 6.
81. Berger, Anderson, and Stringer, *Trends in the World Wine Market*, 187.
82. Echikson et al., "Wine War," 36.
83. UEBL: Belgium/Luxembourg.
84. Usher, "Portugal's Grape Escape," 63.
85. Nichterwitz, "Role of Côtes du Rhône," 8, 14–17; Leah Vyse, "French fight for stake in UK wine market," http://www.food anddrinkeurope.com/news/ng.asp?n=63331-tesco-french-wine -supermarkets.
86. Nichterwitz, "Role of Côtes du Rhône," 15.
87. Echikson et al., "Wine War," 36.
88. Ibid., 37.
89. Nichterwitz, "Role of Côtes du Rhône," 16; Echikson et al., "Wine War," 36.
90. Steiman, "The Wines of Australia." Multipurpose varietals, such as Sultana, Muscat Gordo Blanco, and Waltham Cross account for 40 percent of grape production in Australia, see Oag, "Grape Production in Australia," 1.
91. http://www.abs.gov.au/ausstats/abs@.nsf/Lookup/.
92. http://www.abs.gov.au/ausstats/; for 1998–99 figures, see "Another Record Year for Wine and Grape Industry," http://www .abs.gov.au/ausstats/abs@.nsf/Lookup/NT0000338A.
93. Billy Adams, "Excellent Nose for Business; Matures Well," *The Globe and Mail*, February 13, 2007, E2.
94. http://www.abs.gov.au/ausstats.
95. Echikson et al., "Wine War," p. 38.
96. Ibid., 37–38.
97. Catchpole, "Chairman of the Bordeaux," 9.
98. Shesgreen, "Wet Dogs and Gushing Oranges," B15.
99. Steiman, "The Wines of Australia."
100. http://www.conchaytoro.com/company/devoted.html; http://www .answers .com/topic/baron-philippe-de-rothschild-s-a.

101. http://www.iht.com/articles/1995/04/10/vincon.ttt.php.
102. Oag, "Grape Production in Australia," 12.
103. Ibid., 12.
104. Ibid., 4.
105. Ibid., 1.
106. Usher, "Portugal's Grape Escape," 62–63.
107. http://www.aboutwines.com/home/reference/regions/index.html.
108. Catchpole, "Chairman of the Bordeaux," 9.
109. Baverstock, quoted in Usher, "Portugal's Grape Escape," 63; see also ibid., 62.
110. Per-Henrik Mansson, "Burgundy Faces Another Winemaking Scandal," http://www.winespectator.com/Wine/Daily/News.

# CHAPTER 10

## THE INTERNATIONAL
## WINE MARKET, 1850–1938
### AN OPPORTUNITY FOR EXPORT
### GROWTH IN SOUTHERN EUROPE?

*Vicente Pinilla and María-Isabel Ayuda*

## INTRODUCTION

The purpose of this article is to analyze the international wine market between 1850 and 1938. During this period, the less-developed countries of southern Europe participated in international trade, mainly as exporters of primary products and importers of manufactured goods. For these countries, the export of wine represented a sizeable proportion of this trade. The study of the market for this type of product is essential in order for us to better understand the opportunities made available to these countries from the development of a wine export sector specializing in production to supply the markets of the industrialized countries.

It is a well-known fact that wine, cereals, and olive oil were—toward the middle of the nineteenth century—the major components of the agricultural production of countries such as Portugal, Spain, Italy, and Greece.[1] These countries shared other characteristics, such as their relative economic backwardness in relation to northwestern Europe, the fact that they were not export economies,[2] and an export sector dominated by primary products, mainly raw materials, foodstuffs, and notably wine. Indeed, from the mid-nineteenth century, all three countries emerged as internationally significant wine producers and exporters.[3]

However, research into the history of wine is beset with the problem that statistical sources are sometimes inadequate, and moreover often classify wines generically when in fact they do not constitute a homogeneous product. Table liquor and sparkling wines can each be treated as different products, and on many occasions as substitutes. There are also significant differences in quality.[4]

Our thesis is that from the mid-nineteenth century, southern European wine production responded rapidly to the opportunities that were opening up in the markets of the industrialized nations, particularly France, by increasing both their production and export of wine. For some of these countries this increase was crucial to balance their foreign accounts. However, from the beginning of the twentieth century, wine exports encountered increasing problems, such as a relatively unstable demand and a tendency towards the saturation of the market. These problems were primarily due to three factors: first, French trade policy gave preference to wine imports from its colonial possessions in North Africa; second, the industrialized countries (excluding France) had a low capacity to absorb wine due to the persistence of traditional habits of alcohol consumption, together with a strong prohibitionist movement that reached its peak in the United States; and lastly, the emergence of significant foreign competitors.

Consequently, opportunities for expansion on the part of the Southern European producer were limited. This posed a major problem, for while wine exports had in the second half of the nineteenth century become a crucial source of foreign currency for the developing countries of Southern Europe, the growth—or even the stability—of these exports during the first third of the twentieth century, and thus their ability to contribute significantly to the development of their economies, was highly questionable.

## WORLD CONSUMPTION OF WINE: EVOLUTION AND GEOGRAPHICAL PATTERNS OF CONSUMPTION

Between 1850 and 1945, wine consumption patterns differed significantly from country to country. Wine consumption grew mainly in those countries in which a tradition of such consumption already existed until at least the 1920s. In France, this pattern of growth persisted longer. There, per capita wine consumption more than doubled between 1860 and 1914, from which time it boasted the highest per capita wine consumption in the world. The increase in wine consumption in France and other traditional consumer countries was mostly determined by the growth in per capita income. For example, an examination of per capita consumption in France from 1860 to 1938 gives an estimated long-term elasticity of consumption with respect to income of 0.9; in other words, during these years each 1 percent increase in income translated into a per capita increase in consumption of 0.9 percent. While this elasticity is relatively high—bearing in mind that we are dealing with a food and drinks product—it is nevertheless significantly lower than that of fruit, which belongs to the same group.[5]

Except for those countries that received immigrants from Southern Europe, increase in wine consumption elsewhere in the world was either small or non-existent. In the industrialized countries (excluding France) with higher per capita incomes, the increase in consumption was significant, especially from the 1850s to the 1890s; thereafter, consumption stayed almost constant until 1930.[6] In the economically undeveloped countries, wine consumption remained restricted to a tiny elite, mainly of European origin.

In sum, the growth in wine consumption from the mid-nineteenth century to the 1920s was concentrated in Europe.[7] The following table shows, for those countries worldwide for which we have sufficient data, per capita consumption of wine relative to beer from 1923–27, at the end of this period of growth. Using cluster analysis we have separated the different countries into four groups.[8]

The first group, a very well defined cluster in the Mediterranean region of Western Europe, includes the three main wine consuming countries, with an average annual per capita wine consumption of around 100 liters. These three countries were also, until the Second World War, the world's chief wine producers. It should be noted that beer consumption in those countries was either very small (Italy and Spain) or moderate (France).

The second cluster comprises countries in which wine consumption reaches a medium level and beer consumption is very variable. The moderate wine consumption in Greece can be attributed to its very low income. In Switzerland, the medium level wine consumption and

**Table 10.1** Per capita consumption of wine and beer in various countries, 1923–1927 (five-year averages, pure alcohol in liters)

|  |  | Wine | Beer |
|---|---|---|---|
| High wine-consumption countries | Italy | 12.60 | 0.12 |
| | France | 12.40 | 1.47 |
| | Spain | 12.29 | 0.09 |
| Medium wine-consumption countries | Argentina | 5.80 | 0.72 |
| | Greece | 4.62 | 0.01 |
| | Switzerland | 4.52 | 1.85 |
| Low wine-consumption countries | Hungary | 3.24 | 0.24 |
| | Bulgaria | 2.28 | 0.12 |
| | Romania | 1.48 | 0.18 |
| | Austria | 1.45 | 2.53 |
| Very low wine-consumption countries | Yugoslavia | 1.16 | 0.20 |
| | Belgium | 0.82 | 7.39 |
| | Norway | 0.45 | 1.12 |
| | Germany | 0.44 | 2.36 |
| | Czechoslovakia | 0.34 | 2.47 |
| | Australia | 0.29 | 2.29 |
| | United Kingdom | 0.22 | 3.87 |
| | Denmark | 0.21 | 2.04 |
| | Netherlands | 0.21 | 1.75 |
| | Ireland | 0.15 | 2.02 |
| | Canada | 0.13 | 0.95 |
| | Estonia | 0.09 | 0.30 |
| | New Zealand | 0.08 | 1.94 |
| | Sweden | 0.07 | 0.98 |
| | Russia | 0.06 | 0.12 |
| | Latvia | 0.03 | 0.19 |
| | Lithuania | 0.01 | 0.18 |

*Source: Imperial Economic Committee, Wine, Reports of the Imperial Economic Committee, 23rd Rep. (London, Imperial Economic Committee, 1932), 85.*

medium-high level beer consumption can be attributed to its distinct German, Italian, and French speaking regions, each with their different cultural traditions. Finally, the Argentinean case is characteristic of a country whose Italian and Spanish immigrants possess a tradition of wine consumption.

The third cluster comprises countries with low wine and—with the exception of Austria—very low beer consumption. While enjoying a certain wine tradition, production of wine in these countries is not, as a rule, sufficient to supply their respective domestic markets.

Note should be taken of the medium-low income level of Hungary and the very low-income level of Bulgaria and Romania. By contrast, Austria had a high-income level, and therefore its high beer consumption signified that wine was not the dominant alcoholic beverage.

Finally, Anglophone, Germanic, Scandinavian, and Slavic countries consumed very small quantities of wine. Of these, the Anglophone and Germanic countries were characterized by high beer consumption, Scandinavian countries with medium-level beer consumption, and the Slavic countries—where spirits were the preferred alcoholic beverage—with low beer consumption.

We can conclude that mass wine consumption was characteristic of only the countries abutting the northwestern shore of the Mediterranean, namely Portugal, Spain, France, Italy, and French- and Italian-speaking Switzerland. Wine was also consumed on a significant scale in Argentina, Uruguay, Chile, southern Brazil, and Greece. Elsewhere, wine consumption was restricted to high-income groups. As noted in an official British report in 1932, "today, except in the wine producing countries, wine is a luxury beverage chiefly connected with the ritual of entertainment."[9]

Wine consumption trends from the mid-nineteenth century until the outbreak of the Second World War, together with the levels finally reached in the most developed countries, suggests that initially attractive demand-side prospects tended to evaporate during the first third of the twentieth century. In some developed countries, the rapid development of wine imports, as a consequence of the general increase in international trade, slowed down as wine consumption stagnated, or even declined in some of them. In the less developed countries, wine imports had an insignificant impact. In addition, the strong accumulated increase in consumption in traditional wine-consuming countries proved difficult to sustain until 1939. Finally, the slowing of population growth also induced a gradually slower growth in the demand for wine, even for identical levels of per capita consumption.

Therefore, two kinds of wine demand existed. First, the demand for high quality wine mainly from the high-income sector within the industrialized countries; and secondly, the demand for low or medium quality wines in countries where wine was a product of mass consumption. In the latter case, the strong demand for wine usually coexisted with high domestic production.

## World Production of Wine

During the period under study, global wine production grew at a relatively slow rate when viewed in the long-term. It can be estimated that between 1865–74 and 1935–38, world wine production increased by 65.7 percent, reflecting an average annual growth rate of 0.8 percent. The rate was remarkably constant, at 0.7 percent for the second half of the nineteenth century, and 0.8 percent for the first third of the twentieth century.[10]

In the mid-nineteenth century, wine production was predominantly located in the main consumption areas. In the period 1865 to 1874, France, Italy, and Spain together accounted for 85 percent of world wine production; France alone produced 49 percent. No other country was responsible for even 3 percent of world production.

However, various developments in the second half of the nineteenth century transformed wine production and trade, notably outbreaks of vine diseases affecting European vineyards, techniques of wine handling that enhanced preservation, and above all, transportation improvements that resulted in shorter delivery times and lower transport costs.

In addition, as argued earlier, the process of industrialization and its strong economic and social impact—resulting in higher living standards—led to an increase in wine consumption and in consequence higher demand for wine, chiefly in traditional wine-consuming countries. Similarly, the strong growth in the population translated into a larger number of consumers. All of this acted as an incentive to increase wine production.

The spread of *Phylloxera* in European vineyards had significant consequences for world wine production. Most importantly, France, the world's principal wine producer and consumer, was one of the first countries to suffer the outbreak. The resulting fall in domestic production led to a high French demand for wine imports and to high wine prices. This in turn stimulated some other wine-producing countries, notably Southern European countries such as Spain, Portugal, Italy, and Greece, to expand wine cultivation and production specifically to supply the French market. Spain, the main supplier of the French market during those years, experienced a spectacular increase in wine production, particularly in those regions closest to France or located near ports from which they could easily export their wine.

Other countries took advantage of the fall in French production to develop their own vineyards, even in areas where, despite a tradition of wine consumption, there was no previous history of wine farming. This was the case of some South American countries. At the same time, in Algeria—then a French colony—the metropolitan government applied two policies to encourage French settlers to produce wine: first, in 1884, a customs union that guaranteed the entry of Algerian wine into France free of duties and subject to the same conditions as those enjoyed by metropolitan French producers; second, the provision of cheap credit to wine producers through the Bank of Algeria, which in exchange preserved its right to issue currency from 1880 to 1897.[11]

By the early twentieth century, vine cultivation globally was rapidly expanding as, alongside the traditional Mediterranean producers and the increasingly important Algerian vineyards, other non-European countries such as Chile, Argentina, California, South Africa, and Australia increased their production of wine. As a result, between 1870 and 1900 world wine production grew by an estimated 22 percent. However, this growth was induced not only by external demand, but also by the strong increase in domestic demand in consumer countries, whether traditional or new. Thus, almost all producer countries experienced increased wine production except France, which had not yet recovered from *Phylloxera* that subsequently was to affect almost all other wine-producing countries. They, however, benefiting from the lessons learned from the earlier French experience in the fight against *Phylloxera*, and from buoyant demand, rapidly reconstituted damaged vineyards.

It is important here to indicate the changes in wine growing brought about by *Phylloxera*. All the vineyards affected by the disease had to be replanted with American vines, which in turn required increased care, leading to an increase in production costs. In sum, the post-*Phylloxera* wine-growing sector needed larger amounts of capital in order to prosper.[12]

The existence of serial statistical data on world wine production for the first third of the twentieth century allows us to study its development in detail (Table 10.2). It indicates that wine production grew by 31 percent between the beginning of the century and the end of the 1930s.

In the first third of the twentieth century, the largest increases in wine production took place in countries with previously very low production levels. These countries had propitious climatic characteristics, farmers capable of developing the cultivation of wine (very often immigrants), and internal markets (or metropolitan markets in the case of some colonies) with a sufficient tradition of wine consumption to absorb heavy increases in production.

Thus, world wine production became increasingly geographically diversified. The growth of production in the Maghreb (mainly Algeria) and in South America (mainly Argentina) was especially significant. Wine production in these two regions almost tripled in quantity to more than double their share of world production. Meanwhile, the traditionally dominant producers, notably France and other Southern European countries, experienced a decline in their share of world wine production, and encountered difficult years characterized by chronic overproduction and declining prices.[13] This is partly explicable in terms of the short-run rigidity of supply with respect to price variations—due to the fact that the fall in these prices did not result in the up-rooting of the vines in order to dedicate the land to other crops (vineyards represented a long-term

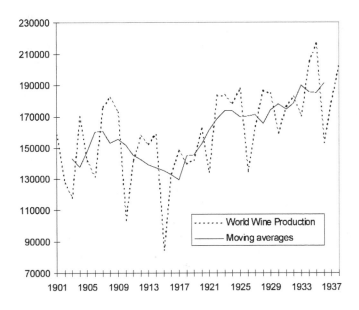

**Figure 10.1** World wine production, 1901–1938 (thousands of hectoliters)
*Sources: See Appendix.*

**Table 10.2** World wine production, 1900–1938 (annual production in thousands of hectoliters, five-year averages)

| | 1900–04 | 1905–09 | 1910–14 | 1915–19 | 1920–24 | 1925–29 | 1930–34 | 1935–38 |
|---|---|---|---|---|---|---|---|---|
| France | 51,614 | 58,322 | 47,524 | 39,038 | 61,861 | 56,845 | 56,940 | 58,771 |
| Italy | 40,400 | 45,299 | 42,271 | 35,628 | 41,690 | 41,193 | 36,397 | 38,926 |
| Spain | 16,040 | 14,928 | 13,638 | 17,827 | 20,785 | 21,215 | 17,809 | 14,852 |
| Algeria | 6,078 | 7,657 | 8,120 | 6,856 | 7,834 | 11,052 | 17,338 | 16,838 |
| Portugal | 5,131 | 5,214 | 4,311 | 4,710 | 5,060 | 5,946 | 7,864 | 7,159 |
| Argentina | 1,708 | 3,028 | 4,597 | 4,435 | 5,718 | 6,098 | 5,139 | 7,395 |
| Romania | 1,156 | 1,608 | 1,295 | 1,930 | 4,345 | 6,384 | 8,233 | 9,438 |
| Southern Europe | 62,965 | 67,199 | 63,157 | 60,867 | 69,346 | 70,684 | 64,856 | 64,218 |
| Central/Eastern Europe | 16,675 | 19,072 | 12,899 | 12,907 | 17,773 | 19,047 | 26,054 | 28,181 |
| North Africa | 6,290 | 8,009 | 8,436 | 7,268 | 8,472 | 12,056 | 19,023 | 19,043 |
| South America | 3,577 | 5,550 | 7,650 | 7,085 | 8,907 | 10,564 | 8,996 | 12,323 |
| World | 143,539 | 160,817 | 142,805 | 129,729 | 168,388 | 171,457 | 178,635 | 188,022 |

*Source: See Appendix.*
*Southern Europe: Greece, Italy, Portugal and Spain; Central/Eastern Europe: Germany, Austria,*
*Bulgaria, Hungary, Luxemburg, Romania, Czechoslovakia, Switzerland, USSR, Yugoslavia; North Africa:*
*Algeria, Cirenaica, French Morocco, Tripolitania, Tunisia; South America: Argentina, Chile, Brazil, Uruguay, Peru.*

investment)—together with the instability of harvests (a common feature of many other agricultural products).

In some countries, the increase in production reflected more of an increase in yields than in the area under cultivation. This can be explained by the changes in cultivation practices implemented after the *Phylloxera* outbreak that entailed greater care of vines and the use of more modern techniques. Moreover, as will be detailed in the following section, variations in wine supply—both quantitatively and geographically—were very closely linked to the changes in consumption, and to the opportunities that international trade offered some producers.

## THE INTERNATIONAL TRADE IN WINE

In the mid-nineteenth century, the international trade in wine was insignificant. The main obstacles to the long-distance trade in wine were both cultural and technological—the transport of ordinary wine was unprofitable due to problems in preserving wine in transit and the high cost of such transportation. Thus, the only trade that existed was in products that traveled better, such as liquor wines (i.e. sherry, port, or similar products), table wine fortified with alcohol to keep it in good condition, and high-quality wine. A significant increase in the wine trade only occurred when the two problems of transportation costs and conservation were solved, although it was facilitated from 1860 by international trade liberalization.

During the second half of the nineteenth century, the main factor underlying the growth in the international wine trade was the huge French demand for table wine, following sharp falls in production due to Phylloxera. French domestic consumption was met by low quality wine that was also, though to a lesser extent, directed to export markets. The *Phylloxera*-induced increase in French domestic demand caused an immediate rise in international wine prices, which encouraged a significant growth in Italian and Spanish exports in the short run and in Algerian exports in the medium run.[14] These imported wines were normally mixed with local French wines prior to sale.

Italian exports were curtailed from 1888 by the onset of a trade war between France and Italy.[15] Initially, the increase in Spanish wine exports to France was very significant, leading to rapid growth in the percentage share of wine in total exports, and particularly in total agricultural exports.[16] However, in the medium-run, Algerian wine progressively dominated Spanish wine in the French market from 1892 when the favorable tariffs on the import of Spanish wines was ended by France (Table 10.3).

It is therefore clear that there were two main forces driving the wine trade during the second half of the nineteenth century: first, for ordinary table wine, the French demand that followed the Phylloxera outbreak; second, for high quality wine, the demand from countries with the highest income levels, such as Great Britain and the United States, where demand was generated by the wealthy elite. As Loubere stated, "Wine was a privileged drink of the privileged class and . . . remained a kind of ideal beverage, a sign of social standing and wealth, or at least of pretension to high status. . . . The general increase of wealth and well being that began in the 1850s amply proved this, for the consumption of wine went up."[17] France was the main beneficiary of the expansion in this elite demand, doubling the value of its exports of table wine between 1855 and 1890.

**Table 10.3** French imports of ordinary wines in casks

|         | Origin of imports (%) | | | % of French production |
|---------|-------|---------|--------|---------|
|         | Spain | Algeria | Others |         |
| 1847–49 | 32.3  | 0.0     | 67.7   | 0.0     |
| 1850–54 | 83.4  | 0.0     | 16.6   | 0.1     |
| 1855–59 | 85.0  | 0.0     | 15.0   | 1.0     |
| 1860–64 | 81.0  | 0.0     | 19.0   | 0.3     |
| 1865–69 | 87.0  | 0.0     | 13.0   | 0.3     |
| 1870–74 | 69.8  | 0.0     | 30.2   | 0.7     |
| 1875–79 | 73.4  | 0.1     | 26.4   | 2.3     |
| 1880–84 | 72.0  | 0.8     | 27.2   | 23.6    |
| 1885–89 | 63.4  | 8.2     | 28.4   | 40.5    |
| 1890–94 | 67.5  | 25.3    | 7.3    | 23.5    |
| 1895–99 | 50.5  | 46.6    | 3.0    | 20.5    |
| 1900–04 | 19.7  | 75.8    | 4.4    | 9.4     |
| 1905–09 | 0.8   | 97.7    | 1.5    | 10.4    |
| 1910–14 | 15.0  | 78.4    | 6.6    | 16.8    |
| 1915–19 | 26.4  | 58.3    | 15.3   | 19.8    |
| 1920–24 | 23.4  | 61.1    | 15.5   | 11.3    |
| 1925–29 | 17.5  | 73.7    | 8.8    | 18.6    |
| 1930–34 | 7.9   | 85.2    | 6.9    | 24.7    |
| 1935–38 | 0.5   | 92.1    | 7.5    | 21.9    |

*Source: Direction General des Douanes,* Tableau du Commerce Exterieur de la France *(Paris, 1850–1938).*

However, it was precisely this "privileged" pattern of consumption—and the preference of the working and medium classes for beer and spirits—that represented the main obstacles to further growth in the wine trade. During the first third of the twentieth century, when demand for wine in other markets stagnated, French demand offered the greatest opportunity to generate an increase in world wine exports. Thus, while between 1909–13 and 1928–32 the wine trade grew by around 20 percent and French wine imports grew by 65 percent, the international wine trade would, without France, have dropped by around 13 percent (Table 10.4).

The economic crash of 1929 caused the international wine trade to fall by 5.6 percent between 1928–32 and 1934–38. During the 1930s, as Loubere indicated, "there was simply too much wine, good and bad, for buyers who lost their jobs or who feared losing them."[18] The depression hit even the wealthy elites who traditionally guaranteed a market for quality wines and increased protectionism did not make things any easier. In the early 1930s, bumper harvests—both in large-scale producers such as France, and in countries outside Europe that had long been expanding their vineyards—accentuated the crisis for wine growers and distributors, although the decline in the wine trade would have been greater had it not been for continued strong demand from the French market.

The result was an over-saturated international wine market. Accordingly, during the first third of the twentieth century, the wine output of the majority of wine producers was directed towards their own domestic markets. Whereas before the 1929 crash the world's seven biggest wine producers exported between 10 and 15 percent of their total yield, for all except Algeria—whose wine industry remained dependent on the French market—those percentages diminished by more than half between 1929 and 1938.[19]

Only in France did wine imports remain at a high level. There, the *Phylloxera* outbreak had resulted in the use of hybrids, which resulted in wines of such low alcohol content that they were unmarketable domestically. The solution was to mix this weak wine with Spanish or Algerian wines that had higher alcohol content, making the wine easier to sell.[20]

French trade policy ensured privileged access to its market to French colonies, thus favoring Algeria and its other colonies in North Africa, for which the French wine market was tariff-free. However, while starting as an imput to French wine, Algerian wine progressively lost its complementary character and increasingly competed with French wines on the French market.[21] Indeed, thanks to the growth of Algerian exports to France, the African continent and Algeria in particular, overtook Europe to become the world's leading wine exporting region (see Table 10.4).

The case of Spain, the second most important wine exporter, exemplifies the difficulties encountered in competing with Algeria due to the discriminatory policies of France, by far the world's largest wine importer (see Table 10.4). These greatly limited the possibilities of expanding wine exports for, for example, other Southern European wine-producing countries. In the long term, every 1 percent increase in the French tariff on foreign wine imports reduced the market share of those imports by 1.8 percent.[22] Had it not been for French tariffs, Southern European wine exports would have probably expanded to meet French demand. However, as a result of French tariff increases from the 1890s, wine imports—from Spain for example—fell, and during the following three decades never reached one third of the peak achieved in the 1880s. By contrast, Algerian wine exports to France, which until 1875 were negligible, thereafter grew rapidly due to privileged access to the French market, and in 1930–34 reached 11.95 million hectoliters (Table 10.3).[23]

An additional problem for Southern European wine exporters was that French demand greatly fluctuated depending on domestic production. Their difficulties were accentuated by growing competition in other markets that were characterized by stagnant demand, and which were traditionally dominated by French wines. They responded by trying to expel French wine from the lower-quality segments, all the while accepting French dominance of the higher-quality segments. Simultaneously, the increase in production in countries with no, or very little, wine-growing tradition—such as Australia and Argentina—meant that their domestic demand was increasingly met by local production. This in turn lowered their need to import wine (see Table 10.4). Thus, whereas South America accounted for almost 10 percent of total world imports before the First World War, they fell dramatically by the end of the period under study to only 0.8 percent. The production increases in these countries were achieved under the umbrella of strong tariff protection, which represented an obstacle to the entry of ordinary table wines coming from Southern Europe.

**Table 10.4** World trade in wine, 1909–1938 (five-year averages)

| Wine Imports | 1909–13 | 1924–28 | 1928–32 | 1934–38 | 1909–13 | 1924–28 | 1928–32 | 1934–38 |
|---|---|---|---|---|---|---|---|---|
| | Thousands of hectoliters | | | | Percentages of total world imports | | | |
| Germany | 1,103 | 950 | 844 | 937 | 6.8 | 5.5 | 4.3 | 5.1 |
| France | 8,237 | 10,565 | 13,603 | 14,343 | 50.9 | 61.1 | 70.0 | 78.1 |
| UK | 574 | 778 | 635 | 745 | 3.5 | 4.5 | 3.3 | 4.1 |
| Switzerland | 1,561 | 1,364 | 1,187 | 942 | 9.6 | 7.9 | 6.1 | 5.1 |
| Europe | 13,079 | 15,375 | 17,696 | 16,823 | 80.8 | 89.0 | 91.0 | 91.7 |
| USA | 331 | 2 | 1 | 131 | 2.0 | 0.0 | 0.0 | 0.7 |
| North and Central America | 770 | 279 | 212 | 267 | 4.8 | 1.6 | 1.1 | 1.5 |
| Argentina | 589 | 62 | 47 | 11 | 3.6 | 0.4 | 0.2 | 0.1 |
| Brazil | 689 | 287 | 167 | 82 | 4.3 | 1.7 | 0.9 | 0.4 |
| South America | 1,526 | 487 | 314 | 143 | 9.4 | 2.8 | 1.6 | 0.8 |
| Asia | 181 | 210 | 198 | 175 | 1.1 | 1.2 | 1.0 | 1.0 |
| Africa | 542 | 890 | 992 | 915 | 3.4 | 5.2 | 5.1 | 5.0 |
| Oceania | 80 | 38 | 32 | 31 | 0.5 | 0.2 | 0.2 | 0.2 |
| World Total | 16,178 | 17,279 | 19,444 | 18,354 | 100.0 | 100.0 | 100.0 | 100.0 |

| Wine Exports | Thousands of hectoliters | | | | Percentages of total world exports | | | |
|---|---|---|---|---|---|---|---|---|
| Spain | 3,106 | 4,078 | 3,712 | 575 | 18.8 | 22.5 | 18.5 | 3.0 |
| France | 1,978 | 1,664 | 1,075 | 833 | 12.0 | 9.2 | 5.4 | 4.3 |
| Greece | 570 | 930 | 850 | 416 | 3.4 | 5.1 | 4.2 | 2.2 |
| Italy | 1,553 | 1,395 | 1,081 | 1,337 | 9.4 | 7.7 | 5.4 | 7.0 |
| Portugal | 1,082 | 1,080 | 957 | 822 | 6.5 | 6.0 | 4.8 | 4.3 |
| **Europe** | **9,406** | **9,412** | **8,129** | **4,735** | **56.9** | **52.0** | **40.5** | **24.6** |
| North and Central America | 78 | 1 | 3 | 3 | 0.5 | 0.0 | 0.0 | 0.0 |
| **South America** | **3** | **33** | **55** | **94** | **0.0** | **0.2** | **0.3** | **0.5** |
| Asia | 59 | 83 | 112 | 97 | 0.4 | 0.5 | 0.6 | 0.5 |
| Algeria | 6,764 | 7,939 | 10,876 | 12,885 | 40.9 | 43.9 | 54.1 | 67.0 |
| Tunisia | 180 | 515 | 714 | 1,114 | 1.1 | 2.8 | 3.6 | 5.8 |
| **Africa** | **6,951** | **8,470** | **11,627** | **14,127** | **42.0** | **46.8** | **57.9** | **73.5** |
| Australia | 43 | 99 | 110 | 168 | 0.3 | 0.5 | 0.5 | 0.9 |
| **Oceania** | **43** | **99** | **110** | **168** | **0.3** | **0.5** | **0.5** | **0.9** |
| World Total | 16,541 | 18,100 | 20,092 | 19,227 | 100.0 | 100.0 | 100.0 | 100.0 |

*Source: Import and export averages made by the International Institute of Agriculture, Annuaire International de Statistique Agricole (Rome: International Institute of Agriculture, 1911–1939), with the exception of the last one period which has been calculated by ourselves with the annual data.*

Furthermore, the international wine market was hit hard by the 1930s Depression and the drop in international trade that resulted from the widespread growth in protectionism. This magnified the fall in global wine consumption at a time when consecutive good harvests produce from new wine-growing countries accentuated problems of over production.[24]

Therefore, with the exception of Algeria, which benefited highly from its direct access to the French market, wine-exporting countries experienced severe problems during the first third of the twentieth century, caused chiefly by falling demand, overproduction, and unfavorable prices.

## Concluding Remarks

It is important to emphasize that the role of wine differed from country to country, especially within Europe. The opportunities to expand wine exports were limited by the fact that wine was a product of mass consumption in only a very small number of countries. In spite of this, during the second half of the nineteenth century wine-exporting countries experienced an authentic golden age. The expansion in the export of high quality wine was due to a growth in demand for these products in industrialized countries, while the rapid rise in the export of medium- and lower-quality wines reflected the problems that affected French vineyards. These problems occurred in a period of rapid growth in domestic and international demand that caused France to increase its imports of wine in order to meet both its growing domestic demand and its growing exports. The global expansion in wine exports was facilitated by improvements in overland and maritime transportation, and in wine preservation technology.

That the lesser-developed countries of Southern Europe reacted quickly to these opportunities demonstrates that their wine-growing and processing sectors were highly sensitive to the signals sent by the market. The growth of liquor wine exports from Portugal and Spain to Great Britain, and of ordinary wine from Portugal, Spain, Italy, and Greece to France, was spectacular. The boom in wine exports partially explains the significant investments made by these producer countries to replant in the years following the outbreak of Phylloxera in France.

However, high expectations in the industry were dampened by the change in French trade policy during the 1890s.[25] In addition, the use of better techniques, and the cultivation of new more productive vines, created a situation of over production in a market in which growth depended primarily on the expansion of French imports. French trade policy was favorable to its colonies, especially to Algeria, with which Southern European wine producers found it increasingly difficult to compete in an export market dominated by France. Moreover, in other markets, Southern European producers had to face the growing competition coming from New World wine producers, chiefly Argentina, Chili, South Africa, and Australia. Finally, the collapse of international trade after 1929 dealt a deathblow to the hopes of Southern European producers. Conversely, Algeria experienced a growth in production and exports without parallel elsewhere in the world.

Consequently, during the first third of the twentieth century, wine prices were generally unfavorable and wine exports highly unstable. Wine exports from some producer countries fell and in others expanded at a far lower rate than during the previous golden age. In the wine-producing countries of Southern Europe, the high expectations generated during the nineteenth century tended to evaporate, as international demand dwindled. This was in turn reflected by the declining importance of wine in their overall exports. Whereas until the end of the nineteenth century, wine exports contributed towards balancing the foreign accounts of these countries by financing the import of manufactured goods, and generally stimulated economic growth, their importance and the benefits accruing from them declined sharply from the beginning of the twentieth century. This underscored the dangers of over-specialization in wine production, and its limitations as a motor for the development of the agricultural sector, the agro-food industry, and foreign trade.

## NOTES

1. The percentage of wine output over total agricultural output oscillated between the highest values for Portugal (around 25 percent), intermediate for Italy (around 20 percent), and somewhat lower for Spain (approximately 10 percent); see Pedro Lains, *A Economia*

*Portuguesa no Século XIX. Crescimiento Económico e Comercio Externo, 1851–1913* (Lisboa: Imprensa Nacional Casa da Moeda, 1995); Grupo de Estudios de Historia Rural, "Un índice de la producción agraria española, 1891–1935," *Hacienda Pública Española* 108/109 (1987): 411–22. In Greece, the vineyard represented 10 percent of the cultivated area; see Georges Dertilis, "Résaux de crédit et stratégies du capital," in idem, ed., *Banquiers, usuriers et paysans: réseaux de crédit et stratégies du capital en Grèce (1780–1930)* (Paris: Fondation des Treilles / Editions la Découverte, 1988), 51.

2. In the sense given by the Kuznets' definition, i.e., in none of these countries were exports larger than 20 percent of their GDP. For levels of openness in the European context see John R. Hanson, "Export Shares in the European Periphery and the Third World before World War I: Questionable Data, Facile Analogies," *Explorations in Economic History* 23 (1986): 93; Giovanni Federico, "El comercio exterior de los países mediterráneos en el siglo XIX," in *El desarrollo económico en la Europa del Sur: España e Italia en perspectiva histórica*, eds. Leandro Prados de la Escosura and Vera Zamagni (Madrid: Alianza Editorial, 1992), 272–73. These countries also had a low level of exports per capita in relation to other European countries; see Paul Bairoch, "European Foreign Trade in the XIX Century: The Development of the Value and Volume of Exports (Preliminary Results)," *The Journal of European Economic History* 2, no. 1 (1973): 16–17.

3. The percentage of Portugal's wine exports over total exports was the biggest, being more than 50 percent until 1900, and approximately 35 percent in the following years; Lains, *A Economia Portuguesa no Século XIX*, 92. In Spain until 1891, this percentage varied between 10 and 40 percent, subsequently falling to between 3 and 15 percent; see Domingo Gallego and Vicente Pinilla, "Del librecambio matizado al proteccionismo selectivo: el comercio exterior de productos agrarios y alimentos en España entre 1849 y 1935," *Revista de Historia Económica* XIV, no. 3 (1996): 619–39. In Italy, it stayed around 5 percent; see Giovanni Federico, "Oltre frontiera: L'Italia nel mercato agricolo internazionale," in *Storia dell'Agricoltura Italiana in età contemporanea, vol. III Mercati e Istituzioni*, ed. Piero Bevilacqua (Venezia: Marsilio Editor, 1991), 216; and in Greece it varied between 5 and 15 percent; see Eloy Fernández-Clemente, *Ulises en el siglo XX. Crisis y modernización en Grecia, 1900–1930* (Zaragoza: Prensas Universitarias de Zaragoza, 1995), 228, and N. Bakounakis, "La vigne et la ville: qui finance la culture?," in Dertilis, ed., *Banquiers, usuriers et paysans*, 92.

4. This makes it very difficult to obtain reliable price series or to be able to distinguish between volume and value in international trade.

5. Vicente Pinilla and María Isabel Ayuda, "Market Dynamism and International Trade: A Case Study of Mediterranean Agricultural Products, 1850–1935," *Applied Economics* (forthcoming).

6. Gema Aparicio, María Isabel Ayuda, and Vicente Pinilla, "World Consumption of Wine, 1859–1938: An Obstacle to the Growth of its Production and Trade?" in *Actas del I Simposio de la Asociación Internacional de Historia y Civilización de la Vid y el Vino, vol. 2*, ed. Javier Maldonado (El Puerto de Santa María: AICHCVV, 2002), 679–94.

7. At the beginning of the 1930s, European wine consumption reached 83 percent of total world consumption. Europe's per capita wine consumption level was almost five times the world average; see International Institute of Agriculture, *Agricultural Commodities and Raw Materials. Production and Consumption in the Different Parts of the World, 1934–38* (Rome: International Institute of Agriculture, 1944), 30, 56.

8. A description of the techniques employed, as well as more details on its interpretation, can be found in Aparicio, Ayuda, and Pinilla, "World Consumption of Wine, 1859–1938," 682–83.

9. Imperial Economic Committee, *Wine. Reports of the Imperial Economic Committee. Twenty-third Report* (London, Imperial Economic Committee, 1932), 10. This was echoed at the end of the same decade in the United States: "In the United States, with the possible exception of California, wine is generally considered a luxury, and its consumption is limited to special occasions." See U.S. Tariff Commission, *Grapes, Raisins and Wines*, 2nd series, Report No. 134 (Washington, DC: GPO, 1939), 286.

10. Wine production data for the second half of the nineteenth century are taken from José Morilla, "La irrupción de California en el mercado de productos vitícolas y sus efectos en los países mediterráneos (1865–1925)," in idem, ed., *California y el Mediterráneo: Estudios de la historia de dos agriculturas competidoras* (Madrid: Ministerio de Agricultura, Pesca y Alimentación, 1995), 303. Table 7.2 shows our reconstruction of production in the twentieth century.

11. H. Isnard, *La vigne en Algérie, étude géographique* (Ophrys: Gap, 1954), 100–17.

12. Tim Unwin, *Wine and the Vine. A Historical Geography of Viticulture and the Wine Trade* (London: Routledge, 1991).

13. Josep Pujol, "Les crisis de malvenda del sector vitivinícola catalá, 1892–1935," *Recerques* 15 (1984): 15–78; Rémy Pech, *Enterprise viticole et capitalisme en Languedoc-Roussillon: du Phylloxera aux crises de mevente* (Toulouse: Publications de l'Université de Toulouse, 1975).

14. French table wine imports jumped from 200,000 hectoliters in the 1860s to almost 11 million at the end of the 1880s; see Vicente Pinilla and María Isabel Ayuda, "The Political Economy of the Wine Trade: Spanish Exports and the International Market, 1890–1935," *European Review of Economic History* 6, no.1 (2002): 65.

15. Leo A. Loubere, *The Red and the White. A History of Wine in France and Italy in the Nineteenth Century* (Albany: State University of New York Press, 1978), 273.

16. D. Gallego and V. Pinilla, "Del librecambio matizado al proteccionismo selectivo: el comercio exterior de productos agrarios y alimentos en España entre 1849 y 1935," *Revista de Historia Económica* XIV, no. 2 (1996): 371–420.

17. Loubere, *The Red and the White*, 265–66.

18. Leo A. Loubere, *The Wine Revolution in France* (Princeton, NJ: Princeton University Press, 1990), 30.

19. Percentages for other significant products were highly variable—around 19 percent of world wheat production was exported; the percentages for barley varied between 9 and 15 percent; the percentage for corn was around 8 percent; for sugar between 40 and 50 percent; and for cotton between 50 and 70 percent; see Gema Aparicio, *El comercio internacional de productos agrarios, 1900–1939*, PhD dissertation, University of Zaragoza, 2000.

20. Loubere, *The Red and the White*, 299; Marcel Lachiver, *Vins, vignes et vignerons. Histoire du vignoble francais* (Lille: Fayard, 1988), 453.

21. Pech, *Enterprise viticol*, 121–22.

22. Pinilla and Ayuda, "The Political Economy of the Wine Trade," 71–75.

23. In the Spanish case, there was a very big difference between the volume of ordinary wine exported between 1880 and 1900, and the much lower volume exported between 1900 and 1935; see Pinilla and Ayuda, "The Political Economy of the Wine Trade," 68.

24. Leon Douarché, *La crise viticole mondiale* (Paris: Librairie Agricole de la Maison Roustique, 1930), 25–27.

25. On the importance of French trade policy and that of other importers, see for Portugal, Lains, *A Economia Portuguesa no Século XIX*, 102–11; and for Spain, Juan Pan-Montojo, *La bodega del mundo. La vid y el vino en España (1800–1936)* (Madrid: Alianza Editorial, 1994); Pinilla and Ayuda, "The Political Economy of the Wine Trade." This would be a good example of Nye's view "that the nature of tariff and tax policy in the West's leading economies imposed substantial economic costs on producer countries with comparative advantage in more heavily and more easily-taxed consumption items";

see John V. Nye, "The unbearable lightness of drink: British Wine Tariffs and French Economic Growth, 1689–1860," in *Political Economy of Protectionism and Commerce, Eighteenth-Twentieth Centuries*, eds. Peter H. Lindert, John V. Nye, and Jean-Michel Chevet (Milano: Proceedings Eleventh International Economic History Congress, 1994), 13.

# CHAPTER 11

# INDIGENOUS ECONOMIC
# DEVELOPMENT
## A TALE OF TWO WINERIES

*Robert B. Anderson, Dianne W. Wingham,
Robert J. Giberson, and Brian Gibson*

## INTRODUCTION

This chapter constitutes one of a number of studies of the reaction of Indigenous peoples[1] to the "new global economy": their participation in the wine-making industry. We first outline the objectives and assess the feasibility of Indigenous economic development. We then discuss two case studies of Indigenous peoples—the Metis and Inuit, an Aboriginal "First Nations" people in Canada; and a Maori collective of tribal nations comprising the members of the Wakatu Incorporation in Nelson, Ngati Rarua Atiawa Iwi Trust in the Nelson/Marlborough area and the Wi Peri Trust based south of Gisborne in New Zealand. Both groups have developed wine-related businesses as key aspects of their economic development strategy. Indeed, they created the world's first and second Indigenous-owned wineries: the Tohu Winery in New Zealand and Nk'Mip Cellars in Canada. Here, we briefly document the creation of these wineries, then describe their contribution to the economic development of the communities involved. Finally, from these case studies, we offer concluding comments about the possibilities for Indigenous economic development in general.

## Indigenous Economic Development

Indigenous peoples worldwide are struggling both to rebuild their "nations" in response to dominant external political authorities that have imposed radically redefined borders, and to improve the socioeconomic circumstances of their people. Economic development is key to their success For example, both the Maori and the Aboriginal people of Canada see participation in the global economy through entrepreneurship and business development as crucial to economy building and nation "re-building." Like Indigenous peoples elsewhere, they want participation in the global economy to be on their own terms. Moreover, as research in Canada has clearly demonstrated, traditional lands, history, culture, and values play critical roles in the process. Entrepreneurship—defined as the identification of unmet or under-satisfied needs and related opportunities—and the creation of enterprises, products, and services in response to these opportunities, lies at the heart of Aboriginal economic development strategy. Through entrepreneurship and business development, Aboriginal and Maori communities believe that they can attain their socioeconomic objectives.

The Aboriginal approach to economic development is predominantly collective, centered on the community or "nation." It has four main objectives: economic self-sufficiency (thus ending dependency); control over economic activity on traditional lands; socioeconomic improvement of the community; and strengthening traditional culture, values, and languages To achieve these aims, Indigenous peoples are in the process of forming business alliances and joint ventures with both Aboriginal and non-Aboriginal partners that can compete profitably over the long run in the global economy. They are also promoting education, training, and institution building. At the same time, they seek to consolidate treaties underpinning Aboriginal rights to land and resources.[2]

It is important to note two things about this approach. First, it involves active participation in the global economy on a competitive business basis. Second, this participation—both the process and the objectives—are shaped by things distinctly Aboriginal. For example, Michael Robinson and Elmer Ghostkeeper, in two papers discussing Indigenous economic development in Canada, suggest that Indigenous peoples are rejecting the industrial development imposed on them from the outside, in favor of development strategies originating within, and controlled by, the community "with the sanction of Indigenous culture."[3] They argue further that "a wide range of cultures may enable entrepreneurship and economic development to flourish," and suggest that the key to success lies in designing development plans around those forces in each culture that are conducive to development.[4]

In his turn, Arun Agrawal contends that the focus on Indigenous knowledge and production systems is due to the failure of neo-liberal (market) and authoritarian/bureaucratic (state) approaches to development.[5] Indigenous groups thus attempt "to reorient and reverse state policies and market forces to permit members of threatened populations to determine their own future."[6]

For the most part, however, these efforts are taking place within the global economy. As Anthony Bebbington notes, "Like it or not, Indigenous peoples are firmly integrated into a capricious and changing market, their well-being and survival depend on how well they handle and negotiate this integration."[7] The Indigenous approach to negotiating this integration is not to reject outright participation in the modern economy, "but rather to pursue local and grassroots control . . . over the economic and social relationships that traditionally have contributed to the transfer of income and value from the locality to other places and social groups."[8] This is certainly the development approach of most Aboriginal peoples worldwide. In the sections that follow, we first explore the theoretical feasibility of Indigenous people negotiating their integration into the global economy in a manner that gives them a reasonable level of control over the terms, conditions, and outcomes of such integration, and how this might be accomplished—with particular attention to the role that entrepreneurship and business development play in the process. Subsequently, we analyze two wine-related cases studies that illustrate the Indigenous approach to participation in the global economy, and assess their success.

## THEORETICAL PERSPECTIVE

Regulation theory is one of the new approaches to development that emphasizes contingency and human agency. According to Paul Hirst and Jonathon Zeitlin, it executes "a slalom between the orthodoxies of neo-classical equilibrium theory and classical Marxism to produce a rigorous but nondeterministic account of the phases of capitalist development that leaves considerable scope for historical variation and national diversity."[9] Concurring with Mark Elam's contention that, in the new global economy, local economic forces and external economic forces are in constant interaction, Ash Amin and Andrew Malmberg argue that the crisis in the global economy has resulted in "new opportunities for the location of economic activities" and that "the geography of post-Fordist production is said to be at once local and global."[10] Similarly, Allen Scott states that new industrial spaces result from a "very specific articulation of local social conditions with wider coordinates of capitalist development in general."[11] In addition, Peter Dicken emphasizes that successful participation in the global economic system "is created and sustained through a highly localized process."[12] This translates into a counter-hegemonic potential in terms of the activities actually undertaken by people as they negotiate their way locally through the global economy. It is not simply a case of conform or fail.

Regulation theory analyzes the global economy "in terms of a series of *modes of development* based on combination of the currently ascendant *regime of accumulation* and a variety of *modes of social regulation.*"[13] Scott states that the regime of accumulation, which determines the general possibilities for the economy, "can be rather simply defined as a historically specific production apparatus . . . through which surplus is generated, appropriated, and redeployed."[14] It is nevertheless global in scale, signifying a "relationship between production and consumption defined at the level of the international economy as a whole."[15]

If the world were peopled by Adam Smith's universal perfectly rational "economic man," no regulation of the global economy beyond the "invisible hand" of perfectly functioning markets would be required. However, people are far from being perfectly rational, and each individual is motivated by a variety of non-economic impulses. The variations from the "perfect" model are thus manifold. As a result, as Scott notes, economic stability is "dependent on the emergence of a further set of social relations that preserve it, for a time at least, from catastrophic internal collisions and breakdowns. These relations constitute a mode of social regulation. They are made up of a series of formal and informal structures of governance and stabilization ranging from the state through business and labor associations, to modes of socialization which create ingrained habits of behaviour."[16] Hirst and Zeitlin add that a mode of social regulation (MSR) "is a complex of institutions and norms which secure, at least for a certain period, the adjustment of individual agents and social groups to the over arching principle of the accumulation regime."[17] While regulation theory does not prescribe the exact nature of a particular mode of social regulation, it is generally agreed that (i) a regime of accumulation does not create or require a particular mode of social regulation: "each regime, in short, may be regulated in a multiplicity of ways";[18] and (ii) because modes of social regulation are based on such things as "habits and customs, social norms, enforceable laws and state forms,"[19] unique modes "can exist at virtually any territorial level—local, regional, national, global."[20]

Another aspect of regulation theory—its historicity—adds to the argument that modes of social regulation, and therefore of modes of development—differing considerably one from another—can and do emerge at every geographic scale. Regulation theory, according to Stuart Corbridge,[21] indicates that the global economic system has gone through four stages in the twentieth century. In stage one, the system was in equilibrium. Stage two was a period of crisis or disequilibrium resulting from a shift from the extensive to the Fordist regime of accumulation. Equilibrium returned in stage three when suitable modes of social regulation emerged. The fourth (current) stage is also one of crisis caused by a failure of the monopolistic mode of social regulation (in all it variants) to accommodate a "selective move from mass production [the Fordist regime accumulation] to various forms of flexible production."[22]

Factors promoting a shift to the new flexible regime of accumulation include: (i) technical limits to rigid fixed capital production techniques; (ii) working class resistance to rigid mass production oriented Taylorist and Fordist forms of work organization;[23] (iii) a change in consumption patterns "toward a greater variety of use values . . . [that] cannot be easily satisfied through mass production";[24] (iv) the increasing mobility of capital and the resulting ability of transnational corporations (TNCs) to move among spatially bounded regulatory jurisdictions in the pursuit of greater profits;[25] and, in the face of this internationalization of capital, (v) the inability of national Keynesian policies (all variants of the of the monopolistic mode of social regulation) to avert crisis.[26]

Everywhere and at every geographic scale—community, subnational region, national, supranational regions, and global—people are struggling to develop modes of social regulation that will allow them to interact with this new, flexible regime of accumulation on their terms. As they do this, they are building the "new economy" and not simply reacting to it. Two related questions come to mind— can they get it right?; and if so, what will this new economy look like? While it is a "work in progress," the nature of the flexible regime of accumulation is becoming clearer, and multiple overlapping modes of social regulation are emerging. Both are briefly described in the paragraphs that follow.

Michael Storper and Richard Walker[27] argue that, in contrast to Fordism, flexible production systems have the following five characteristics: (i) more general purpose equipment and machinery, especially machines based around variable labor processes and/or programmable computerized equipment; (ii) smaller, more specialized workplaces and firms and greater reliance on subcontracting; (iii) greater attention to demand variations, to which the quantity of inputs and outputs can be rapidly adjusted by altering the procedures or the mix of participants; (iv) collective social and institutional order in place of hierarchical control exercised by the mass production corporation; and (v) more temporary and part-time hiring and more relaxed internal rules for assigning workers and managers to various tasks.

Expanding on this, Steven Goldman notes that the flexible regime exhibits, "a distinct set of relationships, interdependencies, and forms of interaction among suppliers, producers, distributors, and customers. It demands new approaches to organizing, operating, and measuring the performance of both individual companies and clusters of cooperating companies."[28] He stresses that in "a competitive environment of continuous and unanticipated change" companies are finding "advantageous on the grounds of cost, speed, or market penetration, to utilize only some company-owned resources, combining them with others available in other companies."[29] Eric Dunning agrees, noting that "we are moving out of an age of hierarchical capitalism and into an age of alliance capitalism. This is placing a premium on the virtues needed for fruitful and sustainable coalitions and partnerships (be they within or among institutions), such as trust, reciprocity, and due diligence."[30] As a result, companies have altered both their conception of which groups they consider to be stakeholders, and their behavior toward these groups. This is particularly reflected in the relationship between companies and their "customer" and "employee" communities. As companies forge networks of suppliers, subcontractors, and marketing channel partners, and seek to control them through "collective social and institutional order in place of hierarchical control,"[31] they increasingly view communities as valued members of networks—which suggests that the emphasis on joint ventures with non-Aboriginal companies in the Aboriginal approach to development is well founded.

This leads us to a discussion of the modes of social regulation that emerge in response to the demands of the flexible regime of accumulation. Conventional accounts have focused on deregulation. However, closer examination of the issue reveals that so-called "deregulation" is, in fact, re-regulation. What has occurred is a shift in the locus of regulation from the nation state on a continuum in two directions—to the supra-national and the local. Thus, Amin and Malmberg state that the crisis in the global economy has resulted in "new opportunities for the location of economic activities" and that "the geography of post-Fordist production is said to be at once local and global" (wealth generated through movement in organizations along the continuum).[32] Scott concurs, noting that "new industrial spaces result from a very specific articulation of local social conditions with wider coordinates of capitalist development in general."[33]

Finally, Peter Dicken emphasizes that successful participation in the global economic system "is created and sustained through a highly localized process" and that local "economic structures, values, cultures, institutions and histories contribute profoundly to that success," leading to successful participation in global business through Aboriginal ownership and philosophies.[34] Our two Indigenous wine-growing businesses provide examples of successful participation in the new re-regulated economy shaped by the convergence of the characteristics of the wine industry (global market structures), and their respective sets of values, cultures, institutions, and histories.

Local modes of social regulation can be, in Gramscian terms, both hegemonic and counter-hegemonic to the extent to which they consent to the forces of the capitalist global economy, or attempt to transform or dissent from that economy—responses associated with three different ideological starting-points. The first claims that peripheral communities have been excluded from, but should aim to integrate into, capitalism; the second that capitalism is in part culturally alien and that those "alien" aspects of it must be transformed in order to participate in it; and the third, that capitalism is exploitative beyond redemption and should be resisted or avoided. These viewpoints, and the beliefs about the economy associated with them, are present in varying combinations and strengths in all human communities.

Figure 11.1 illustrates a group's response to the global economy on two continua. The first reflects the degree to which it opts into or out of the global economy. The second addresses the nature of such choices; for example, does a decision to opt in signify a blanket acceptance of the global economy, or does it imply the desire to modify aspects of that economy? A combination of the continua results in four extreme possibilities. The first two occur when a group chooses to opt out of the global economy. At one extreme (1) opting out can be passive: a desire to be isolated, even protected from the impact of the global economy. Alternatively (2), opting out can be active and aggressive: the desire to reject, resist, or even undermine the global economy through protest or "revolution." The other two extreme positions (3 and 4) occur when a group chooses to "opt in" and actively participate in the global economy. Again, that participation can be characterized by the degree to which the group accommodates itself to the requirements of the global economy. Indigenous people in Canada and in New Zealand have generally "opted in," in a dynamic rather than passive fashion. They have, for example, continued their struggle for land and other rights to ensure participation "on their own terms."

Each community's perspective on the global economy is formed less in isolation than in response to direct experience, with actors in the global economic system, notably (i) the businesses (here termed "corporations") with which they interact as suppliers, customers, and/or employees, (ii) the "state" (local, sub-national, national, and international), and (iii) a myriad of civil sector groups including non-government agencies (NGOs) and special interest groups such as Amnesty International, the World Council of Indigenous People, and the Sierra Club (see Figure 11.2). Corporations are for many Indigenous communities closely associated with, if not the "face" of the regime of accumulation, while the "state" at all its levels is most closely tied to the mode of social regulation. The organizations that comprise the "civil" sector also play an important role directly and through their influence on the state and on corporations. In Australia there is a strong relationship between the Indigenous Peoples and Business Australia (IBA)—part of the governmental

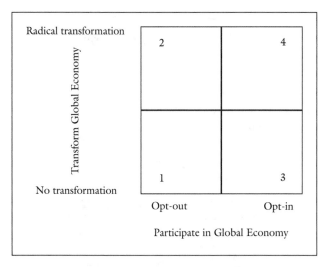

**Figure 11.1** Indigenous responses to the global economy[35]

Indigenous Economic Development program—that creates business opportunities for Aboriginal and Torres Strait Islander individuals and communities. A similar role is played in New Zealand by Bio diversity strategy (administered by the Parliamentary Commissioner for the Environment), in Canada by the National Aboriginal Business Association and the Aboriginal Human Resources Development Strategy (AHRDS), and in the United States (for Native Americans and Indigenous peoples of Alaska and Hawaii) by the Environmental Protection Agency.

The approach (integrating, transforming, or excluding mechanisms) adopted by a particular community in reaction to the forces of the global economy, and therefore the mode of development that emerges, is heavily influenced by local circumstance, and occurs within the context of multiple, overlapping, and often conflicting modes of social regulation.

## THE GLOBAL ECONOMY

What the Osoyoos Indian Band "sees" as its particular collage within its Nk'Mip Project differs in certain important respects from the viewpoint of other winery and eco tourism operators in the Okanagan Valley, just as the perspective of the Maori of the Wakatu

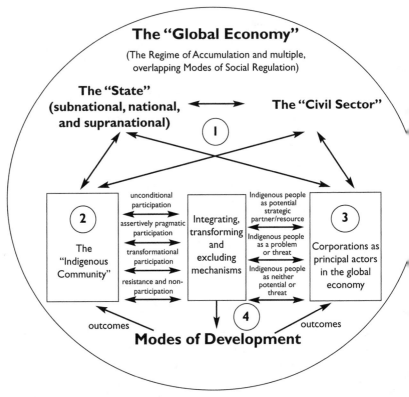

**Figure 11.2** Modes of development[36]

Incorporation in Nelson, the Ngati Rarua Atiawa Iwi Trust in the Nelson/Marlborough area, and the Wi Peri Trust based south of Gisborne in developing their Tohu Wines company differs significantly from that of non-Indigenous wineries.

Indigenous groups "opting in" to the global economy find themselves at the beginning of a long process of interaction with the chief representatives of that economy. To succeed on their own terms they must identify business opportunities that satisfy their economic and other development objectives, and then marshal the requisite resources and develop the necessary organizations to realize those objectives. This is the process of entrepreneurship—defined broadly in Schumpeterian terms as an economy-building process rather than narrowly as the creation of a small business. As Macdonald Morris states, "entrepreneurship is a universal construct that is applicable to any person, organization (private or public, large or small), or nation [that] is critical for the survival and growth of companies as well as the economic prosperity of nations."[37] Closer to the Indigenous model is Raymond Kao's definition of entrepreneurship as, "not just a way of conducting business; it is an ideology originating from basic human needs and desires . . . entails discovering the new, while changing, adapting and preserving the best of the old."[38]

## WINE, WINE TOURISM, AND INDIGENOUS TOURISM

We examine here the nature of the encounter between entrepreneurial Indigenous groups and the chief actors of the global economy, and the developmental models that emerge, through two case studies involving Indigenous development of wineries: the Osoyoos Indian Band's Nk'Mip Project in the Okanagan Valley in Canada, and the Tohu wine project of three Maori communities in New Zealand. The latter project includes the Wakatu Incorporation in Nelson, the Ngati Rarua Atiawa Iwi Trust in the Nelson/Marlborough area, and the Wi Peri Trust based south of Gisborne.

Both the Osoyoos Indian Band (OIB) and the Maori see considerable opportunities in the global economy for the production and sale of their wine through the global marketing system and wine tourism. Their strategy is to produce limited quantities of high quality wine and market it through restaurants, a few high-end distributors, and at the cellar door. They also stand to gain from wine tourism as wine lovers increasingly seek opportunities to sample wines in unique settings in both the Old World and New World.

Successful wine tourism regions fulfill three criteria. First, in order to successfully create brand awareness of wineries, wines, and the wine country, a wine region must employ effective marketing techniques. Second, they must possess a critical mass of wineries in relatively close proximity. This enables visitors to tour several facilities with ease, and provides the capacity to organize wine festivals and other events that help attract a large customer base to a region.[39] Third, the complete wine tourism experience must involve complementary services and events, including a gamut of tours and tourist attractions, accommodations, recreational activities, and dining facilities, as well as a good transport network, and communication and regional information sources. Wineries and complimentary services must be well signposted to assist tourists. Given intense international competition, each wine region needs to differentiate its product in order to attract high yield tourists, a small number of whom can provide sufficient income to support a region.

Indigenous wine growers from New Zealand and Canada recognize that they can offer unique wine tourism experiences based on their Aboriginal culture—from management and cultivation of vineyards held under native title to Indigenous philosophy. They also participate in a related and growing specialty market—Indigenous tourism. The synergies are obvious. The cultural component allows them to differentiate their wine and their wine tourism "product," which grants them a competitive advantage in the wine/wine tourism industry. At the same time, the wineries and related projects, all imbued with a strong cultural component, will appeal to those tourists seeking the "Indigenous" experience.

In Canada, the vast majority of tourists currently utilizing Aboriginal tourism businesses are from Canada and the United States. In the year 2000, according to the Government of Canada's Department of Industry, the tourism industry in Canada was valued at $54.1 billion, employing almost 550,000 people. Aboriginal tourism with around 1 percent of this total generates $300 million annually and employs 16,000 people through an estimated 1,500 Aboriginal-owned and operated businesses. Moreover, Canadian Aboriginal tourism has recently been generating significant interest from European travelers—a reflection of its growing international profile.[40] Forecasts predict that the annual revenue from Aboriginal tourism in Canada will rise to $1.9 billion within a decade.[41] Growth prospects are similar for New Zealand's 150 Maori-owned[42] tourism businesses and Australia's 200 Aborigine-owned businesses (annual sales currently totaling $130 million).[43]

## Case Study 1: Nk'Mip Cellars

The OIB lands are in the southern Okanagan Valley in British Columbia, the westernmost province in Canada. The Okanagan Valley is one of two principal wine areas in Canada (the other is the Niagara Peninsula in the province of Ontario). Over the past four decades wine-related businesses have played a key role in the economic development of the OIB. The OIB owns and operates nine other profitable enterprises: a construction company, a sand and gravel company, a forestry company, a campground, a recreational vehicle park, golf course, two housing developments, and a grocery store. The motto of the OIB development corporation is "working with business to preserve our past by strengthening our future." Two of its development objectives are to achieve full employment for OIB members, and become economically self-sufficient by 2010.

In 1994, the OIB generated $1.3 million in revenues from its commercial activities. By 2002, this had increased more than tenfold to $14.3 million. Whereas in 1994, this self-generated revenue was less than the value of federal funds flowing to the OIB, by 2002 it was seven times greater than federal government payments. Source of income data from the 1986 and 2001 censuses confirms the increasing importance of employment income as a percentage of total household income. Employment income as a percentage of total household income increased from 28.1 percent in 1986 to 44.5 percent by 2001. This represented clear progress towards the goal of self-sufficiency. Success on the employment front has been equally impressive: between 1986 and 2001, the OIB participation rate increased from 34.6 percent to 46.2 percent, the unemployment rate fell from 29.6 percent to 9.3 percent, and the employment rate increased from 25.6 percent of the potential labor force (those aged 15 years and older) to almost 42 percent. However, rates of OIB employment income economic activity participation and employment remains far below the rates for British Columbia as a whole, where the 2001 figures reveal rates of employment income at 75.8 percent of total income, participation at 65.2 percent, and employment at 60 percent.

Building on the foundation provided by these successful development activities, the OIB's current activities and future plans centre on a group of business activities together called the Nk'Mip Project. Included in this forty-million-dollar project are the nine-million-dollar Nk'Mip Desert and Heritage Interpretive Centre, the Nk'Mip Cellars and associated vineyards, a recreation vehicle park and campground, a residential resort, and the Sonora Dunes golf course, which opened in 2004. These ventures are located on a 1,200-acre parcel of band land that adjoins the town of Osoyoos and fronts on Osoyoos Lake. The nine-million-dollar Nk'Mip Desert and Heritage Interpretive Centre[44] is being developed to appeal to the growing Aboriginal/ecotourism market by educating visitors about the three thousand years of history of the Osoyoos band, and the unique nature of the community's desert environment. Chief Clarence Louie stated that "the Desert and Heritage Centre is probably going to be our biggest business venture, and it's going to combine all of those things that you see in a first class desert interpretive centre–the educational stuff, the scientific stuff, the desert trails, the walks, the scientific interpretive stuff . . . the other major component of it, which is really special, is the uniqueness of the Okanagan First Nations, with the language and the heritage and the cultural component to it."[45] With the cultural ecotourists in view, the centre will preserve up to one thousand acres of the band's unique dessert ecosystem. It will also work to restore habitat, and reintroduce species at risk to the area.

The center began operation in the temporary facility on June 13, 2002, with the gift shop half-stocked and admission by donation. By July 15, the retail store was fully stocked and the center began charging full admission. As well, a start has been made on the interpretive trails and a traditional Okanagan village. Construction of the permanent building began in early 2005 and the new building opened for the 2006 season. From its opening in June to September 30, 2002, the Nk'Mip Desert and Heritage Interpretive has attracted 3,865 visitors. Nk'Mip Cellars did not open until September 2002, six months later than planned, so the visitors that came were attracted solely by the centre. There were approximately 7,000 visitors to the Centre during the 2003 season in spite of serious forest fires, which limited tourism in the region in late summer; 9,000 in 2004; and a projected 20,000 in 2006.[46]

Nk'Mip Cellars[47] opened on September 13, 2002. The seven-million-dollar project includes an eighteen-thousand-square-foot winery and a twenty-acre vineyard. It is North America's first Aboriginal winery, and the world's second (a Maori-owned winery opened in New Zealand in 1998). The OIB provided an operating line of almost one million dollars and two to three million dollars from various federal agencies and, as a result, owns 51 percent of the venture. Vincor invested three million dollars and owns 49 percent, but as important is Vincor's expertise. As Don Triggs, Vincor's chief executive states: "We have shared with them everything that we know in design of the winery, in processing and in managing hospitality."[48] Vincor will be the managing partner in Nk'Mip for ten years, after which it can sell its interest to the OIB.

With a capacity of eighteen thousand cases, the Nk'Mip Winery's objective is to make small quantities of high quality wine. Nk'Mip—which currently produces Chardonnay, Pinot Blanc, Pinot Noir, and Merlot exclusively from grapes from the Inkameep Vineyard—expects to sell at least 40 percent of its output to visiting wine tourists. It received almost six thousand visitors between September 13, 2002 (opening day), and December 31, 2002 (the off-season for tourism in the Okanagan Valley), when the interpretive center was closed. During the 2003 season to the end of September, the winery hosted more than twenty thousand visitors who spent more than $240,000 while at the winery. Nk'Mip Cellars sold at total of seven thousand cases of wine during the 2003 fiscal year, generating revenues of $900,000. The grape crush for 2003 increased to eighteen thousand cases—full capacity—and has remained at this level since. Most of the remainder of its production will be distributed through Vincor's marketing channels to restaurants, specialty wine stores, and the international market. Nk'Mip wines have won over fifty international wine awards (thirty in 2005 and 2006), a clear indication of success.

Expanding on its original resort plans, the Band has developed a strategic alliance with Bellstar Hotels & Resorts to develop the Spirit Ridge Vineyard Resort and Spa, a twenty-two-million-dollar four-star resort—one of only nine four-star rated resorts in British Columbia.[49] Located adjacent to the winery and interpretive center, it will play an integral role in the success of the Nk'Mip Project. Construction is underway. The resort and spa, which opened thirty villas for operation in the fall of 2005, was booked solid in late 2005. In the spring of 2007, a full service spa will open in the Spirit Lodge Building, and construction will begin on an additional 132 suites and villas.

## CASE STUDY 2: TOHU WINERY

For centuries, the Maori—a convocation of the Indigenous people of New Zealand—worked on, lived around, and loved the rugged yet fertile lands of their ancestors. Through the awareness of the earth as the giver of all life came a respect for sustaining the land's fertility and value. The belief that the Indigenous people born on that land inherited both the right to produce from it, and the duty to protect it for the benefit of all, is reflected in the tenets of the Native Land Titles. Iwi Wakatu Incorporation of Maori is made up of individual shareholders possessing kinship ties and *mana whenua* (the mana that the gods planted within "Papa-túã-nuku"—"Mother Earth"—to give her the power to produce the bounties of nature) over their lands. The Indigenous landholdings in Marlborough and Gisborne are among the foremost wine growing regions in New Zealand and Tohu Wines Ltd. is the first Indigenous branded wine from New Zealand to be produced for both the domestic and export markets. One hundred percent Maori-owned, Tohu incorporates "global" wine-making skills and economic advisers, within five years was amongst the top rated wineries nationally, and proclaims itself as "one of New Zealand's finest achievements created from a mutual vision of harmony and respect of our people and our place."[50]

The company has three main goals: to turn a profit; put Maori culture on to the labels and thus export that culture around the world; and produce unique quality wines (in 2002 it produced only 25,000 cases). Tohu's director, James Wheeler (whose grandmother was an original board member), believes that while making money is the key to being a successful Maori organization, it must be tied to the principles of *tikanga* ("the Maori way of doing things"—derived from the Maori word *tika* meaning "right" or "correct"). He emphasizes the importance of creating jobs for Maori people—and the export market as a key to providing employment. In this respect, Tohu is performing remarkably well. Its Marlborough Sauvignon Blanc and Pinot Noir, Gisborne Chardonnay, Reserve Chardonnay, and Unoaked Chardonnay wines, exported to both individuals and high quality restaurants, have won a number of prizes and earned Tohu an international reputation, and fast growing markets in the United States, Canada, the United Kingdom, Ireland, the Netherlands, Germany, Belgium, and Denmark. Tohu moved to diversify when in 2004 it purchased a 19 percent stake in *Davies*, a specialist American importer of New Zealand and Australian wines. Ownership in this company ensures Tohu has secured an importing structure within the lucrative United States market. Tohu Wines is a good example of a successful Maori organization succeeding in an extremely competitive international market by utilizing a formula of excellent business sense and skill, all the while adhering to the traditional virtue of *tikanga*.[51]

Another example of Indigenous "wine" enterprise is the Wi Pere Trust, a major caretaker of Maori-owned land. The traditional official approach to Indigenous groups was to encourage dependence on state assistance. However, in the late nineteenth century, Wi Pere, a chief of the Te Aitanga a Mahaki and Rongowhakaata tribes near Gisborne, determined to break the impoverishment that this encouraged. In April 1899, he founded the Wi Pere Trust to commercially manage their land and thus encourage the self-sufficiency of Maori people. The Trust, which currently administers lands and considerable assets, is involved in farming (sheep, beef, and wine), horticulture (citrus fruits, flowers for export), and forestry. Moreover, in partnership with another Indigenous trust—the Ngati Rarua Atiawa Iwi Trust, which administers sixteen million dollars worth of lands and assets—it is involved in other ventures, including wine growing; apple packing; apple, kiwi fruit; and pear cultivation; deer and sheep raising; and forestry.[52]

A third example of successful Indigenous development strategy in New Zealand is the Wakatu Incorporation, a body of Maori shareholder-owners formed in 1977 that adds value to many of its primary products by processing, packaging; and marketing. From an eleven-million-dollar base in 1977, it grew to a value of over two hundred milliondollars in 2005—to date showing an annual growth of around 15 percent. It offers training, scholarships, and employment to members of its shareholders' families, and now is firmly established as an Indigenous consortium of businesses—including commercial property and property development, leased lands, horticulture, seafood, forestry, and the wine industry—that has deliberately involved itself in the mainstream global economy, and has done so on its own terms.[53]

## Conclusion

It is apparent that the Osoyoos Indian Band in Canada and the Maori of the Wakatu Incorporation in Nelson, the Ngati Rarua Atiawa Iwi Trust, and the Wi Peri Trust of New Zealand have opted to participate in the global economy. As articulated by Tohu's Chief Executive, James Wheeler, "Without trade we would die."[54] However, they have "opted in" on their own terms, safeguarding their culture, values, traditions, and histories. Both groups of people have chosen to use the best of their own and of foreign cultures to maximize group benefits, create successful business ventures, and take their success to the global marketplace without sacrificing their traditions. They have demonstrated a truly Indigenous path to economic development.

## NOTES

1. "Indigenous" within this study relates to peoples who are of or pertaining to the family of native global aboriginal nations.
2. Robert B. Anderson, *Economic Development among the Aboriginal Peoples of Canada: Hope for the Future* (Toronto: Captus University Press, 1999), 9–14.
3. M. Robinson and E. Ghostkeeper, "Native and Local Economies: A Consideration of Economic Evolution and the Next Economy," *Arctic* 40, no. 2 (1987): 173.
4. M. Robinson and E. Ghostkeeper, "Implementing the Next Economy," *Arctic* 41, no. 3 (1988): 173.
5. A. Agrawal, "Dismantling the Divide between Indigenous and Scientific Knowledge," *Development and Change* 26, no. 3 (1995): 414.
6. Ibid., 432.
7. A. Bebbington, "Modernization from Below: An Alternative Indigenous Paradigm," *Economic Geography* 69, no. 3 (1993): 275.
8. Ibid., 281.
9. P. Hirst and J. Zeitlin, "Flexible Specialization versus Post-Fordism" in *Pathways to Industrialization and Regional Development*, eds. Michael Storper and Allen Scott (London: Routledge, 1992), 84.
10. Ash Amin and Andrew Malmberg, "Competing Structural and Institutional Influence of the Geography of Production" in *Post-Fordism: A Reader*, ed. Ash Amin (Oxford: Blackwell, 1984), 222.
11. Allen J. Scott, *New Industrial Spaces: Flexible Production Organization and Regional Development in North America and Western Europe* (London: Pion, 1988), 108.
12. Peter Dicken, "International Production in a Volatile Regulatory Environment" *Geoforum* 23, no. 3 (1992): 307.
13. Hirst and Zeitlin, "Flexible Specialization," 84–85.
14. Scott, *New Industrial Spaces*, 8.
15. Hirst and Zeitlin, "Flexible Specialization," 85.
16. Scott, *New Industrial Spaces*, 9.
17. Hirst and Zeitlin, "Flexible Specialization," 85.
18. Scott, *New Industrial Spaces*, 9.
19. J. Peck and Adam Tickell, "Local Modes of Social Regulation," *Geoforum* 23, no. 3 (1992): 349.

20. Michael Storper and Richard Walker, *The Capitalist Imperative: Territory, Technology and Industrial Growth* (New York: Basil Blackwell, 1989), 215.
21. S. Corbridge, "Post-Marxism and Development Studies: Beyond the Impasse," *World Development* 18, no. 5 (1989): 623–39.
22. Glen Norcliffe, "Regional Labor Market Adjustments in a Period of Structural Transformation: The Canadian Case," *The Canadian Geographer* 38, no. 1 (1994): 2.
23. Bob Jessop, "Conservative Regimes and the Transition to Post-Fordism," in *Capitalist Development and Crisis Theory*, eds. M. Gottdiener and N. Komninos (New York: St. Martin's, 1989), 261–99.
24. Ash Amin, 1984. "Post-Fordism: Models, Fantasies and Phantoms of Transition," in Amin, ed., *Post-Fordism*, 12.
25. Andrew Leyshon, "The Transformation of a Regulatory Order," *Geoforum* 23, no. 3 (1989): 347–63.
26. Nicos Komninos, "From National to Local: The Janus Face of Crisis" in Gottdiener and Komninos, eds., *Capitalist Development*, 348–64.
27. Storper and Walker, *Capitalist Imperative*, 152.
28. Steven Goldman, *Agile Competition: The Emergence of a New Industrial Order* (Hamilton, Ontario: Society of Management Accountants, 1995), 1.
29. Ibid., 6–7.
30. J. H. Dunning, *Making Globalization Good: The Moral Challenges of Global Capitalism* (Oxford: Oxford University Press, 2003), 24.
31. Storper and Walker, *Capitalist Imperative*, 152.
32. Amin and Malmberg, "Competing Structural and Institutional Influence," 222.
33. Scott, *New Industrial Spaces*, 108.
34. Dicken, "International Production," 307.
35. Source: Robert B Anderson, Leo Paul Dana, and Teresa Dana, "Aboriginal Land Rights, Social Entrepreneurship & Economic Development in Canada: 'Opting-In' to the Global Economy," *Journal of World Business* 41, no. 1 (2006): 50.
36. Source: Robert B Anderson et al., "Indigenous Land Rights in Canada: The Foundation for Development?" *International Journal of Entrepreneurship and Small Business* 2, no. 2 (2005): 116.
37. Macdonald Morris, *Entrepreneurial Intensity: Sustainable Advantages for Individuals, Organizations and Societies* (Westport: Quorum Books, 1998), 2.
38. R. W. Y Kao, K. R. Kao, and R. R. Kao, *Entrepreneurism for the Market Economy* (London: Imperial College Press, 2002), 44. Several

other writers express similar views; see, for example, Ken Blawatt, *Entrepreneurship: Process and Management* (Scarborough: Prentice Hall Canada, 1998); Peter F. Drucker, *Innovation and Entrepreneurship* (New York: Harper & Row, 1985); James O. Fiet, *Systematic Search for Entrepreneurial Discoveries.* (Westport: Quorom Books, 2002); Peter Moran and Sumantra Ghoshal, "Markets, Firms, and the Process of Economic Development," *The Academy of Management Review* 24, no. 3 (1999): 390–412.

39. D. W. Wingham and B. Gibson, "Wine as a Small Business: A Cross Regional Preliminary Study of Cellar Door Sales Issues," paper presented at the *USASBE Conference*, Hilton Head, South Carolina, 2003.

40. D. Williams and G. Richter, "Developing and Supporting European Tour Operator Distribution Channels for Canadian Aboriginal Tourism Development" *Journal of Travel Research* 40 (2002): 404–15.

41. Margret Brady, "The Fine Art of Selling Culture: Aboriginal Tourism," *National Post*, August 27, 2001, p. 16.

42. Edwin McDowell, "Aussies Tout Aboriginal Culture" *Times— Colonist*, February 12, 2000, Victoria, B.C., p. c3.

43. Heather Zeppel, "Maori Tourism Conference 'Te Putanga Mai,'" *Journal of Travel Research* 36, no. 2 (1997): 78–80.

44. See http://nkmipcentre.osoyoos.com.

45. Cheryl Petten, "Economic Development Meets Cultural Preservation in Project," *The Province*, September 11, 2001, Vancouver, B.C., p. C6.

46. Figures as yet unavailable.

47. see http://www.nkmipcellars.com/home.

48. John Schreiner, "Grape Expectations: Osoyoos Indian Band Thought to Have First Aboriginal Winery in North America," *National Post*, July 18, 2002, FP9.

49. http://www.nkmip.com/spirit.htm.

50. http://wakatu.org/.

51. http://www.tohuwines.co.nz/.

52. http://governance.tpk.govt.nz/share/tohuwines.aspx.

53. http://www.auckland.ac.nz/.

54. Quoted on http://wakatu.org/horticulture/.

# CHAPTER 12

## SOUTH AFRICA
### WINE, BLACK LABOR, AND
### BLACK EMPOWERMENT

*Gwyn Campbell*

## INTRODUCTION

In 1988, Nelson Mandela conducted a series of negotiations with the white government of South Africa from the Victor Verster Prison Farm in South Africa's wine-producing region near Paarl[1] that a few years later led to his own release, the fall of apartheid, and the inauguration of a fully-fledged, black-dominated democracy. However, Mandela also negotiated a deal whereby the new African National Congress (ANC) government renounced its intentions to nationalize industry and embraced capitalism and globalization. White-dominated business was urged to encourage black participation, but this has proved a slow and arduous process that was particularly strongly resisted in the rural sector. This was the case of South Africa's wine industry.

During the last decade of the apartheid regime, Mary Rayner wrote, "The habits of domination one associates with racial slavery in the eighteenth and nineteenth centuries are startlingly evident to a researcher visiting farms in the Western Cape in the 1980s. Despite the considerable capitalization of the region's agriculture . . . the labour system appears to be grounded in a combination of derisory wages, tied housing, chronic indebtedness, alcohol addiction, and social relationships marked by deference and racism."[2] Almost a decade later in 2005, following the dismantling of apartheid and the inauguration of an ANC government in 1994, the lifting of sanctions and an explosion in South African wine exports (wine production quadrupled between 1994 and 2004),[3] Tom Cannavan commented of South Africa's wine country: "The ugly townships still sprawl for mile after mile alongside major roads and motorways, signaling that poverty, and its spectral bedfellows of crime, disease and lack of education, are still acute problems for huge numbers of mostly black and coloured South Africans. Whole cities of corrugated iron shacks and basic government-provided shelters peter out within a few hundred yards of the five-star hotels and multi-million pound wine estates."[4] Most academic writing on labor issues in South Africa has focused on the industrial—notably the mining—sector, and in agriculture on the sugar plantations of Natal. This paper explores the history of black labor and of recent black empowerment on the wine farms of the Western Cape.

## BACKGROUND

Wine making in South Africa, concentrated in the Western Cape,[5] is closely associated with white colonists. Cape Town was settled in 1652, and the first grapes were pressed in 1659, making South Africa the first New World wine producer. Thirty years later, Huguenot refugees imported French grape-growing expertise from their homeland.[6] However, the industry was initially afflicted by a lack of labor and domestic and foreign markets so restricted that the government curbed production to avoid wine gluts.[7]

From the end of the seventeenth century, the wine industry expanded rapidly largely due to the influx of imported slave labor, and a small but significant export market, chiefly passing ships (provisions) and European trading settlements in the East.[8] The majority of slaves working on wine farms originated from Indonesia, India, and Madagascar until the 1780s, the time of the first peak in the wine industry, when slave imports from India and Indonesia dropped, and African slave imports—notably from Mozambique—increased substantially.[9] The vast majority of wine farms were white-owned, although there were some exceptions. For example, in the early eighteenth century, Louis van Bengaal—a "free black"—owned the Lanzerac Vineyard.[10]

The rhythm of work on the wine farms was, as with other agricultural work, highly seasonal. During the winter and early spring (June to August) the vines were pruned—a specialist task; in August and September, the ground was dug, cleared of weeds and stones, and planted with new vine shoots; from September to February, the vineyards were weeded and guarded against birds and other pests—a task traditionally allotted to children; and from February to March the grapes were harvested and pressed, and the wine bottled and stored.[11] Work in the fields necessitated constant bending for adults, leading to premature ageing and physical deformation.[12] Slaves filled a variety of roles, from menial farm labor, domestic service, and cooking, to craft work (smiths, carpenters, and coopers), the skilled activities of distillers and vintners, and overseers.[13] Workers were often given daily rations of "dop beer" made from the husks of pressed grapes and water—the so-called "dop system"—that encouraged addiction and later formed a core element of worker wages.[14]

In off-peak seasons, winegrowers hired their slaves to grain farmers, notably from April to June when oats, rye, barley, and wheat were sown, and November to late December when the grain crops were harvested.[15] It was probably during these periods when adult workers were away that slave children assumed most wine farm tasks. The workload was heavy and mortality high. In 1826, one wine farmer complained that of some sixty to seventy slaves he had amassed a decade earlier, twenty "young and old" had died of causes other than accidents and epidemic disease.[16] Some slaves sought to escape the work regime through flight: in 1834, in the wine-farming sub-district of Stellenbosch, 1.3 percent of all slaves had run away. However, with little prospect of finding a safe haven, most slaves remained on the farms, to which the majority of fugitive slaves also returned.[17]

Following their takeover of the Cape in 1806, the British suppressed the slave trade, which boosted the value of slave labor. However, they simultaneously encouraged commercial wine farming through promoting exports. In 1813, tariffs on the import of Cape wines into Britain were reduced to a third of that imposed on Portuguese and Spanish wines.[18] As a result, the wine sector entered its second phase of prosperity. Wine output jumped by 151 percent, and by 1823, wine comprised 72 percent by value of all exports (those to Britain more than doubled between 1813 and 1824).[19] In 1817 alone, 1,621 tuns (1 tun = approximately 954 liters) of wine left the Cape, whereas in the eighteenth century annual wine exports were often less than a tun.[20] Moreover, greater care was taken to produce quality wines than in the eighteenth century, when Cape wines had a generally poor reputation.[21]

In the absence of technological innovation and a good transport system, increased wine production was achieved on the backs of slaves.[22] Some 80 percent of slaves lived in the Western Cape where wine farmers each owned an average of sixteen slaves, double the number owned by three quarters of slave-owners.[23] Slaves formed an important part of the collateral upon which farmers could raise bank finance. For instance, in 1823, about 18 per cent of Cape wine-growers' mortgages comprised slaves,[24] while the following year Charles Henry Somerset, governor of Cape Colony from 1814–26, stated that slaves "are the only property of value in this colony; land is of none in comparison."[25]

Although total slave numbers remained largely static because of negligible natural increase (0.8 percent), the slave population on wine farms in the Stellenbosch and Cape districts increased by 18 percent between 1814 and 1823. However, the number of adult male slaves increased by only 4 percent, compared to 55 percent for adult females, 44 percent for slave girls, and 19 percent for slave boys—reflecting the importance of child labor in the wine industry.[26]

The wine boom did not last long. In 1825 and again in 1831, the differential between duties paid by Cape wines and other wines entering the British market narrowed, plunging South African wine farmers into a crisis of overproduction that made access to cheap labor even more vital.[27] The overall stagnation of the slave population and the abolition of slavery in 1834—before abolition elsewhere in the British Empire in 1837—pushed the colonial government into attempting to find alternative supplies of cheap labor.[28]

Fresh sources of labor were initially sought well before abolition from "Prize Negroes"—slaves seized aboard ships by British anti-slave trade squadrons, landed at the Cape, and forced to work off 14-year indentures. The total number landed after 1808 amounted to 2,100, but relatively few were assigned to wine farms: in 1823, 54 (36 were men) worked on Stellenbosch wine estates and 116 on Cape wine estates.[29] Farmers generally treated the Prize Negroes as slaves, and there were numerous cases of ill treatment. Some Prize Negroes reacted by trying to escape, while most—at least in the first years—followed the example of slaves in adopting Islam, which according to Christopher Saunders, offered them "membership of new socio-economic networks and a belief-system which gave them a new sense of self-worth."[30] It appears that conditions for Prize Negroes improved in the 1820s due to more lenient legislation; and most later Prize Negro arrivals adopted Christianity rather than Islam.[31] From the late 1820s, with the end of their apprenticeship, they gained freedom, intermarried into the free black and ex-slave population, and gradually became an indistinguishable part of the ensuing "colored" population.[32]

The state also enforced on the indigenous Khoi and San the 1809 Pass Law, restricting their geographical mobility, and the 1812 and 1817 legislation obliging Khoi and San children born to workers on settler farms to become apprentices on those farms until they reached the age of eighteen.[33] From 1828, this system was maintained on a "voluntary" basis and, for male children, was in 1836 extended to the age of twenty-one years.[34] The commercial opportunities offered by grape growing, in one case at least, enabled a bonded laborer to gain his freedom. In the 1830s, Adam, an apprentice of a Uitenhage farmer, accumulated sufficient funds to purchase his liberty by selling the produce—including grapes from a small vineyard he started—from the plot his master had given him.[35]

Nevertheless, Prize Negroes, Khoi, and San formed a small minority of the wine workforce. Thus, the authorities also stipulated that all emancipated slaves continue to serve their former masters as "apprentices" until 1838.[36] Farmers then seized the opportunity to rid themselves of old, infirm, or difficult ex-slaves.[37] However, they were surprised when many former slaves—notably women—also profited from their newly acquired liberty, left their masters, and migrated to the towns, to remote areas to farm independently, or to settle on government land. By 1848, an estimated six thousand of the twenty-five thousand former slaves in the Western Cape had migrated to mission stations, and an additional one thousand had settled on public land.[38]

The post-1838 exodus of workers, combined with smallpox and measles epidemics in 1839–40,[39] caused a labor shortage on farms that forced up the mean cash wage of agricultural workers in the Western Cape from ten to fifteen shillings a month in the 1840s. To attract labor, farmers also increasingly rented plots of farmland to workers, and "dop" rations were increased.[40] Farmers also agitated successfully for restraints on worker movement, and for a disciplinary code. The Masters and Servants Ordinance of 1841 enabled employers to extend oral contracts from one month to one year, and written contracts from one to three years.[41] In some cases, farmers established retail shops on their farms, which extended credit designed to indebt workers and thus tie them to the workplace.[42]

These measures proved largely insufficient and labor shortages undermined the industry at precisely the time that wine production recovered spectacularly from a major slump in the early and mid 1830s. From 1838–41, more wine was pressed than in any other four-year period between 1806 and 1855. However, as the production of quality wine required heavy inputs of labor—which was lacking—the result was poor quality wine, used chiefly for brandy.[43] Wine exports continued to fall: those to Britain fell from a peak of about 5,500 leggers per annum in the late 1820s, to 3,500 leggers by the early 1830s (in 1831 the tariff differential between continental European and Cape Colony wine imports was reduced), to 3,365 leggers by 1840–44.[44] In consequence, vine land values also fell— sometimes by up to 46 percent—pushing a number of wine farmers into bankruptcy.[45] From the 1840s, wool succeeded wine as the Cape's major export, a trend accentuated from 1860 when imperial preference for Cape wines was abolished and Cape wine exports to Britain collapsed,[46] a calamity seemingly symbolized by the 1865 shipwreck of the steamship *Kadie* that transported wine from the Overberg region to the Cape.[47]

Nevertheless, the domestic, notably Cape Town, market for wine expanded and grape growing remained the most important economic activity in the southwestern Cape. Indeed, the number of vines in the Western Cape increased from 13 million in 1819 to 55.3 million in 1865 to 69.9 million in 1875.[48] The districts of Paarl and Stellenbosch were particularly dependent on wine farming.[49] Production remained heavily labor-intensive compared to grain production, which became steadily more mechanized.[50] By 1880, about one-third of the economically active population of the Western Cape was involved, directly or indirectly, in wine farming[51]—a figure that excludes the seasonal and largely unremunerated labor of the wives and children of adult male farm workers.[52]

Despite the *Masters and Servants Act* (1856) designed to tie workers to the land, the discovery of alluvial diamonds on the Vaal

River in the late 1860s, and the expansion of other sectors of the Cape economy, resulted in a continued labor exodus from the wine farms—which competed with one another and with wheat farms, for labor.[53] Indeed, conditions were so favorable to workers that an "explosion" in small commercial black farming activity occurred in the 1870s.[54] Moreover, while the meteoric rise of Kimberley, diamond exports, and subsequently gold discoveries and exploitation on the Rand protected some sectors of the Cape economy against the international depression of the 1880s, wine farmers faced competition in the domestic market from both foreign imports (following the 1878 excise) and Transvaal brandy distillers.[55] In 1887, work was started on a railway line (Worcester to Roodewal) intended to facilitate the export of wine and fruit, but *Phylloxera* hit in 1886, and the railway company went bankrupt in 1892.[56]

The government assisted farmers affected by *Phylloxera* with monetary compensation, the provision of American and grafted vines to replace infected vines, and regulatory inspections.[57] However, this had little effect on the recession in the wine sector that, with brief interludes of prosperity (as from 1894–1903), lasted until the 1920s.[58]

In consequence, wine farmers continued to squeeze their labor force in a desperate attempt to avoid bankruptcy. One important consequence of this was the maintenance of the "dop" system and imbedded alcoholism among "colored" farm workers.[59] Another was the emergence of Afrikaner nationalism among the wheat and wine farmers of the Western Cape between 1870 and 1915. This, Hermann Giliomee argues, arose less in response to events in the Transvaal than to the widening rift between two Western Cape factions: the British merchant class in Cape Town, which promoted economic liberalism, cheap imports of foodstuffs and beverages, and limited political representation for blacks; and Afrikaner-speaking farmers who advocated protectionism, guaranteed access to cheap black labor, white supremacy, and the promotion of the "Afrikaner" language and culture.[60] One result was the founding of the Afrikaner Bond which agitated for a clear distinction between the descendants on the one hand of slaves, and on the other hand of the slaveholding class. It pushed for the exclusion of "coloreds" from education, land-ownership and squatting, and the franchise in order to create a cheap pool of subservient labor.[61] As P. D. Hahn declared in 1883, "There is a feeling, which you will generally find prevailing among all farmers: they do not like to see anyone else occupying their lands and deriving profit therefrom. They think that on their lands there should be only two classes, 'Baas,' that is, themselves, and the others, servants."[62] British aggression against the Boer Republics in 1877, 1895, and especially in the war of 1899–1902 helped cement Afrikaner nationalism in the Western Cape. However, the wine farmers' immediate concerns were access to cheap credit and labor, and a protected market for their wine.[63] Following Union in 1910, farmers started to mobilize Afrikaner capital in the form of rural financial institutions, but speculative bubbles and bankruptcies continued to characterize the industry.[64] More important was the political influence of wine farmers, notably on the National Party, founded in 1914, that outflanked its Afrikaner rival, the South African Party, through concentrating on protectionism for farmers.[65]

From 1910 to 1935, eighty-seven Acts were passed by the Union parliament offering permanent assistance to farmers.[66] However, a durable recovery for the Cape wine sector only came following political victory for the National Party in 1924 under J. B. M. Hertzog. The new government immediately approved subsidies to wine farmers and support for the Cooperative Wine Farmers' Association of South Africa (Koöperatiewe Wynbouers-Vereniging [KWV]), a cartel formed in 1918 to regulate output and fix prices. Exports were few and largely restricted to grapes,[67] but the KWV, to which most wine farmers sold their grapes, dominated the industry and the domestic market until 1997.[68] The government promoted wine exports further through the Land and Agricultural Bank (established in 1912), specifically to channel loans to farmers and cooperatives, and—in the 1930s—a wine control board that was maintained throughout the post–World War II era to restrict imports, fix minimum prices, guarantee (often through subsidies) the disposal of all output, and maintain quality.[69]

The Hertzog government also took firm action to control labor. The *Native Land Act* (1913) prevented black land purchases and the *Native Urban Areas Act* (1923) declared urban areas to be "white," and forced all black African men in those areas to carry passes. Those found without a pass were arrested and sent to a rural area. The *Colour Bar Act* (1926) further undermined choices for black labor by restricting skilled positions in the Transvaal mines to Europeans.[70] In 1930, the government boosted the white electorate (which already constituted over 90 percent of the total electorate) at the expense of the "coloreds" through extending the franchise to white but not to "colored" women. At the same time, however, it sought to woo "colored" men through promising to extend the "colored" male franchise to other provinces (where only whites had the vote) and thus undermine attempts from "black" unionists to recruit "colored" workers.[71]

Government backing and economic recovery also led to the re-establishment of traditional labor relations, and black vineyard workers became effectively the first fully landless, proletarianized rural workers in South Africa; in most other rural sectors, share-cropping and labor tenancy persisted until recently.[72] Wine farm labor became intimately bound up in the Afrikaner paternalist nexus, characterized by extreme subservience of "colored" workers to the white farm owner.[73] In 1928, Raymond Buell wrote that "Those natives living on European farms are without the protection of government inspection, and their condition approximates that of serfs."[74] As Andries du Toit noted:

> every aspect of life is bound up with the world inside the wit hekke (white gates). Agricultural workers depend on the farm for every aspect of their material survival: money, housing, water, electricity— often even food and drink. To lose your job, in Western Cape farming, is to lose your home. . . . This relationship in fact brought some advantages for workers: it institutionalised farmers' obligations, and probably lessened the degree of naked exploitation and brutality that existed. But it also brought dependence and vulnerability. Farmers control almost every aspect of farm life, from movement on the farm to the labour power of male workers' wives and children.[75]

The paternalist-dependency nexus was so enclosed that trade unionists failed to make the slightest impression on farm workers.[76] The wine farming interest also fought against a strong prohibitionist movement that emerged in the Cape from the end of the nineteenth century and which crystallized around the "dop" system.[77]

Apartheid from 1948 codified racialist policies based on a hierarchy dominated by whites, in which people classified as "coloreds" were treated more favorably than those classified as "blacks." Thus, whereas the KWV possessed a few black members in its initial years, they were, under apartheid, excluded.[78] The prevalent white pretext for such exclusion was that Africans were bound in a static traditional economy, dominated by primitive social structures and religious values that

blocked the emergence of individual entrepreneurship, private ownership of property, and the profit motive. In the mind of the
apartheid state, rural black communities, including those working
on wine farms, were considered to have maintained a "traditional
self-sufficiency."

This viewpoint justified the payment of sub-standard wages to
black workers, thus helping to keep costs of production down and
profits up.[79] Further, white wine farmers tied "colored" workers and
their families to their farms through payments redeemable in company stores—which frequently resulted in worker indebtedness—
and through alcoholism (farmers continued to "give" wine to
workers even after the "dop" system became illegal in 1962).[80] This
ensured not only cheap adult male labor, but also continued access
to adult female and child labor during the peak periods in the agricultural year. As ever, the small size and nimble fingers of children
were particularly valued in grape picking.[81] Indeed, Susan Levine
considers that child labor, while largely unrecognized, is still central
rather than peripheral to the wine industry, is at most poorly paid,
and is often unremunerated.[82]

## BLACK EMPOWERMENT

Despite some domestic advantages, the overall costs of apartheid for
the wine industry were large. First, on the international stage, South
Africa became a pariah increasingly subject to boycotts that undermined its position in foreign wine markets. Moreover, by the time
export restrictions were lifted in the mid-1990s, it found itself pitted
against technically more advanced and market-savvy newcomers,
such as Australia and Chile. Second, apartheid policies denied the
industry the resources of the majority of its employees; blacks
were critically under-trained and denied entrepreneurial opportunities. Moreover, reliance on cheap labor to generate profits agitated against the capital investment and R&D (Research and
Development) required to be internationally competitive. In adopting liberal economic policies that reduced central subsidies to farmers, and by introducing minimum wages, the new ANC-led
government encouraged white farmers to cut back on their permanent work force and increase the labor of seasonally employed workers. Thus, the huge post-apartheid increase in wine production from

38.9 million liters in 1994 to 153.4 million liters in 2004 was largely due to labor-intensive methods.[83] At the same time, the dismantling of the "homelands" has led to a considerable migration of blacks into the Western Cape, where they have in many cases competed successfully against "coloreds"— who comprise some 60 percent of the population of the Western Cape—for skilled jobs in the wineries. By contrast, "coloreds" form the vast majority of field workers.[84]

White-dominated economic sectors proved hesitant and sometimes openly hostile to change, pushing the government to formalize its black economic empowerment policy. The mining sector—the core of the economy—was the first to be targeted: mining firms must ensure that 15 percent of their equity is black owned by 2009, with a further boost to 26 percent by 2014.[85]

For rural sectors, the government pledged to redistribute 30 percent of the country's agricultural land by 2014,[86] and in 1997 to replace the Wine Board by the National Agricultural Marketing Council in order to promote small-scale producers. Additional pressure on white farmers has come from the Black Association of the Wine and Spirit Industry (BAWSI), formed in 1998, whose members are drawn from trade unions, civil and social organizations, and black businessmen in the wine sector. Its aim is twofold: firstly, to make the Wine and Spirit Industry fully representative at all levels, and secondly, to enable black South Africans to become farmers and farm owners in their own right: "We, the members of Bawsi, declare for all to know: That the Wine and Spirit Industry is owned and managed by whites. That people of colour had been deliberately excluded from participation as capitalists in the industry, but to participate as exploited workers. That formal and/or technical skills are primarily vested in whites and that the industry is managed by whites . . . We pledge ourselves as members of Bawsi to strive together, sparing nothing of our strength and courage, until the changes for transformation as set out below have been achieved."[87]

Some white winemakers adapted to government pressure relatively swiftly. Thus, at Fairview estate in Paarl, the owner Charles Back had allowed black workers to buy some of the land, and by 2000 they were making and selling their own labels internationally.[88] Other blacks entered the wine industry as vintners. In 2001, Mzokhona Mvemve became South Africa's first black winemaker at Cape Classics, and by 2004, he was appointed manager of the Indaba vineyard, deciding how and when to harvest the grapes, and controlling the winemaking process through to the finished product.[89] Since then, other blacks have gained oenology degrees at Stellenbosch University and have entered the wine industry, including Nontsike Biyela, the first black woman oenology graduate, and South Africa's first black female winemaker, who in 2004 started work at the boutique Stellekaya Cellars (founded in 1999).[90] She has since nurtured to perfection four prize-winning wines. [91]

However, Cape Classics is an odd man out in an industry dominated by whites as an import company cofounded by Jabulani Ntshangase, a black South African wine wholesale distributor in New York, and Andre Shearer, a white South African who is devoted solely to high quality South African wines.[92] Indeed, overall, voluntary measures were piecemeal and too limited to satisfy black aspirations, and in 2003, the government introduced Black Economic Empowerment (BEE) legislation.[93] Also in 2003, BAWSI formed its own black economic empowerment company, Bawsi-i, to facilitate substantial black investment and ownership, and target the participation of historically disadvantaged people at all levels in the wine industry.[94]

Most BEE projects comprise joint ventures into which black wine-farm workers buy using the money given by the government ($3,080 per person) to enable them to purchase farmland. It is only through forming groups of fifty to one hundred people and pooling this money that black workers are able to purchase a share of farmland—which is rapidly increasing in value.[95] At the end of 2003, 30 percent of Boschendal estate was transferred to a BEE consortium in a deal valued at R323 million, [96] while in July 2004 Phetogo Investments, a black empowerment consortium, acquired a 25.1 percent stake in KWV, which had controlled the South African wine industry for almost a century.[97]

By the end of 2004, only 5.51 percent of South African wine grape producers were engaged in BEE shareholding schemes; 5 percent had introduced profit-sharing programs for their workers; and some 13 percent claimed that their employees participated in strategic and policy decision-making.[98] By the end of 2005, the Black Vintners Alliance embraced over twenty black-owned vineyards.[99] Moreover, in 2006, after two years of negotiations pressed by the government, the wine sector as a whole adopted a BEE charter with the target of 10 percent black ownership of land by 2014.[100] The BEE initiative has been backed by the 2005 decision by the South

African Wine Industry Council (which in 2003 replaced the South African Wine and Brandy Company) to include on its advisory forum—in order to accelerate transformation in the wine industry—representatives from labor (SALBA), farm workers (VinPro), Wine Cellars of South Africa, the South African Wine Industry Trust (SAWIT), BAWSI, NAFU, and the Rural Development Network.[101]

The charter was a major success given embedded white-farmer fear of BAWSI ambitions, which they considered would lead to a transfer of their land into black hands.[102] Indeed, Charles Erasmus, chief executive of the South African Wine Industry Trust (SAWIT), recognized the moral, political, and economic imperatives for black empowerment: "We need to get the industry to understand that it also makes good business sense. BEE is not simply about giving away land, but about enlarging the economic cake to include others as well. If white farmers were to give shares in their businesses to black workers, all will benefit at the end of the day."[103]

## CONCLUSION: THE FUTURE FOR THE SOUTH AFRICAN WINE INDUSTRY

Currently, South Africa has 4,360 primary wine grape producers and 581 wine cellars, of which 51 percent crush 100 tons of grapes or less a year, and which produce over 5,000 different labels.[104] However, whereas under 10 percent of South Africa's 44 million population is white, in the winemaking sector—the world's eighth largest producer of wine, brandy, and grape juice concentrate (1 billion liters)[105]—less than 1 percent of the 257,000 people employed in any way own, manage, or control aspects of that industry.[106] Moreover, Erasmus doubts that the wine industry's target of 10 percent black ownership of land by 2014 can be met, due to the lack of black management skills and inability of blacks to access the funds necessary to survive in a capital intensive industry.[107] These were major factors in the failure of Phetogo, which collapsed after Sawit called in its R135 million loan to the consortium.[108]

Nevertheless, some joint-partnerships with majority black-worker ownership have succeeded, despite the odds. One of these is the Bouwland partnership trust between renowned vintner Beyers Truter, and Jan Hendriks—founder of the Stellenbosch Farm Workers Association—on the one hand, and on the other hand, sixty black workers, half of them female, representing some forty families who own a 76 percent majority share paid for out of land redistribution payments. The venture, started in 2003, raised a ten million rand bank loan. Just breaking even because of repayments to the bank, it aims to quickly become a profit-making enterprise through increasing output from its fifty-six hectares of vineyards outside Stellenbosch from 12,750 liters in 2006 to 225,000 liters per annum by 2014. Its major long-term difficulty is not so much climate—2004, for example, was a drought year—or loan repayments at high interest rates, as a total dependence on white know-how and equipment.[109]

However, schemes are being launched to provide the necessary skill and capital to transform the industry. In 2004, Cape Classic established the Indaba Scholarship to help black South Africans study areas of the wine industry,[110] while agreements were signed— in 2001 with France[111] and in 2006 with the United States—to send black South African viticultural students overseas to "develop skills and create a new class of owners and entrepreneurs in South Africa's wine industry."[112]

There are also aims to generate finance for black wine enterprises in the United States,[113] although a recent deal has demonstrated that probably the best way to provide for successful black empowerment in wine businesses is through the raising of finance locally. In a 2006 joint venture between black workers and white owners, Solms-Delta, Lübeck, and Deltameer—three Western Cape wine farms in Franschhoek covering seventy-six hectares—was transferred to over two hundred people in twenty-two worker families, making them owners "after generations of tilling vineyards on which they had no claim."[114] Financial services group Investec funded the Deltameer acquisition—for which Solms-Delta and Lübeck provided the necessary collateral—and provided development capital for upgrading. The initiative raised the value of the assets in the joint venture to R62-million with R23-million in liquid capital. The farm workers' Wijn de Caab Trust is sustained by a profit share in Solms-Delta, formerly owned by Mark Solms and Richard Astor, who remain directors of the trust. It will purchase the active portion of Deltameer from Solms and Astor either via grant funding or bank financing, with any loan repaid through profits.[115]

Another new factor is the virtually untapped domestic black market (blacks traditionally drink beer). Potential domestic black demand for wine is increasingly important, given the ferocity of global competition and the fact that in 2006 for the first time since the fall of apartheid (the volume of wine exported rose from 22 million liters in 1992 to 282 million liters in 2005), wine exports fell in 2006 by about 5 percent.[116] Thus, Andrew Moth, editor of the South African trade guide *Hotel & Restaurant*, highlights as the number one characteristic of the performance in 2006, that domestic wine consumption had fallen for the fourth consecutive year and that recovery depended on new brand growth in the black market where wine is perceived as a "highly aspirational category."[117] It is in response to this need to re-orientate market aims that *Wines of South Africa*, the industry's international marketing arm, has been given the mandate to promote wine as a lifestyle product on the local market.[118] Should black South Africans be persuaded to switch from beer to wine, the future of the South African wine industry would be assured.

## NOTES

1. Scott Macleod, "South Africa Meeting of Different Minds," *Time Magazine*, December 25, 1989, http://www.time.com/time/magazine/article/0,9171,959432,00.html.
2. Mary Isabel Rayner, "Wine and Slaves: The Failure of an Export Economy and the Ending of Slavery in Cape Colony, South Africa, 1805–1834," PhD dissertation, Duke University, 1986, p. 2.
3. William G. Moseley, "Post-Apartheid Vineyards," *Dollars & Sense*, January/February 2006, p. 16.
4. Tom Cannavan, "South African Update, Part I," May 8, 2005, http://wine-pages.com/features/sa2005.htm.
5. Currently over 90 percent of wine grapes in South Africa are grown in the Western Cape; see Gavin Williams, "Black Economic Empowerment in the South African Wine Industry," *Journal of Agrarian Change* 5, no. 4 (2005): 477.
6. Susan Levine, "In the Shadow of the Vine: Child Labor in Post Apartheid South Africa" PhD dissertation, Temple University, 2000, p. 78; Jamie Robertson, "Black Vintners Face Challenges in SA," BBC News, October 9, 2006, http://news.bbc.co.uk/2/hi/business/6035711.stm.
7. P. L. Wickins, "Agriculture," in *Economic History of South Africa*, ed. F. L. Coleman (Pretoria: HAUM, 1983), 52, 54.
8. Rayner, "Wine and Slaves," 4, 36; Timothy Keegan, "The Dynamics of Rural Accumulation in South Africa: Comparative and Historical

Perspectives," *Comparative Studies in Society and History* 28, no. 4 (1986): 631; Maurice Boucher, *The Cape of Good Hope and Foreign Contacts 1735–1755* (Pretoria: University of South Africa, 1985), 59, 95.

9. Rayner, "Wine and Slaves," 61–66; see also John Iliffe, "The South African Economy, 1652–1997," *Economic History Review* LII, no. 1 (1999): 88.

10. Williams, "Black Economic Empowerment," 481.

11. Rayner, "Wine and Slaves," 68.

12. Ibid., 68–69.

13. John Edwin Mason, "Fortunate Slaves and Artful Masters: Labor Relations in the Rural Cape Colony During the Era of Emancipation, ca. 1825 to 1838" in *Slavery in South Africa. Captive Labor on the Dutch Frontier*, eds. Elizabeth A. Eldredge and Fred Morton (Boulder: Westview, and Pietermaritzburg: Univesity of Natal Press, 1994), 73–74.

14. Rayner, "Wine and Slaves," 17–18.

15. Ibid., 69.

16. Pieter Cloete, quoted in Rayner, "Wine and Slaves," 70–71.

17. Mason, "Fortunate Slaves and Artful Masters," 74–75.

18. Wickins, "Agriculture," 65.

19. Susanne Newton-King, "The Labour Market of the Cape Colony, 1807–28" in *Economy and Society in Pre-Industrial South Africa*, eds. Shula Marks and Anthony Atmore (Harlow, Essex: Longman, 1985), 173; Rayner, "Wine and Slaves," 4; Wickins, "Agriculture," 65.

20. C. W. de Kiewiet, *A History of South Africa, Social & Economic* (London: Oxford University Press, 1957), 36.

21. Boucher, *Cape of Good Hope*, 41.

22. Rayner, "Wine and Slaves," 66–67; V. E. Solomon, "Transport," in Coleman, ed., *Economic History of South Africa*, 95–96.

23. Rayner, "Wine and Slaves," 4.

24. Ibid., 35–36.

25. Somerset to the Colonial Office, February 1, 1824, quoted in R. L. Watson, *The Slave Question. Liberty and Property in South Africa* (Johannesburg: Witwatersrand University Press, 1991), 17.

26. Rayner, "Wine and Slaves," 4, 37–42, 59.

27. Wickins, "Agriculture," 65; de Kiewiet, *History of South Africa*, 38.

28. Slave owners had received compensation in 1834, but not at market values: e.g. for an emancipated field worker, the sum paid out averaged just over £54, whereas the market value of such a slave averaged almost £133. In total, some £1.25 million in compensation flowed to the Cape; see Rayner, "Wine and Slaves," 4, 37–42; Wayne Dooling, "The Decline of the Cape Gentry, 1838–c.1900," *Journal of African History* 40 (1999): 223, 225.

29. Christopher Saunders, "'Free, Yet Slaves.' Prize Negroes at the Cape Revisited," in *Breaking the Chains. Slavery and its Legacy in the Nineteenth-Century Cape Colony*, eds. Nigel Worden and Clifton Crais (Johannesburg: Witwatersrand University Press, 1994), 110; Rayner, "Wine and Slaves," 51–56.

30. Saunders, "'Free, Yet Slaves,'" 113; see also ibid., 110–12.

31. Ibid., 114–15.

32. Ibid., 115.

33. Rayner, "Wine and Slaves," 56–58.

34. Nigel Worden, "Between Slavery & Freedom. The Apprenticeship Period, 1834 to 1838" in Worden and Crais, eds., *Breaking the Chains*, 122.

35. Mason, "Fortunate Slaves and Artful Masters," 81.

36. Ibid., 67.

37. Worden, "Between Slavery & Freedom," 143; "The Liberal Cape," http://www.anc.org.za/books/ccsa01.html.

38. Dooling, "Decline of the Cape Gentry," 220–21.

39. "The Liberal Cape."

40. Robert Ross, "Pre-Industrial and Industrial Racial Stratification in South Africa, "https://www.openaccess.leidenuniv.nl/bitstream/1887/4213/1/1246876_037.pdf; Dooling, "Decline of the Cape Gentry," 222.

41. Ross, "Pre-Industrial and Industrial Racial Stratification in South Africa"; "The Liberal Cape."

42. Dooling, "Decline of the Cape Gentry," 222.

43. Robert Ross, "'Rather Mental than Physical' Emancipations & the Cape Economy" in Worden and Crais, eds., *Breaking the Chains*, 153–54.

44. Ibid., 159.

45. Dooling, "Decline of the Cape Gentry," 225–26.

46. Wickins, "Agriculture," 65; Ross, "'Rather Mental than Physical,'" 159; Hermann Giliomee, "Western Cape Farmers and the Beginnings of Afrikaner Nationalism, 1870–1915," *Journal of Southern African Studies* 14, no. 1 (1987): 39.

47. Solomon, "Transport," 123.

48. Wickins, "Agriculture," 65; Ross, "'Rather Mental than Physical,'" 159; Giliomee, "Western Cape Farmers," 39.

49. Giliomee, "Western Cape Farmers," 40.

50. Dooling, "Decline of the Cape Gentry," 228–33.

51. Giliomee, "Western Cape Farmers," 39.

52. Ibid., 40.

53. Pamela Scully, "Criminality and Conflict in Rural Stellenbosch, South Africa, 1870–1900," *Journal of African History* 30 (1989): 289–91, 293.

54. David J. Webster, "The Political Economy of Food Production and Nutrition in Southern Africa in Historical perspective," *Journal of Modern African Studies* 24, no. 3 (1986): 455.

55. Giliomee, "Western Cape Farmers," 46; Scully, "Criminality and Conflict," 289–90.

56. Rayner, "Wine and Slaves," 3–4; Wickins, "Agriculture," 66; Solomon, "Transport," 110.

57. Giliomee, "Western Cape Farmers," 47.

58. Scully, "Criminality and Conflict," 289–90; Giliomee, "Western Cape Farmers," 46, 53.

59. Stanley Trapido, "'The Friends of the Natives': Merchants, Peasants and the Political and Ideological Structure of Liberalism in the Cape, 1854–1910" in Marks and Atmore, eds., *Economy and Society*, 266.

60. Giliomee, "Western Cape Farmers," 38, 41–44, 46.

61. Ibid., 44–45.

62. P. D. Hahn, *Select Committee on Colonial Agriculture and Industries, 1883*, quoted in Giliomee, "Western Cape Farmers," 47.

63. Giliomee, "Western Cape Farmers," 48.

64. Ibid., 49–58.

65. Ibid., 61–62.

66. De Kiewiet, *History of South Africa*, 253.

67. Wickins, "Agriculture," 66.

68. Williams, "Black Economic Empowerment," 478, 481–82.

69. Wickins, "Agriculture," 80–81.

70. Raymond Leslie Buell, "Black and White in South Africa," *Annals of the American Academy of Political and Social Science* 140 (1928): 300–301.

71. Jeremy Creighton Martens, "Conflicting Views of 'Coloured' People in the South African Liquor Bill Debate of 1928," *Canadian Journal of African Studies* 35, no. 2 (2001): 331–32; Buell, "Black and White in South Africa," 301–4.

72. Andries Du Toit, "The Micro-Politics of Paternalism: The Discourses of Management and Resistance on South African Fruit and Wine Farms," *Journal of Southern African Studies* 19, no. 2 (1993): 315.

73. Andries Bernadus Du Toit, "Paternalism and Modernity on South African Wine and Fruit Farms: An Analysis of Paternalist Constructions of Community and Authority in the Discourse of Coloured Farm Workers in the Stellenbosch Region," PhD dissertation, University of Essex, 1996.

74. Buell, "Black and White in South Africa," 302.

75. Andries Du Toit, "The Micro-Politics of Paternalism: The Discourses of Management and Resistance on South African Fruit and Wine Farms," *Journal of Southern African Studies* 19, no. 2 (1993): 315–36.

76. Andries Du Toit, "The Micro-Politics of Paternalism: The Discourses of Management and Resistance on South African Fruit and Wine Farms," *Journal of Southern African Studies* 19, no. 2 (1993): 316.
77. Martens, "Conflicting Views," 317–27.
78. Williams, "Black Economic Empowerment," 481.
79. Keegan, "Dynamics of Rural Accumulation," 628–50.
80. Williams, "Black Economic Empowerment," 481; Levine, "In the Shadow of the Vine," 110–11, 132; Moseley, "Post-Apartheid Vineyards," 17
81. Levine, "In the Shadow of the Vine," 134; Moseley, "Post-Apartheid Vineyards," 17.
82. Levine, "In the Shadow of the Vine."
83. Williams, "Black Economic Empowerment," 479; Moseley, "Post-Apartheid Vineyards," 17–18.
84. Levine, "In the Shadow of the Vine," 79–80; see also Moseley, "Post-Apartheid Vineyards," 17.
85. Shola Olowu, "South Africa Encourages Black Vintners," BBC News, May 6, 2004, http://news.bbc.co.uk/1/hi/business/3687615.stm.
86. Moseley, "Post-Apartheid Vineyards," 16.
87. BAWSI, "Transformation of the Wine Industry."
88. http://archives.cnn.com/2000/FOOD/news/04/21/south.africa.wine/index.html.
89. Olowu, "South Africa Encourages Black Vintners."
90. Tom Cannavan, "South African Update, Parts I and II," May 8, 2005, http://wine-pages.com/features/sa2005.htm.
91. Cannavan, "South African Update, Part I."
92. Eunice Fried, "The Great Wines of Southern Africa: Now that the Embargo is Lifted, South African Wines are Making a Strong Comeback," *Black Enterprise*, May 1995, http://www.findarticles.com/p/articles/mi_m1365/is_n10_v25/ai_16827588.
93. Robertson, "Black Vintners Face Challenges in SA."
94. BAWSI, "Transformation of the Wine Industry."
95. Moseley, "Post-Apartheid Vineyards," 18.
96. Cannavan, "South African Update, Part I."
97. Williams, "Black Economic Empowerment," 476–504; Cannavan, "South African Update, Part I"; http://www.wosa.co.za/SA/bee.htm.
98. Cannavan, "South African Update, Part I."
99. Joshua Hammer, "Grapes of Power and Frustration; South African Blacks Get Into the Wine-making Biz," *Newsweek* 146, no. 19, November 7, 2005, p. 63.
100. Robertson, "Black Vintners Face Challenges in SA"; Olowu, "South Africa Encourages Black Vintners"; Cannavan, "South African Update, Part I."

101. Ronnie Morris, "Vineyards Make Inroads into Tight Global Market," *Business Report,* January 15, 2007, http://www.busrep.co.za/index .php?fSectionId=2515&fArticleId=3627315; "SAWIT Restructures SAWB—Makes Way for New Representative Wine Industry Muscle," http://www.sawit.co.za/news/news_articles_07.asp.
102. Cannavan, "South African Update, Part I."
103. Cannavan, "South African Update, Part I."
104. BAWSI, "Transformation of the Wine Industry"; Graham Howe, "The Premiumisation of Wine," February 5, 2007, http://www.wine .co.za/news/news.aspx?NEWSID=9660&Source=News; Morris, "Vineyards Make Inroads."
105. 2004 figures.
106. Moseley, "Post-Apartheid Vineyards," 18–19; Mariette le Roux, "Praise for S. Africa's First Black Woman Winemaker," *Middle East Times,* November 20, 2006, http://www.metimes.com/storyview .php?StoryID=20061120-065150-8549r; BAWSI, "Transformation of the Wine Industry"; Morris, "Vineyards Make Inroads."
107. Cannavan, "South African Update, Part I"; Robertson, "Black Vintners Face Challenges in SA."
108. Morris, "Vineyards Make Inroads."
109. Hammer, "Grapes of Power," 63; Moseley, "Post-Apartheid Vineyards," 16, 19–20; http://www.wine.co.za/directory/winery.aspx ?PRODUCERID=4296.
110. Olowu, "South Africa Encourages Black Vintners."
111. http://www.avenuevine.com/movabletype/archives/001815.html, September 12, 2006).
112. Judy Chambers, quoted in Carolee Walker, "South African Winemakers Apprentice in United States. U.S. wineries host interns in first exchange with South Africa," September 27, 2006, http://pretoria .usembassy.gov/wwwhpress060927.html.
113. Morris, "Vineyards make inroads."
114. Paula Wilson, spokesperson for the farms, quoted in "Wine Workers in Innovative BEE Deal," October 16, 2006, http://www.southafrica.info/ doing_business/businesstoday/empowerment/285485.htm.
115. "Wine Workers in Innovative BEE Deal," October 16, 2006, http:// www.southafrica.info/doing_business/businesstoday/empowerment/ 285485.htm.
116. De Kock Communications, "2006 A Tough Year for SA Wine Industry," January 1, 2007, http://www.wosa.co.za/news.aspx; Cassie du Plessis, "Excesses and shortages," *Wineland,* February 2007, http:// www.wineland.co.za/.
117. Howe, "Premiumisation of Wine."
118. Morris, "Vineyards make inroads."

# Chapter 13

## Wines of the Farthest Promised Land from Waipara, Canterbury, New Zealand[1]

### *Rupert Tipples*

*Antipode*, noun, masculine. Place on the earth's surface diametrically opposed to another. New Zealand is the antipode, at
the antipodes of France[2]

## Introduction

Since settled largely by Britons in the nineteenth century, New
Zealand has been economically dependent on its pastoral farming
exports. The need for export diversification was highlighted by the
United Kingdom's entry to the European Economic Community
(EEC) in 1972, when the former export markets were restricted by
EEC quotas and tariffs. Growing crops have formed an important
part of the subsequent diversification. Horticulture, New Zealand's
sixth largest primary industry, contributed $NZ2.1 billion in exports
in 2004.[3] Wine exports, as part of that, have grown almost tenfold

since 1995 to $NZ434.9 million in 2005, representing one percent of global wine exports. New Zealand's largest wine export market is the United Kingdom, worth $NZ162 million in 2005. Unlike Australia, which has focused on heavily discounted bulk sales to supermarkets, New Zealand exports are unique, niche quality wines that, in the UK, have the highest landed bottle price of all imported wines.[4]

This study examines the development of successful vineyards in the Canterbury region of the South Island. Vineyard developments in New Zealand were the product of small individual initiatives, compared to Australia where they were heavily influenced by public policy.[5] French settlers were the first to plant grapes in Canterbury—at Akaroa in 1840—for their own consumption.[6] Indeed, the first commercial vineyard in Canterbury was established as late as 1978, about twenty kilometers north of Christchurch. This chapter first explores the reasons for such a late development, and subsequently traces the modern development of grape growing and winemaking in Canterbury.

## EARLY DEVELOPMENTS

Romeo Bragato (1858–1913), Viticulturist to the Government of Victoria, Australia, visited New Zealand in 1895 to assess New Zealand's viticulture potential. He looked at existing vineyards, tasted their wines, and evaluated which were the appropriate areas where grapes might be grown for wine production. He reported that the Akaroa district of Canterbury was "splendidly suited to the cultivation of the vine," but warned that vineyards there were in decline:

> The wine industry (at Akaroa) prospered as long as those by whom it was started remained at the helm, but immediately they began to die off, the vineyards became neglected, and the vines died out. . . . It would seem that the pioneer French settlers of Akaroa failed to communicate to their offspring even a small percentage of that enthusiasm over the cultivation of the vine which they were in such large measure possessed of, or it may be their descendants suspended work by reason of the vines becoming attacked with *oidium*, thus causing the disappearance of vineyards which had been to their forebears as a bit of the fatherland.[7]

Bragato proposed a remedy for the situation: "If capitalists could be induced to invest some of their money, encouraged and assisted in their enterprise by the Government, they would undoubtedly be richly rewarded, and Akaroa acquire world-wide fame."[8]

The failure of a wine industry to develop at Akaroa may be attributed to both natural and human factors. First, despite a favorable environment, the vine was damaged extensively by birds and, from the 1870s, by *Oidium*. Also, the area was remote, far from the nearest market on the Canterbury plains. Moreover, the population of the plains was mainly of British ancestry, with a cultural tradition that favored beer over wine. In addition, the early French settlers—who had escaped poverty in France in the hope of a better life in the Antipodes—were not capitalists, and produced for home consumption rather than for the market.[9] Few had the background, capital, and entrepreneurial desire to establish a wine industry. Nor did they have many children to carry on winemaking after them.[10]

## Developments 1895 to 1973

Dalmatian immigration, which played a large part in the development of the New Zealand wine industry in the North Island, had no impact in Canterbury.[11] Moreover, the impact of the early French wine growers of Akaroa remained local and limited, while the government turned a deaf ear to Bragato's advice in 1895 that they invest in what he considered to be an industry of enormous potential. In a largely pastoral economy, new crops received little encouragement. In addition, the times were unfavorable for a new venture. The turn of the century was a period of national concern over the evils of drink, and the virtues of abstinence. Another factor was the place of wine as a drink in society. Fortified ports and sherries were most in demand. Even the more prosperous classes in New Zealand were uninterested in poor New Zealand wines. After World War II, attitudes to drink and familiarity with wine changed. Many returning servicemen had experienced wine while overseas. Attitudes to licensing became more relaxed, the number of sales outlets increased, demand expanded, and with the increase in travel after 1945 and the growth of tourism, the market for grapes and wine began to exhibit more possibilities.[12]

However, the twentieth century history of wine in Canterbury is largely the product of the chance meeting of two very different men, one an academic fruit scientist and the other a Central European visitor of complex background, classical winemaking skills, and entrepreneurial tendencies.

## The Role of Lincoln College

In Canterbury, a lot of interest was expressed about the possibility of growing grapes and making wine in areas such as around Akaroa. Lincoln College, the University College of Agriculture for Canterbury, was not concerned with horticultural courses until 1949. The pastoral dominance in New Zealand agriculture did not encourage too much effort being put into marginal and speculative crops such as grapes, but interest in grape production did come to Lincoln with the appointment of Dr. David Jackson as a Lecturer in Fruit Production in 1968. Jackson became involved with grapes. One of the differences between grapes and the other fruits fascinated Jackson. Most pip and stone fruits flower soon after bud break, but grapes flower some six to eight weeks later. This gave the grape berry a relatively short period in which to ripen, a contrast which stimulated Jackson's scientific imagination.

Jackson, a fruit scientist and teacher without practical experience of grape growing and winemaking, was fortuitously introduced to Danny Schuster, a visiting Czech Research Fellow who had been contracted to solve some fermentation problems in cider production. Danny—who had trained in grape growing and winemaking at the Melnik Institute, situated in a small Bohemian wine-producing district about fifty kilometers north of Prague—was enlarging his overseas experience in New Zealand before moving on to South Africa for the next vintage.[13]

The encounter between the two men created a synergy that led to the revival of grape growing and winemaking in Canterbury—something that Bragato had dreamed of for Akaroa in 1895. A winemaking seminar that the two men organized in May 1973 attracted many participants, reflecting a much greater level of serious public interest in wine than had been anticipated. This encouraged Jackson to plant his first wine grapes in order to assess their suitability for Canterbury, and to begin a series of related promotional activities. He and Schuster coauthored a new range of publications that highlighted the path-breaking developments at Lincoln, and placed the growing of grapes and making of cool-climate wines in a world context. In addition, they organized a series of seminars to highlight the potential in Canterbury for growing grapes and making satisfactory wines.[14]

The first planting of trial grape varieties in the winter of 1973 nearly came to grief due to a late frost. At first, the trials focused on cool-climate varietals in order to test whether Canterbury's dry cool season was amenable to producing grapes for a German-style white wine. Subsequently, warm-climate varietals were tested. Jackson concluded that any grape that ripened in the exceptionally bad 1975/76 season when the total degree days[15] at Lincoln were only 630, compared with an average level of 973 over the ten years 1965–1975 (and there was an early frost causing leaf drop and killing some berries), could be successfully adopted by wine growers in similar or warmer climates.[16]

Of the varietals suitable for the Canterbury climate, initial results suggested Gewürztraminer, Pinot Blanc, two forms of Chasselas, and Sylvaner produced reasonable sugar and acid levels. Pinot Noir and Gamay de Beaujolais were rather high in acid but still showed potential. Chardonnay, Riesling, and Hermitage were all too high in acid, but allowing for the poor year still exhibited some potential. Jackson's conclusions included a caution for those wishing to grow grapes in South Island conditions that considerable finance, skill, and flexibility were vital attributes given the still largely experimental conditions and uncertain yields and markets.[17]

By the time of Jackson's second report in 1978, the trials had expanded to cover forty wine grape varieties[18] and fourteen different systems of pruning and training. That season, many of the grapes in the variety collection first matured and so were evaluated in a series of procedures that Schuster played an important role in setting up. First, the mature grapes were comparatively assessed for sugar and acid levels. As microvinification[19] had begun, taste or sensory evaluation panels were introduced. Assessment of the output was also reported for the first time.

The sensory evaluation panels, which operated from 1978 to 1984, each comprised fifteen members with some expertise in wine, from wine producers and merchants to adherents of wine appreciation societies and professional oenologists. All were instructed how to evaluate wine in terms of alcohol content, color, flavor, aroma and age. Drawn from all over New Zealand, they were well placed to convey to their peers in the industry the results of experiments at Lincoln.[20]

By 1979, preliminary conclusions could be made. First, Canterbury was on a par in terms of heat accumulation with areas of

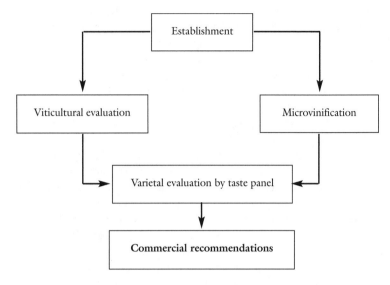

**Figure 13.1** Stages in the cultivar evaluation research program

the world that produced excellent white wines. Second, due to insufficient precipitation, Canterbury might need irrigation in order to establish new plantings. Wind was also a problem, necessitating the provision of adequate shelter for grapes. In addition, while the buds of grapes and apples burst at about the same time, grapes were closer to the soil and thus more susceptible to ground frosts. In consequence, the value of frost-free sites or a system of frost protection was emphasized.[21] Sloping sites were generally frost free due to natural air drainage and greater exposure to the sun, but machine cultivation of slopes was more difficult, necessitating higher—and more expensive—labor inputs.[22] However, the most serious problem encountered was bird and wasp damage (wasps attacking grapes already punctured by birds).[23]

By 1976 Schuster was back in New Zealand after supplementing his experience in South Africa and Bordeaux, and was working in Marlborough as a Viticulture Advisor for Montana Wines, which in 1973 had started a large propagation and planting program. He chose to work there to be close to developments at Lincoln, which he regularly visited.

While its experimental program was proceeding, Lincoln organized seminars, workshops, and courses to give interested parties an insight into developments and help them with their own growing plans. Courses offered in 1976–78 were largely Jackson and Schuster affairs, supplemented by local and national speakers according to subject.[24] Regular interaction between researchers and potential growers and winemakers was encouraged, there being none of today's concerns about commercial sensitivity. As many participants were, by the early 1980s, playing significant roles as grape growers and winemakers, David Jackson believed that by then the initial aims of educating the industry had been largely achieved. Those wanting further information could continue to directly contact the experts at Lincoln. Jackson, discouraged at the lack of non-technical literature to assist grape farmers, decided to write his own guides. In 1971, early in his teaching days at Lincoln, Jackson had published his *Notes on Fruitgrowing*, a distillation of information about a range of fruit crops, including grapes, to accompany his horticultural courses.[25] He subsequently coauthored with Schuster two works: "Possibilities for Grape Growing and Wine Making in the South Island of New Zealand" and *Grape Growing and Wine Making: A Handbook for Cool Climates*, now in its fourth edition and with a world-wide market.[26]

## Spin-offs from Lincoln: Regional Commercial Wine Production

Jackson and Schuster's "odd ball" idea of planting grapes in Canterbury was taken up quicker than they could have imagined, stimulated by the desire of local producers to rival Auckland wine growers. Much of the early interest centered on Banks Peninsula, the remnants of volcanic cones rising to nearly a thousand meters to the southeast of Christchurch, and site of the earlier French plantings at Akaroa. A 1975 Lincoln experiment with the planting of grapes near Akaroa[27] failed as a result of the area's drought prone character, Schuster's inexperience with the locality, and the remoteness of the area from Lincoln. With hindsight it is also clear that irrigation at the time of planting was necessary. Schuster had long held the view that vines should not be nursed too much at planting but be encouraged to get their roots down deep even if some plant losses were the consequence.[28]

Unfortunately, when farmers realized that establishing vineyards on Banks Peninsula would restrict their use of hormone herbicides for controlling weeds, such as gorse and broom, vineyards became a prohibited form of land use.

Another early center of grape cultivation was just north of Christchurch on the Canterbury Plains where two plantings followed directly from involvement with Lincoln. One of these comprised a two-hectare plot planted with Riesling, Gewürztraminer, Pinot Gris, and Pinot Noir located on the orchard of Bill Turner, the sponsor of the cider fermentation research for which Schuster had originally been contracted. This inspired Ernie Hunter—a local hotel manager and friend of Turner who became enthralled with the possibilities of New Zealand wine—to purchase land in Marlborough for grape production. Using improvised equipment, he and Turner made wines—their first—that won three silver and three bronze medals in the National Wine Competition. Before Ernie's early death in 1987, the Hunter family built their own winery in Marlborough and became significant promoters of the export of New Zealand wines.

The Mundy brothers initiated the second Plains planting after their vegetable growing operation was undermined by a devastating attack of the potato cyst nematode. Inspired by developments at Lincoln, from where they obtained cuttings, they planted four hectares of grapes in 1978, which had increased to twelve hectares by 1981 when their first vintage sold out in one day.[29] In 1983, their St. Helena Winery won a national gold medal at the *Air New Zealand Wine Awards* for its 1982 Pinot Noir. This provoked national interest in Canterbury as a wine-producing area. As with the composite Hunter wines, the St. Helena Pinot Noir combined Mundy's St. Helena grapes with a small quantity of grapes from Banks Peninsula. They came from a small area of vines planted by Jackson's technician assistant, Graeme Steans, with Danny Schuster's help. There were too few of them to be classified as a vineyard and thus prohibited[30].

Two other wine-growing initiatives were founded by members of Lincoln's Sensory Evaluation Panel: one by the Giesen brothers from Germany—who wanted to produce cool climate Riesling and became the largest of the early Canterbury growers—and the other by John Thom and July Wagner, from Rolleston, who established the first winery restaurant. Their project was the first step in setting up what is now an important wine tourism industry in Canterbury.[31]

In the Waipara district, Sophie Fox (née Glasman), who had sufficient experience in wine growing from her native Alsace to recognize the geological potential of Waipara, initiated the first vineyard
in the 1880s.[32] The wine potential of Waipara's limestone soil also
led, in the late 1950s, to an initial planting in a Weka Valley nurs-
ery of ten thousand cuttings from the Mission Vineyard in Hawkes
Bay.[33] A third experiment was tried by John McCaskey, using
hybrid cuttings in an attempt to find a viable alternative to sheep
farming.[34] However, none of the three initiatives succeeded. One
major problem was drought. Rainfall was reasonable during the
1960s, but the region experienced bad droughts from 1970 to
1973, and in 1972 the New Zealand Agricultural Engineering
Institute at Lincoln College was asked by local farmers to carry out
a feasibility study for an irrigation scheme. The result was the government subsidized Glenmark Irrigation Scheme, which harvested
water from floods and other high flow levels and stored it in a
range of ring and gulley dams for use when moisture shortages
began to impede plant growth.[35] It was envisaged that the chief
beneficiaries of the scheme would be producers of wheat, barley,
lamb, and wool, but it was noted that wine growers would also
benefit.[36]

John McCaskey was first to take advantage of the irrigation
scheme, when in 1981 he planted four hectares of land with Riesling,
Chardonnay, Muller Thurgau, Cabernet Sauvignon, Pinot Noir, and
Gewürztraminer vines that he cultivated along Lincoln lines. Each
vine on his plot received approximately one liter of water weekly from
a small ring dam that had originally been built to water tomatoes.
When agricultural subsidies were removed in 1984, the Glenmark
Irrigation Scheme was terminated prematurely. Consequently
only half of the potential area was irrigated, but it included
McCaskey's farm, which produced a Waipara Red wine that in
1985 won a Bronze Medal, a presage of future success for the new
wine-producing district.[37]

Four other viticulture enterprises founded in 1982 that also benefited from the Glenmark irrigation scheme became contract growers for Corban's Wines in Marlborough. Their grapes won Rhine
Riesling wines gold medals in competitions in 1986, 1988, and
1989.[38] In addition, in 1986, specifically to grow Pinot Noir grapes,
Danny Schuster founded the Omihi Hills Vineyard there on an elevated wind-protected hillside, with soils reminiscent of Burgundy of
heavy clay loam, rich in ironstone and chalk.[39]

## DEVELOPMENTS SINCE THE LATE 1980S

Vine plantings in Canterbury have increased since 1990, notably in the Waipara area, which has also received significant American investment at Canterbury House Winery, developed by an American Radiologist, Dr. Michael Reid. On the Plains, Danny Schuster established a second vineyard, of Chardonnay and Pinot Noir, on gravelly soils in mid Canterbury to complement his Waipara production.[40]

Banks Peninsula also witnessed developments in wine growing from the late 1980s, when a severe rural recession led to a withdrawal of the prohibition on vineyards. Some farmers were persuaded to profit from climate, aspect, and slope advantages favorable to vines and to establish vineyards around Akaroa Harbor, the location chosen for the first plantings by the original French settlers. In a further development in 1990, a vineyard restaurant was opened at Waipara Springs that has helped to promote Waipara as a tourist destination, and has acted as a model for others established at Glenmark and Pegasus Bay.[41]

By 2005, Canterbury had 853 hectares under vine—a figure that is predicted to reach 980 hectares by 2008. This currently represents only 4 percent of the total area under vines in New Zealand. Of the area under vine in Canterbury, 33 percent—projected to increase to 36 percent by 2008—is planted with Pinot Noir, almost one-third with Riesling and about one-seventh with Chardonnay.[42] Following its acquisition of Corban's award-winning Amberley Rhine Riesling wine vineyards in Canterbury in 2000, Montana Wines, then New Zealand's largest wine company, also established major Pinot Noir and Riesling plantings in the province. This signaled the beginning of significant corporate wine production in Waipara.[43] In total, it is estimated that by 2008, the area under wines in Waipara will increase to 245 hectares for Pinot Noir, 234 hectares for Riesling, and just 53 hectares for Chardonnay.[44]

While the viticulture area was expanding, developments continued at Lincoln where a one-year postgraduate diploma in dedicated viticulture and wine science was established in 1989. The course immediately became extremely popular, and experts from all over New Zealand—and one from California—were recruited to help with the teaching.[45] In 1998, the program was expanded with the addition of a three-year Bachelor of Viticulture and Oenology degree. By 2006, nearly 120 students were enrolled in the undergraduate, and over 40 in associated postgraduate programs. From 1993, there was also a renewed interest in short-term courses that provided an opportunity for local grape growers and winemakers to meet students and to catch up with the latest research and technological developments.

## CONCLUSION

Recent entrepreneurial developments have led to a significant expansion of the wine industry, wine tourism, and wine exports in the Canterbury region of New Zealand. This chapter has outlined the early beginnings and subsequent successful establishment of the wine industry. Initially based on a small number of individual initiatives, it required a supportive research and educational institution, and the unrelated backing of government policy from the early 1980s to prove successful.

Wine has made a considerable visual and economic impact on Waipara. In visual terms, irrigation and vines have added greens and autumnal reds to the formerly uniform pale straw colors of late summer and autumn. Also, a thriving new sector has been added to the economy as, in addition to the vineyards and wineries, wine tourism has developed. Waipara has become part of the Hurunui Tourist Triangle (which also includes the thermal resort of Hanmer Springs, and the whale watching centre of Kaikoura), attracting increasing numbers of local and international tourists—all of which has a multiplier effect on other sectors of the economy: The winery tourism multipliers for Canterbury, for example, have been calculated at between $NZ1.48 and $NZ1.91.[46]

Moreover, the future of winemaking in Canterbury looks rosy. Montana Wines, currently owned by Pernod Ricard, New Zealand, has made a substantial commitment to the district, with huge new plantings of 220 hectares of Pinot Noir, Riesling, and Pinot Gris.[47] Again, the creation of Waiata Vineyard Waipara, which has long-term supply contracts with Villa Maria and Nobilo's, will lead to a further planting of 330 hectares.[48] Such investment is well founded. At the 2003 International Wine Challenge in London, Sherwood Estate was awarded Gold for its 2002 Reserve Riesling.[49] Canterbury, and Waipara wines have truly become internationally established.

# NOTES

1. I wish to acknowledge David Jackson for viticulture and oenology advice. Recording recent history has depended upon the reminiscences of many of those involved. My grateful thanks are extended to all. John Lay, my boss and the director of the Applied Management and Computing Division, Lincoln University, facilitated the work and publications produced through liberal injections of funds, for which I thank him.

2. Author's translation of "Antipode" in *Le Nouveau Petit Robert—Nouvelle édition du Petit Robert de Paul Robert*, ed. Michel Legrain (Paris: Dictionnaires Robert, 1995).

3. HORTNZ, "Horticulture—Our Growth Industry" (2005), http://www.hortnz.co.nz/about/industrystats.html.

4. Rachel Alembakis, "Challenges to Australia's Strength in the UK Marketplace," *The Australian and New Zealand Grapegrower and Winemaker* 473 (2003): 75–76.

5. T. Unwin, *Wine and the Vine: A Historical Geography of Viticulture and the Wine Trade* (Routledge: London and New York, 1991), 296–300.

6. Jason Mabbett, "Prehistory of the New Zealand Wine Industry," *Journal of Wine Research* 8, no. 2 (1997): 103–14.

7. Romeo Bragato, *Report on the Prospects of Viticulture in New Zealand Together with Instructions for Planting and Pruning*, New Zealand Department of Agriculture (Wellington: Government Printer, 1895), 6.

8. Ibid., 6.

9. Rupert Tipples, *A History of Grape Production and Winemaking in Canterbury, New Zealand (1840–2002)*, Research paper no. 1, Applied Management and Computing Division, Lincoln University, Canterbury, New Zealand, 2002, pp. 3–4.

10. S. Lowndes, " The French Connection," in Akaroa Symposium 2000, *Antipodes* 6 (2000): 42.

11. Jason Mabbett, "The Dalmatian Influence on the New Zealand Wine Industry: 1895–1946," *Journal of Wine Research* 9, no. 1 (1998): 15–23.

12. J. Barker, N. Lewis, and W. Moran, "Reregulation and the Development of the New Zealand Wine Industry," *Journal of Wine Research* 12, no. 3 (2001): 199–221.

13. Danny Schuster, interview at Omihi Hills Vineyard, October 19, 2000.

14. Tipples, "History of Grape Production," 14–15.

15. A degree day is a measure used in assessing the growth potential of a district through the heat accumulated during a growing season. The

method of calculation is discussed in D. I. Jackson and D. F. Schuster, *The Production of Grapes and Wines in Cool Climates* (Lincoln, New Zealand: Lincoln University Press, 1997) 5–7; see also D. I. Jackson and N. J. Cherry, "Prediction of a District's Grape-Ripening Capacity Using a Latitude-Temperature Index (LTI)," *American Journal of Enology and Viticulture*, 39, no. 1 (1988): 19–26.

16. D. I. Jackson, "Experiments in Viticulture at Lincoln College," Unpublished manuscript, Department of Horticulture, Lincoln College, 1976, p. 4.

17. Tipples, "History of Grape Production," 12.

18. D. I. Jackson, "Report from the First Major Grape Crop at Lincoln College," Unpublished manuscript, Department of Horticulture, Landscape and Parks, Lincoln College, June 30, 1978.

19. "A specialised microvinification unit for the production of small volumes of wine was set up in time for the 1978 vintage, using methods of standardized wine production similar to those successfully used in other research centers. The main principle involved was the need to produce small volumes of wine, which retain the natural balance and varietal character of the harvested fruit"; see Danny Schuster and Graeme Steans, "Evaluation of Grape Cultivars Reaches Sensory Stage," *Southern Horticulture Grapegrower and Winemaker* 1 (1983/84): 67.

20. Tipples, "History of Grape Production," 12–14.

21. Anon., "The Grape Experiments at Lincoln College and Preliminary Results to 1979," Unpublished manuscript, Department of Horticulture, Landscape and Parks, Lincoln College, 1979.

22. Tipples, "History of Grape Production," 14.

23. Ibid., 14.

24. The papers from these courses were published in a two volume collection: Anon., "Papers in Winemaking and Wine Evaluation," Department of Horticulture, Landscape and Parks, Lincoln College, 1978).

25. David I. Jackson, "Notes on Fruitgrowing," Unpublished typescript, Department of Horticulture, Lincoln College, 1971.

26. David I. Jackson and Daniel F. Schuster, "Possibilities for Grape Growing and Wine Making in the South Island of New Zealand," Unpublished typescript, Department of Horticulture, Lincoln College, 1973; idem., *Grape Growing and Wine Making: A Handbook for Cool Climates* (Martinborough: Alistair Taylor, 1981).

27. Tipples, "History of Grape Production," 18.

28. Michael Cooper, *The Wines and Vineyards of New Zealand* (Auckland: Hodder and Stoughton, 1993), 170; Rosemary George, *The Wines of New Zealand* (London: Faber and Faber, 1996), 288.

29. Collins, Ian "'Odd Ball' Idea Now a Winning Industry," *Lincoln University News* 6 (1991): 1–2.
30. Tipples, "History of Grape Production," 18.
31. Rosemary George, *The Wines of New Zealand* (London: Faber and Faber, 1996), 281, 287; Liz Grant, *Weekends for Wine Lovers in the South Island* (Auckland: New Holland, 2000), 100–102; C. Michael Hall, E. Sharpies, B. Cambourne, and N. Macionis, *Wine Tourism around the World: Development, Management and Markets* (Oxford: Butterworth Heineman, 2000), 150–74.
32. Danny Schuster, David Jackson, and Rupert Tipples, *Canterbury Grapes and Wines 1840–2002* (Christchurch: Shoal Bay), 60–61.
33. Ibid., 61.
34. Ibid., 61–64.
35. Filomeno de Jesus Hornay, "A Case Study of the Effect of a Key Innovation on Farmers Adoption Behaviour," Master's thesis, Lincoln University, 1996, pp. 13–15.
36. T. D. Heiler, R. D. Plank, and G. T. Daly, "Glenmark Irrigation Scheme-Final Design, Vol.1, Summary," New Zealand Agricultural Engineering Institute, Lincoln College, Canterbury, New Zealand, 49.
37. Schuster, Jackson, and Tipples, *Canterbury Grapes and Wines*, 64.
38. Ibid., 66.
39. Danny Schuster, personal communication, 2000; Michael Cooper, *Wines and Vineyards of New Zealand* (Auckland: Hodder and Stoughton, 1994), 170.
40. Tipples, "History of Grape Production," 24.
41. Schuster, Jackson, and Tipples, *Canterbury Grapes and Wines*, 67–69.
42. New Zealand Winegrowers, *Statistical Annual* (2005), 23—24, http://www.nzwine.com/statistics/.
43. Caroline Courtenay, *Wine in New Zealand* (Auckland: Montana and Godwit Books, 2003), 165.
44. New Zealand Winegrowers, *Statistical Annual*, 2005, pp. 23–24.
45. Ian Collins, *Lincoln College News*, March 1989, p. 5.
46. H. Bigsby, M. Trought, R. Lambie, and K. Bicknell, "An Economic Analysis of the Wine Industry in Marlborough," A Report to Marlborough Winemakers, Agricultural and Economics Research Unit, Lincoln University, 1998.
47. Courtenay, *Wine in New Zealand*, 165.
48. Bristow, Robin "Newest vineyard a hi-tech creation," *The Press*, Christchurch, New Zealand, January 5, 2006,p. 3; Chris Turner (project manager, Waiata Vineyard Waipara), personal communication January 31, 2006.
49. Found at Dayne Sherwood, "Sherwood Estate wins GOLD," Sherwood Estate News Archive, September 1, 2003, http://www.sherwood.co.nz/news/news.asp?ReID=57.

# APPENDIX

# SOURCES AND CALCULATION METHOD FOR WORLD WINE PRODUCTION (TABLE 10.2)

We have made our calculation of world wine production on the basis of data collected from the International Institute of Agriculture, *Annuaire International de Statistique Agricole* (Rome: International Institute of Agriculture, 1911–1939). Data missing from the above source has been completed using the following sources: B. R. Mitchell, *International Historical Statistics. Africa and Asia* (London: Macmillan,1986); B. R. Mitchell, *International Historical Statistics. Europe, 1750–1988* (London: Macmillan,1992); B. R. Mitchell, *International Historical Statistics. The Americas, 1750–1988* (New York: Stockton, 1993); United States Tariff Commission, *Grapes, Raisins and Wines, (Washington, 1939)*; and Office International du Vin, *Annuaire International du Vin* (Paris: Office International du Vin, 1928–1939).

Data that could not be obtained from any of the above sources has been estimated as an average of the available data on previous and subsequent years. The percentages of estimated production of total world production in each period are: 1.5 (1900–04); 2.8 (1905–09); 3.9 (1910–14); 3.5 (1915–19); 2.4 (1920–24); 1.0 (1925–29); 1.1 (1930–34); 4.9 (1935–38).

# Author Biographies

## Editors

GWYN CAMPBELL, COEDITOR
(McGILL UNIVERSITY, DEPARTMENT OF HISTORY)
Gwyn Campbell is a Canada research chair and the director of the Indian Ocean World Centre in the Department of History, McGill University. He holds degrees in economic history from the universities of Birmingham and Wales and has taught in India, Madagascar, Britain, South Africa, Belgium, France, and Canada. As author, editor, or coeditor, he has over one hundred publications, including *An Economic History of Imperial Madagascar, 1750–1895: The Rise and Fall of an Island Empire* (Cambridge: Cambridge University Press, 2005); and *The Impact of Globalisation on the Wine Industry*, special edition of the *British Food Journal* 108. 4 (2006), coedited with Nathalie Guibert.

NATHALIE GUIBERT, COEDITOR
(UNIVERSITY OF AVIGNON, DEPARTMENT OF BUSINESS)
Nathalie Guibert is professor of business and management at the University of Avignon, France, where she is director of the Wine Management and International Trade Research Laboratory, and of the master's program in management and international trade. She is coeditor, with Gwyn Campbell, of *The Impact of Globalisation on the Wine Industry*, special edition of the *British Food Journal* 108. 4 (2006).

# Other Contributors

## Marianne Ackerman
### (Independent Writer)

Marianne Ackerman holds an MA from the University of Toronto. A Montreal-based writer, she has published two novels and four plays. As a journalist she has published widely in leading newspapers and magazines, including *The Globe and Mail, Saturday Night Magazine, The Guardian Weekly*, and the *Montreal Gazette* (also see http://www.marianneackerman.com).

## Robert B. Anderson
### (University of Regina, Faculty of Business Administration)

Robert B. Anderson, professor in entrepreneurship and management accounting at the University of Regina, Canada, is the author or coauthor of numerous articles on entrepreneurship and economic development. He is editor of the *Journal of Small Business and Entrepreneurship* and coeditor of the *Journal of Enterprising Communities*.

## María-Isabel Ayuda
### (University of Zaragoza, Department of Economic Analysis)

María-Isabel Ayuda, an associate professor in the Department of Economic Analysis at the University of Zaragoza, is the author or coauthor of numerous publications in the field of econometric theory and cliometrics.

## Linda Bramble
### (Attached to Brock University, St. Catharines, Ontario, Canada)

Wine educator Dr. Linda Bramble is a wine writer and broadcaster and former professor in wine appreciation at the Cool Climate Oenology and Viticulture Institute at Brock University in St. Catharines. As adjunct professor to the Faculty of Business, she taught courses in creativity and entrepreneurship. Among several books, she has written two about Ontario wine country and Ontario wines—*Discovering Ontario's Wine Country* and *Touring Niagara Wine Country*—and a third on the industry's history is in preparation. She is also the Canadian correspondent for the *Oxford Companion to Wine*. She was a lecturer in philosophy and education at Brock University, professor at Concordia University in Montreal, and a program director with the Niagara Institute, a think tank bringing together leaders from business, labor, government, and academia, now part of the Conference Board of Canada. Her interest in wine became professional when she cofounded a Niagara region magazine, which brought her into contact with the Ontario wine industry. She is also a recent former member of the Board of Directors of the Liquor Control Board of Ontario. She currently conducts research in wine tourism and leadership in wine.

KATHLEEN BROSNAN

(UNIVERSITY OF HOUSTON, DEPARTMENT OF HISTORY)

Kathleen Brosnan is an associate professor of history and research director of the Center for Public History at the University of Houston. Dr. Brosnan holds a JD from the University of Illinois and a PhD from the University of Chicago. She is the author of *Uniting Mountain and Plain: Cities, Law, and Environmental Change along the Front Range* (2002). Brosnan is finishing a book on the environmental history of the Napa Valley wine industry and editing a four-volume *Encyclopedia of American Environmental History* for Facts On File.

PATRIC CHOFFRUT

(UNIVERSITY OF AVIGNON, DEPARTMENT

OF COMMERCE AND APPLIED LANGUAGES)

Patric Choffrut, *Maître de Conferences* in the Department of Commerce and Applied Languages at the University of Avignon (American studies), is also a linguist and expert in Provencal, the tongue of the troubadours and a language that once dominated the entire region from Catalonia through Southern France to adjoining regions of Italy. His research interests are minorities in general, Jewish and Occitan histories in particular.

### CARMAN CULLEN
(BROCK UNIVERSITY, DEPARTMENT OF MANAGEMENT, MARKETING)

Carman Cullen is an associate professor of marketing and a three-time winner of the Faculty of Excellence Award in the Faculty of Business at Brock University. Carman has an extensive background in consumer research and retailing, both as practitioner and as a consultant. Dr. Cullen has offered numerous seminars and conducted research throughout North America and Europe, with a most recent focus on wine marketing. He is coeditor (with G. Pickering and R. Phillips) of the *Conference Proccedings Editors—Bacchus to the Future, The Inaugural Brock University Wine Conference*, Brock University Press, St. Catharines, Ontario, 2002.

### ROBERT J. GIBERSON
(UNIVERSITY OF REGINA, FACULTY OF ADMINISTRATION)

Robert J. Giberson is associate dean of undergraduate and international programs and is associate professor (of marketing) at the University of Regina, Canada. He researches and publishes in enterepreneurship.

### BRIAN GIBSON
(MURDOCH UNIVERSITY, MURDOCH BUSINESS SCHOOL)

Brian Gibson is an associate professor of accounting at the Murdoch Business School in Western Australia, where he researches and publishes in small business practice and entrepreneurship.

### JOSEPH KUSHNER
(BROCK UNIVERSITY, DEPARTMENT OF ECONOMICS)

Joseph Kushner is a professor of economics and director of business economics at Brock University and was formerly with the Royal Military College of Canada. His publications have appeared in the following journals: *Advances in Industrial and Labor Relations, Antitrust Bulletin, Applied Economics Letters, AREUEA Journal, Atlantic Economic Journal, Canadian Business Economics, Canadian*

*Journal of Administrative Sciences*, *Canadian Journal of Economics*, *Canadian Journal of Political Science*, *Canadian Journal of Public Health*, *Canadian Journal of Urban Research*, *Canadian Public Administration/Administration Publique du Canada*, *Canadian Water Resources Journal*, *Cost and Management*, *Dalhousie Review*, *Engineering Economist*, *Health Services Research*, *Science Forum*, *Journal of the Midwest Finance Association*, *National Tax Journal*, *Quarterly Journal of Business and Economics*, *Review of Financial Economics*, and *Utilities Policy*. He is a co-recipient of the Douglas C. Mackay Outstanding Paper Award in Finance.

GARY PICKERING

(DEPARTMENT OF BIOLOGICAL SCIENCES AND COOL CLIMATE OENOLOGY & VITICULTURE INSTITUTE, BROCK UNIVERSITY)

Educated and trained as an oenologist in New Zealand and Australia, Gary holds a PhD in wine science and has a very active research program focused on wine flavor and perception. He is the author of over one hundred research papers, is an international wine judge, and is the North American editor of the *Journal of Food, Agriculture & Environment*. He is currently chair and professor in the Department of Biological Sciences at Brock University, and a research scientist in the Cool Climate Oenology & Viticulture Institute, also at Brock.

VICENTE PINILLA

(UNIVERSITY OF ZARAGOZA, DEPARTMENT OF APPLIED ECONOMICS AND ECONOMIC HISTORY)

Vicente Pinilla, professor of economic history in the Department of Applied Economics and Economic History at the University of Zaragoza, has published widely in the field of economic history, notably of nineteenth- and twentieth-century Spain and international trade in agricultural and food products.

STEVE STEIN

(PROFESSOR OF HISTORY, UNIVERSITY OF MIAMI)

Dr. Stein's research area is modern Latin American history, focusing on Peru and Argentina. He is presently conducting a multi-faceted research project on the history of wine in Argentina and is writing a comprehensive history of the Argentine wine industry. His major scholarship has been in the social and cultural history of Peru, concentrating on the evolution of the Lima popular sectors from the early twentieth century through the contemporary period. Dr. Stein's publications on the early twentieth century include "Populism in Peru: The Emergence of the Masses and the Politics of Social Control" (1980) and "Lima obrera 1900–1930," Vol. 1 and 2 (1986 and 1988). He has also written on Peru—"La crisis del estado patrimonial" (1988)—which analyzes the impact of Peru's most profound economic crisis on social, political, and cultural changes in the country. He has recently completed two co-edited works, entitled *Popular Art and Social Change in the Retablos of Nicario Jiménez Quispe* (with Professor Carol Damian of Florida International University), published by the Edwin Mellen Press in 2005, and *El vino y sus revoluciones: Una antología histórica sobre el desarrollo de la industria vitivinícola argentina* (with Professor Ana Maria Mateuof the Universidad Nacional de Cuyo, Argentina). In addition to his work in the History Department, Dr. Stein is the director of the Center for Latin American Studies at the University of Miami. He is also a member of the Tasting Board of the Miami International Wine Fair and teaches wine seminars in the South Florida area.

### Rupert Tipples

#### (Lincoln University, Canterbury)

Rupert Tipples, senior lecturer in employment relations at Lincoln University, New Zealand, is author of several primary industry histories, most recently *Canterbury Grapes and Wines 1840–2002.*

### Julie Holbrook Tolley

#### (University of South Australia, School of Social Work and Social Policy)

Julie Tolley is currently employed at the School of Social Work and Social Policy at the University of South Australia. She recently completed her PhD on the history of women in the South Australian wine industry. Her current research is compiling data from an online survey on the relationship between teaching, learning, and grading students' assignments to present at a conference in Georgia (United States) in November.

## Robert C. Ulin
(Western Michigan University)

Robert Ulin is a professor and chair of the Department of Anthropology. His research interests include the anthropology of Europe, social and cultural theory, political economy, ethnohistory, globalization, nationalism, wine growing, commodities, notably in France. His most recent book is *Understanding Cultures: Perspectives in Anthropology and Social Theory*, 2nd edition, Blackwell Publishers, 2001.

## Dianne W. Wingham
(The University of Newcastle, College of Business and Law)

Dianne Wingham, PhD, is an associate professor, teaching online courses and researching in entrepreneurship and strategy at the University of Newcastle, Australia (Grad School.com.au). She is CEO of Wingham Aplied Synergy, a Global Professional Development Company.

# INDEX